Autobiography of George Dewey

*Admiral of the United States Navy, and Hero of
the Spanish-American War*

Published by Pantianos Classics

ISBN-13: 978-1-78987-112-8

First published in 1913

Contents

Appendices 144

Preface

It was my fortune to be in command on May 1, 1898, of an American squadron in the first important naval action against a foreign foe since the War of 1812. The morning that we steamed into Manila Bay marked an epoch in the history of our navy and in that of our country in its relations with other great nations. A battle in a harbor whose name was unknown to our average citizen made us a world-power, with a resultant impetus to the national imagination and a new entail of national responsibilities. My orders were to capture or destroy the enemy's force, and to conduct offensive operations in the Philippine Islands. These orders I endeavored to obey with all possible expedition, in keeping with the traditions of our navy.

After the battle I received so many requests from publishers and editors for contributions in any form under my name that I might well have concluded that the victory which had come as the climax of my naval career was about to embark me on a literary career, toward which I naturally had the disinclination of a man of action. Urgings from many quarters to write my reminiscences have continued to the present time. My answer invariably has been that my record up to the time of the battle had not in itself sufficient personal significance to warrant an autobiography; for the life of every naval officer doing his duty as it comes to him, under the authority of the President and of Congress, merges into the life of the whole navy as a unit of service in preparedness for national defence in a crisis.

In keeping with the decision made when I was at Manila, my official reports have been thus far my only public account of the battle. However, after my return to Washington, for the sake of historical accuracy I wrote, with the assistance of my aide, the late Commander Nathan Sargent, U. S. N., a complete account of my command of the Asiatic Squadron from the time I hoisted my commodore's pennant until my return home in 1899. My plan was not to have this published until after my death. But now, fifteen years after the battle, I am yielding to the arguments of my friends, not only to have it published, but also to write my recollections of my career before Manila Bay brought me into prominent public notice.

It is fifty-nine years since I became an acting midshipman. Thanks to the creation of the grade of admiral of the navy by Congress in 1899, I was not retired at the usual retiring age, but kept on the active list for life. My memory stretches from an apprenticeship under the veterans of the War of 1812, those heroes of the old sailing-frigates and ships of the line; from the earlier days of the steam-frigates through the Civil War; from the period of inertia in the 'seventies, when our obsolete ships were the byword of the navies of the world, to the building of the ships of our new navy, which I was to give its first baptism of fire; and, finally, to my service as head of the general board of the navy since the Spanish War.

I have been through many administrations and many political changes, and have known many famous men both at home and abroad. When I entered the Naval Academy, in 1854, Commodore Perry was just opening Japan to civilization; it was only six years since California had become United States territory; while there was as yet no transcontinental railroad. At seventy-five I am writing in the hope of giving some pleasure to my countrymen, from whom I have received such exceptional honors, and in the hope that my narrative may be of some value and inspiration to the young men of the navy of to-day, who are serving with the same purpose that animated the men of Decatur's, Macdonough's, and Farragut's day, and later, the men of our squadrons which fought at Manila and Santiago.

I may add that in everything that refers to my command of the Asiatic Squadron in 1898-9 the greatest pains have been taken to insure the correctness of every detail; but in the reminiscences of a more remote period I must often depend upon my recollection of incidents which were not recorded at the time that they came under my observation. I narrate them as I remember them. In this part particularly, as well as for his literary advice and assistance in the whole work, it is a pleasure to acknowledge my indebtedness to Mr. Frederick Palmer, a friend of Manila days.

George Dewey

May 12, 1913.

Chapter One - Early Years

During my long stay in the heat of Manila Bay after the battle, certain angles of view of the irregular landscape of *Luzón* from the deck of the flagship *Olympia* often recalled the Green Mountains of my boyhood days. Indeed, I never look across a stretch of rolling country without a feeling of homesickness for Vermont. My ancestors were reared among the New England hills. They were of the old Pilgrim stock whose character has so eminently impressed itself on that of the nation.

A desire for religious freedom brought the French Huguenot family of Douai to Kent, in England, in the latter half of the sixteenth century. There the name became Duee. In a later time a desire for religious freedom sent one Thomas Duee, the founder of the American family, from Sandwich, in Kent, to Massachusetts, where the name was changed to Dewey. He settled at Dorchester in 1634, and mention of him appears in the old town records as follows:

It is granted that Thomas Duee shall have 2 acres of mowing ground, neere the Fresh Marsh, which he hath formerly mowen, in satisfaction for an acre of ground, which he left in common at his house.

Later he became one of the founders of Windsor, Connecticut. He had five children. My branch is that of Josiah, the second son, who had the rank of sergeant in King Philip's War.

My great-grandfather, William Dewey, was one of the volunteers at the battle of Lexington, and his brother, Simeon Dewey, was with Ethan Allen at the taking of Fort Ticonderoga by the Green Mountain Boys. My grandfather, Simeon Dewey, born in 1770, formed a connecting link for me with the Revolution, of which he had many youthful memories. He was particularly fond of telling how, as a boy of nine, he had taken a team of oxen to the woods, felled a tree, drawn the log to the house, and cut it up into firewood without any assistance. He was a farmer in the days when much of the soil of Vermont was still virgin, before competition from the opening up of the prairie land of the West had led to the abandonment of so many New England farms. I recollect him as the embodiment of the old Puritan qualities, with his lip and cheeks shaven and a beard about his chin and throat, in the fashion of his time. On my first cruise in the Mediterranean I sent him an olive-wood walking-stick from the Holy Land, which he used until the day of his death, in 1863, when I was a lieutenant in Farragut's command in the Gulf.

My father. Doctor Julius Yemens Dewey, after his graduation from the medical department of the University of Vermont, settled for practice in Montpelier, where, in a comfortable frame house of the type which you may see in any New England town, I was born, December 26, 1837, the youngest of three brothers. My mother I hardly remember, as she died when I was only five. To my father's influence in my early training I owe, primarily, all that I have accomplished in the world. From him I inherited a vigorous constitution and an active temperament. He was a good deal more than a successful practising physician. He was one of those natural leaders to whom men turn for unbiassed advice. His ideas of right and wrong were very fixed, in keeping with his deep religious scruples.

My early life was that of the boys of the neighborhood of a quiet street in an American town, which, to my mind, is about as healthy a life as a growing boy can lead. I went early to the district school, and they say the nature of my disposition led me into a great many adventures. Certainly I was full of animal spirits, and I liked things to happen wherever I was. Probably I had a gift for stirring up the other boys to help me in my enterprises. A life of Hannibal which I had received as a present fired my imagination. In winter it was easy to make-believe that in storming a neighboring hill I was making the passage of the Alps. If there were no other soldiers to follow me, I might draft my sister Mary, who was two years my junior.

Doctor Julius Yemens Dewey

My memory has kept no account of the number of boyish battles that I was in. The first day that the legislature sat was always a great occasion in the State capital, and boys used to come in from near-by towns for the gingerbread and sweet cider festivals, counterparts of the pea-nut and lemonade festivals of to-day, while their elders were shopping, trading horses, and talking politics. For the phalanx of our street it was an occasion for proving whether or not the outsiders were more valiant than we.

One of my favorite deeds of bravado was descending the old State-house steps blindfolded, with the on-lookers wondering whether I would slip on the way and take the rest of the flight head first. I was a good swimmer and had plenty of opportunity for practice in the waters of the Onion River, since called the Winooski, which was near our house. Perhaps some boy may have since excelled me in the length of time that he could hold his head under water, but my record was unbeaten in my day. It gave me the authority of leadership in all water functions.

On one occasion, when the river was swollen to a flood, I thought that it would be a grand exploit to drive a horse and wagon across the current. The wagon was submerged. I crawled over the dashboard onto the horse's back, and he brought me drenched to the shore. I was less worried over what I had escaped than over the reckoning that was to come with a father whose discipline was so necessary to a nature that was inclined to rebel against sedate surroundings. When he returned from a professional call he found me in bed in my room, shivering very determinedly.

"You ought to be glad that I am alive!" I told him reproachfully. He seemed to take the same view, for I was not punished, though he had lost his wagon.

THE BIRTHPLACE OF ADMIRAL DEWEY AT MONTPELIER, VERMONT

As I grew older the masters of our district school had such a difficult time in keeping order that they were frequently changed. Some of the boys of my age regarded it as their business to test each new appointee. Such rebellious manifestations were not uncommon in district schools of that time and certainly did not contribute to scholarship. My father doubtless saw that I was in need of discipline, and he

THE SCHOOL-HOUSE AT MONTPELIER

sent me, at the age of fourteen, to the old Military Academy at Norwich, Vermont. It had been founded by the first superintendent of West Point, Captain Alden Partridge. At one time its reputation had been so high that it was considered superior to West Point, and many boys from the South, where the military spirit was more common in those days than in the North, had been among its pupils. We lived in dormitories and had regular military drill. As an institution in keeping with its original purpose, Norwich had greatly deteriorated. I am glad to say it has now recovered its former excellence.

Not long ago in Woodstock, Vermont, where I spend my summers, the judge of the district court there invited me to sit on the bench with him and see how the cases were conducted. I answered him that I already had a pretty good idea of court proceedings in Woodstock from personal experience, for the docket of the old court-house in Woodstock records the following in expression of the view that might be taken of a school-boy's pranks in a staid academy town in the early fifties:

WINDSOR COUNTY COURT
Dec. Term, 1854.

| The State | Converse & Bassett |
| *vs.* | *For* Comstalk. |

Lloyd E. Bowers,
Gordon S. Hubbard,
Daniel Comstalk,
George Dewey *and*
Martin V. B. Wasson.

As will be seen, Comstalk was the only one of us who had a lawyer. The five culprits had stood outside the window of a room where hymns were being sung and broken up the meeting by a rival concert of our own, made up mostly of negro melodies. Life in that school provided us with little relaxation. The very insistence of the authorities on continual study in a solemn manner was bound to awaken the spirit of mischief. Our invention of a means of amusement to make up for the absence of any in the curriculum brought our arrest and an order to appear before the court at Woodstock.

My allowance being pretty small, I worried terribly over how I was going to pay my hotel and travelling expenses; and also as to what my father, with his strict ideas, would say about it all. However, I summoned the courage and wrote him the truth. Of course, he sent me the money, but the letter accompanying the remittance was rather tart. He declared that in the start of my educational career away from home I had accomplished more than he had expected. Indeed, I had made such progress that he was convinced that I needed no further education, and my evident knowledge of the ways of the world should make me equal to undertaking the battle of life at once.

Chapter Two - At Annapolis

At the time that I left Norwich, 1854, West Point had a great name as a disciplinary institution. There boys had to obey. Annapolis was not then so well known as West Point, being only nine years old. We owe the efficiency of the personnel of our navy to Annapolis; and we owe Annapolis to George Bancroft, a man of singular versatility of talent and singular sturdiness and decisiveness of character. He not only wrote the standard history of the United States which bears his name, but he was also minister to Berlin and secretary of the navy.

When he saw that, with the development of naval science, a school was as necessary for training officers for the navy as one for training officers for the army, his proposition met with the immediate opposition of the veteran officers of the service. Their disparagement was sufficient to prevent Congress from appropriating money to give the new institution a start. But this did not discourage Mr. Bancroft. He went right ahead with what resources he could command. At Annapolis there was old Fort Severn, which had been deserted. In want of funds for buildings, he secured the use of the buildings which had been occupied by the force that formerly manned the fort. The barracks which had housed privates of artillery became the dormitories of the future officers of the navy. Henry H. Lockwood, a former army officer and a graduate of West Point, was appointed professor of mathematics and became the chief instructor. Most of the other instructors were civilians. Their assistants were young officers of the navy.

While the majority of the old officers poked fun at the idea, one of the progressives, *Franklin* Buchanan, a Marylander, was Bancroft's energetic aid in the organization of the academy. Buchanan resigned from the navy at the outbreak of the Civil War; but when he found that his own State, Maryland, had not seceded, he tried to withdraw his resignation. This being refused, he joined the enemy. He commanded the *Merrimac* in her raid in Hampton Roads, at which time he was wounded. This made him the hero of the Confederate navy. He was in command at Mobile Bay against Farragut. It is one of the anomalies of history that one who had such strict loyalty to State's as opposed to national rights should have been the most conspicuous organizer of that school whose graduates, in the Spanish War, struck the blows which did so much to unite the North and the South in a new feeling of national unity before the world.

Too frequently credit for the Naval Academy has been given to Buchanan rather than to Bancroft. It is related that Bancroft used to get much out of patience with the old officers. In those days the men on the captain's list received their assignments to ships in rotation, without regard to their fitness. A great many of the captains were not only old, but their habits, as the legacy of the hard-living days of the War of 1812, scarcely promoted efficiency in their declining years. Indeed, it was still the custom to serve out two rations of grog every day to the sailors, while officers of the broadside school did not limit themselves to any stated number. One of the veterans was so conspicuously unfit that Bancroft passed him by when it came his turn to have a ship. He wrote to the secretary in great indignation, wanting to know what he had done that he should have been overlooked in that fashion after a long career in his country's service. Bancroft wrote back, "Nothing!" which was exactly what that captain had been doing for a good many years.

Competitive examinations were not yet the rule in my time in choosing candidates for either West Point or Annapolis, Appointments were due entirely to the political favor of representatives in Congress. There was no vacancy for West Point from Vermont. Otherwise, I might have gone into Manila Bay on an army transport instead of on the *Olympia.*

But it happened that there was a vacancy at Annapolis. A boy by the name of George Spaulding, of Montpelier, received the appointment at first, but decided that he would not take it. My father, through his influence with Senator Foote, had me made Spaulding's successor. Spaulding became a distinguished clergyman. Perhaps he was better suited for that than to be a sailor. Certainly I was better suited to be a sailor than a clergyman. I recollect that he preached a sermon in honor of the victory of Manila Bay at his church in Syracuse.

My father accompanied me to Annapolis, where I was to try the entrance examination. That was quite a journey into the world for a Vermont youngster of ante-bellum days. We went by rail to New York, where we stopped at the Irving House, which was kept by a Vermonter and was situated on Broadway, opposite A. T. Stewart's great store, which was then regarded as a kind of eighth wonder of the world by all women shoppers.

Father took me to the theatre, where Burton, a famous comedian of the period, was playing. I had never seen a real stage comedian before, and I laughed so hard that I fairly lost control of myself, and my father made me leave the theatre.

The next day we started for Annapolis, which was then twelve hours' journey from New York. First we took a steamer to Perth Amboy. From there we went by train to Philadelphia. Horses drew the car in which we went through the streets of Philadelphia, and we left this car at Havre de Grace. I recall that we had luncheon on the steam ferry crossing the Susquehanna.

We went through Baltimore in the same way that we had through Philadelphia, in a railroad car drawn by horses at a trot, with a brakeman blowing a horn for people and vehicles to get out of the way of the through express.

The entrance examinations to the Naval Academy were very simple in those days, consisting chiefly of reading, writing, and arithmetic. I had the good fortune to pass. Before he started home my father said to me:

"George, I've done all I can for you. The rest you must do for yourself."

This advice I have always tried to keep in mind.

Although the entrance examinations were easy, the process of elimination was even more rigorous through that stiff four years' course than at present. Sixty of us entered the academy in '54, and only fifteen of us were graduated in '58. By the end of the first year twenty-three had been plucked. I was number thirty-three out of the remaining thirty-five. That old faculty for making things happen had given me one hundred and thirteen demerit marks. Two hundred meant dismissal.

I was very poor in history and geography, but excellent in mathematics, which had pulled me through. In the second year, when nine more had been dropped, I was ninth among the survivors. My conduct marks had improved, and I was even better now in French and Spanish than in mathematics, but still low in history. On leaving the academy I was fifth among the fifteen who remained out of the original sixty. As for geography, I was to learn something of that in the harbors of the world. My weakness in history I overcame later in life, when I grew fond of reading. As for tactics and gunnery, in which I had also been low, I had practice in the Civil War which was far more valuable than any theory. Moreover, the tactics and gunnery which I had been taught at the academy were soon to become quite antiquated as more progressive officers already understood. I flatter myself that this accounted partially for my lack of interest in this branch.

The academy at that time had not yet settled in its traditions, and naval science was in a transition period from sails to steam. All the graduates of the academy were as yet juniors and not of any considerable influence in the service. No retirement provision existed. The old captains, many of whom had been in the War of 1812, were brought up in wooden frigates and ships of the line. Their ideas were very fixed. They had little charity for the innovations suggested by their juniors. To them a naval officer must ever remain primarily a sailor. But from them through the War of 1812 the navy had a proud inheritance. The history of that war on land, with its untrained volunteer troops, in which our Capitol was burned and our effort at the invasion of Canada proved a fiasco, hardly makes pleasant reading for any American who has the right kind of patriotism, which never closes its eyes to facts.

But the ships of our little navy, keeping to the traditions of our fast clippers and of Decatur at Tripoli, by outrunning the enemy in overwhelmingly superior numbers, closing in on him when terms were equal, gave an account of themselves that thrilled the nation. They fought the veterans of Trafalgar according to their own methods. These were terrible, bloody encounters at close quarters. That of the *Constitution* and the *Guerrière* was over in an hour; that of the *United States* and the *Macedonian* in an hour and a half; and that of the *Hornet* and *Peacock* in fourteen minutes. The spirit of the lesson which the British learned in the Napoleonic wars, they met in us. It meant boarding with the cutlass when. the ships were alongside, after they had been raked fore and aft with gun fire. Tactics and gunnery were very simple then compared to the present, when action may begin at a distance of six or seven miles.

The boys who came to Annapolis from all parts of a big expanse of a country not yet nationalized by the broad community of thought and intelligence of to-day had to be welded by the spirit of corps into a common life and purpose. When you enter the academy you cease to be a Vermonter or a Georgian or a Californian. You are in the navy; your future, with its sea-service and its frequent changes of assignment, makes you first a man of the country's service and only secondly a man of the world. Your associations all your life are with the men of your first comradeship of study and discipline. My fellow-midshipmen at Annapolis were the officers who, rising grade by grade, held the important commands of squadrons and ships afloat, and were the commandants of navy-yards and the heads of bureaus ashore during the Spanish War.

In the fifties we were still almost exclusively an agricultural nation. Our population was hardly a third of what it is at present. Personal wealth and luxury were limited to a few of the older cities. The midshipman of to-day, with his fine quarters, his shower-bath, his superior and varied diet, his football stadium, his special trains to the annual army and navy games, expresses the change that has come over the life of the nation as a whole. We now practise as well as preach the precept that all work and no play makes Jack a dull boy.

In my day at Annapolis we had no system of athletics except our regular military drill. There was no adequate gymnastic apparatus. The rule was one endless grind of acquiring knowledge. Our only amusement within the walls of the academy was the "stag hop" on Saturdays, held in the basement of the old recitation hall. We were all vigorous boys or we could not have passed the physical entrance examination; and we were being trained for a career that required dash and physical spirits. Under such restraint there were bound to be outbreaks and such infractions of discipline as not only would not be tolerated but would not occur to-day. Every midshipman had his nickname, of course, as every one has had from the inception of the academy and still has, and mine was "Shang" Dewey. I confess that I do not know how it originated. Hazing was rife. It was accepted as a part of the curriculum in whipping raw youths, whose egoism may have been overdeveloped by fond parents, into the habit of comradeship and spirit of corps. The excuse for it in its rigor of my time no longer exists under the present organization, however. I fear, too, that the faculty did not always receive the respect that they should have received. An assistant professor called "Bull Pup" was at one time captured and imprisoned in a glass wall-case in the chemical laboratory as an expression of midshipman disapproval.

Such actions, if inexcusable, had the palliation of a course which was without athletics or amusement and of the youth of the academy, which had not yet found itself as an institution. However, I believe that rowdyism was then far more common in civilian colleges than it is to-day; and if, in later times as instructors, the men of my day would not permit such infractions, it was proof of our realization of their utter subversion of military principles, while in recollection of our own close confinement we did provide for athletics and other forms of relaxation which left no excuse for ebullitions of an insubordinate nature.

Fistic arbitration of grievances between two midshipmen, I believe, still prevails under the supervision of upper-class men as the court of honor, in spite of the close observation of the commandant. There were numbers of them in my time. They were privately acknowledged, if openly discouraged, by the instructors as the manly way to settle differences. I looked after an affair of my own without waiting on any formality. A cadet who sat opposite me called me a name at mess which no man can hear without redress. I did not lose a second, and, springing around the table, I went for him and beat him down under the table before we were separated. That was a pretty serious infraction of discipline at mess. The combatants were brought up before the superintendent. Captain L. M. Goldsborough, later the well-known rear-admiral of the Civil War, who asked me why I had made the attack. I told him the name which my classmate had called me. He said that I could not have done anything else, fined me ten demerits, and assured the fellow whom I had thrashed that he had got exactly what he deserved. That I thought was a very sensible decision.

Captain George S. Blake, who was superintendent for the last three years that I was at Annapolis, married a daughter of Commodore Barron, who, it will be remembered, killed Decatur in a duel. Mrs. Blake had a warm place in the hearts of all the Annapolis graduates of my time. She was very kind to us in a day when the acting midshipmen saw little of home life. Thanks to Captain Goldsborough, Blake's predecessor, we had our barracks heated by steam and also the luxury of gas lamps. We lived two in a room and had to make our own beds and sweep our own rooms, but negro women who came in at stated intervals did the scrubbing. There were, as a rule, less than a hundred midshipmen all told; so that we came to know one another well.

Of course, all the under-class men looked forward to the glorious day when they should go on furlough at the end of their second year, as has ever been the custom. We had a song that expressed the feelings, in anticipation of that long-leave absence, of boys who had known an unremitting grind far from home:

"Come all ye gallant middies
    Who are going on furlough;
We'll sing the song of liberty;
    We're going for to go.

"Take your tobacco lively
    And pass the plug around;
We'll have a jolly time to-night
    Before we're homeward bound.

"Our sweethearts waiting for us.
    With eyes brimful of tears,
Will welcome us back home again
    From an absence of two years."

The reference to the plug of tobacco is to a habit in the United States which readers of Dickens's "American Notes" will recall excited the author's fervent comment. I always joined in the song heartily, and I also chewed tobacco. It was the habit of the acting midshipmen, in keeping with the universal male habit of the time. However, when I went to the Mediterranean on my midshipman cruise and found that the British and other foreign officers did not chew, I became convinced that it was a filthy, vulgar habit in which no officer or gentleman should indulge. So I declared that I would chew no more. It required a good deal of fortitude to overcome this habit, more, I think, than to give up smoking. But I kept my pledge to myself, and never took another chew after I had made up my mind on the subject.

The fifteen in my class who were finally graduated were well grounded. The things that we knew we knew well. This has always been the character of Annapolis, which fashions a definite type of man for a definite object in life. The relentless examinations permit of no subterfuge of mental agility and no superficial familiarity with a variety of subjects to take the place of exact knowledge of a limited number of subjects. I think I may say that no four years' course in any institution gives its students more in mind and character than the school from which the officers of our navy are drawn.

Chapter Three - The Midshipman Cruise

On our graduation from the academy on June 18, 1858, we passed from the rank of acting midshipmen to that of midshipmen, with two years' experience in practical cruising ahead of us before we actually got our commissions. We were now to have our reward for the four years' grind. We were to see the world. With three of my classmates I was assigned to the *Wabash*, a steam-frigate of over four thousand tons, with a powerful battery for her day and one of a class of six that had been built in 1855. The *Merrimac* of this class, which fell into Southern hands in the Norfolk Navy Yard at the outbreak of the Civil War, became the famous iron-clad which the Confederates called the *Virginia,* but which was always known in the North by her original name. The *Wabash* was the flag-ship of the Mediterranean Squadron, bearing the flag of Flag-Officer E. A. F. La Valette. At that time the highest rank in the navy was captain, so that the commander of a squadron was known as the flag-officer.

Flag-Officer La Valette, a veteran of 1812, had been in the battle of Lake Champlain. He was a white-haired, fine-appearing old officer and a very worthy representative to take a squadron abroad. On a number of occasions he had the young officers in to dinner. It was inspiring to us to hear his experiences in a war that had been fought forty-five years previously.

The *Wabash* had two horizontal engines, and her maximum speed under steam was nine knots, with an average of about five. We sailed from Hampton Roads on July 22, 1858, arriving at Gibraltar on August 15. Altogether, some fourteen months were spent in the Mediterranean, cruising from port to port. We youngsters of the "steerage," as the junior mess is called in distinction from the senior or wardroom mess, had close quarters, but ours was the happiest period that comes to a naval officer's career. In every important port from Gibraltar to Turkey and Egypt we had glimpses of life ashore; and we were introduced for the first time to the exchange of official calls and salutes between nations, which becomes routine to older officers, but to us had the charm of novelty. No conducted tourist excursion can quite equal that under official auspices.

I recall that President Cleveland once said to a friend of mine that he considered that the commander of a man-of-war on the European station had about as lordly a position as could fall to the lot of an American citizen. He. is the king of a little world of his own, subject only to squadron orders and to those from Washington.

But the midshipman at the bottom round of the official ladder has one advantage over all his superiors, and that is youth. On my cruise homeward from Manila in 1899, when I needed rest before the overwhelming public reception that awaited me, I spent several weeks in the Mediterranean, of whose climate and associations I had always been very fond. I enjoyed myself almost as well as I did when I was a midshipman.

The *Wabash* was a ship of which we could be justly

The U. S. Steam Frigate "Wabash"

proud, which means a great deal to any naval officer when he is in foreign waters. He does not like to feel that his country's flag is flying over an antiquated craft, which was the case throughout the depressing years of the seventies and eighties. Many visitors in every port came on board the "Yankee" and marvelled at her trimness and particularly at her cleanliness, which has always been characteristic of American men-of-war.

At this period France, after England, was far and away the preponderant naval power, and of course the next greatest influence in world politics. The German Empire and a United Italy were yet to be born. The leading ships of all the nations were in the Mediterranean, in view of a war impending between France and Italy and Austria. Besides, the situation in the Near East was always the ticklish one in the policy of foreign chancelleries, which, of late years, has yielded its place in that respect to the Far East.

Every navy was largely represented in the Bosphorus in October, 1858, in celebration of the births day of Mohammed, This was my first introduction to Constantinople and the Orient. On account of the Crimean War, in which the French and the English had been allies of the Turk, both were friendly to the Sick Man of the East, and they made the most of the demonstration as a political manoeuvre against Russia.

The *Wabash* was quite the finest ship of the foreign fleet and also the largest. Her tonnage was in excess of that allowed for foreign men-of-war in the Bosphorus by an international agreement which had its origin in the mutual jealousy of the powers lest one should get advantage of the others. Of course the United States had no interest in the interplay of European politics, and morally the fact of the size of the *Wabash* did not matter at all. But Lord Stratford de Redcliffe, the British ambassador, did not see it that way. In his position as spokesman for the British in a period of preponderant British influence in the Orient, he was in the habit of giving the Sultan orders. So the word came to Flag-Officer La Valette that the *Wabash* must depart.

Meanwhile our very able American minister, Mr. Williams, had become a little weary, as had the other foreign ministers, over Lord de Redcliffe's autocratic methods. We were already making the *Wabash* ready for departure when I went with Flag-Officer La Valette as his aide to see the Selemlik, when the Sultan makes his weekly public visit to the mosque. Those who have witnessed this brilliant and picturesque ceremony in later times, so pregnant with meaning to Mohammedans, tell me that it is little changed. The Sultan of Turkey, who is also Padishah of all Moslems, drives from the palace to the mosque between banks of soldiers, surrounded by his brilliantly uniformed staff and followed by some of the ladies of the harem.

When he came out of the mosque he did a very unusual thing, we were told, for so formal an occasion. He came over toward the little group of American naval officers among the contingent of foreigners and, addressing Flag-Officer La Valette, he said that he had heard we were about to depart and he asked us to remain; otherwise he would be deprived of the privilege of seeing our fine ship. As he spoke as the head of the government of Turkey, and we were in Turkish waters, Flag-Officer La Valette changed his plans.

No doubt Abdul Mejiid, who, like later sultans, was beset by European chancelleries and never missed an opportunity of playing one power against another, enjoyed this little hit at the officious guardianship of the British ambassador. At all events, nothing further was heard from Lord de Redcliffe, and the honors of the affair were with the Sultan and the *Wabash*, while all the other diplomats were probably chuckling. When his Majesty came on board we dressed ship most elaborately, and of course we flew the Turkish imperial flag in his honor. He saw to it that we had many special favors shown us. Among others was a trip up the Bosphorus on a government vessel.

I imagine that back of the Sultan's action was the prompting of Mr. Williams, our minister. Moreover, I know that his charming daughters did much to make the stay of the *Wabash* pleasant for the midshipmen attached to her. When I was in the harbor of Trieste on the way home from Manila, a Princess Mary de Ligouri, who lived there, asked the consul to take off her autograph album to secure my signature. In looking over the signatures, which dated back forty years, I saw many Turkish ones, probably pashas and beys, and among the many Europeans those of some officers of the *Wabash*. I looked at her card. Princess Mary de Ligouri! Was it possible that this was Mary Williams, one of the daughters of the former minister?

I sent off word to the consul that, if she were, my barge was at her service; and that afternoon she came off to call. Much water had passed through the Bosphorus since we had last met, and both of us had white hair. She confessed that she did not remember me among the officers of the *Wabash*, and expressed her regret, in view of the fact that I had remembered her. I answered that this was only natural, as there were a good many American naval officers with our squadron, while there had been very few American girls in Turkey in 1858. Though she had lived so long abroad she was still a good American at heart, and she declared that she had fairly crowed when she heard of our victory at Manila, because she was surrounded by Austrians who had strong Spanish sympathies and thought that Spain would win.

But to return to the midshipman cruise and to Constantinople. On the eve of Mohammed's birthday the foreign fleet and the Turkish batteries fired a salute, and many of the minarets of the twin cities on either side of the Bosphorus were illuminated, making a beautiful sight. Before the festivities, which lasted for some days, were over we sailed for Beirut in Syria, with Minister Williams on board. At Beirut we made up a party for a journey overland to Jerusalem, and our itinerary of sights was finally complete when, later, we visited Alexandria and had a glimpse of an Egypt whose backwardness, in contrast with the present Egypt of order and improvement, is an unanswerable argument in favor of British occupation.

Returning across the Mediterranean on the leisurely homeward leg, we were at Genoa when Prince Napoleon arrived from Marseilles on the steam-yacht *Reine Hortense,* to conclude his marriage contract. From Genoa we went to Civita Vecchia, where we saluted the Pontifical flag, which was soon to cease to be recognized as an emblem of the Pope's temporal power by other nations.

We were in the harbors of Italy, enjoying the privilege of onlooking neutrals, when the war between France and Italy and Austria was in progress. Here it was, watching keenly for the news from day to day, that we heard of the victory of Solferino, which was a crushing blow to the Austrian power which the skilful machinations of Metternich had built. Napoleon III was in the zenith of his career. When I consider what a grand figure he was in the imagination of Europe when we fired salutes in honor of his birthday two months after this battle, it seems hard to realize what a small figure posterity has made of him.

In spite of the diplomatic officiousness of Lord de Redcliffe at Constantinople, any memory of this Mediterranean cruise would not be complete without some mention of our pleasant relations with the British Navy. It has been a rule that wherever a British and an American ship meet their officers and their crews fraternize. The two services speak the same language; they have a common inheritance of naval discipline and customs. Exchanges of visits which are ceremonial where other navies are concerned become friendly calls in a congenial atmosphere. When the 28th Regiment of British infantry passed out of the Bosphorus on H. M, S. *Perseverance,* I remember that we gave them a hearty cheer; and as we left the Bay of Naples we played the British national air in honor of the British ships at anchor and they answered with ours.

Curiously enough, it was the summer of 1859 that the celebrated "Blood is thicker than water" incident occurred. Flag-Officer Josiah Tatnall, who had won fame by a brilliant exploit at Vera Cruz in the war with Mexico, and won more later as a Confederate officer, witnessing the heavy fire which the British chartered steamer *Toey-wan* was suffering from the Chinese forts in the Pei River, could not keep out of the fight. Turning to a junior officer he exclaimed, "Blood is thicker than water," and ordered his boat manned, and with his own crew took the place of fallen British gunners in firing on the Chinese.

Afterward he used the *Toey-wan* in towing up the British reserves for the storming party that attacked the forts. This is a service that the British navy has never forgotten. In the trying days at Manila after the battle. Sir Edward Chichester, as we shall see, exemplified the spirit of that stirring phrase of Tatnall's in a manner that was deeply gratifying. True international friendship is best tested in time of trial, and the British proved theirs in 1898.

Aside from the great educational influence of that Mediterranean cruise, it had left a profound impression on the minds of the younger officers in their talks with the juniors of the British ships that the world was on the threshold of a revolution in navy-building. We little thought it was to come in our own land in a civil war which foreigners were then telling us was inevitable, while we, with our perspective dulled by familiarity with the events gradually bringing the cleavage between the North and the South to a crisis, were still fairly confident that a peaceful solution would be found. For two centuries there had been little change in naval science, in which the British had led; so that the older British officers, in common with ours, held that the old wooden frigates and ships of the line were still invincible.

To the French belongs not only the honor of inventing the first shell guns, but also that of putting the first armor-clads afloat and in action. However, in 1842 the United States Congress had authorized the secretary of the navy to contract for "the construction of a war steamer, shot and shell proof, upon the plan of the said Stevens," who was the Colonel John Stevens for whom Stevens Institute was named. This vessel was begun, but never finished.

In the engagement of Sinope, in the Crimean War, 1853, shell guns had been used for the first time. The Russian shells set the Turkish ships on fire and destroyed them with almost no Russian loss. In 1854 the French brought out to the Crimea three armored vessels which were little more than floating batteries. Though they were placed close under the enemy's guns in the attack on the Russian forts at Kinburn in 1855, they were the deciding factor in the battle without having their armor once pierced.

This, rather than the *Monitor* and *Merrimac* duel, was the first convincing evidence to progressive officers that the future of naval warfare was with the iron-clad. The British in their conservatism still hesitated, held by sentiment to their tall frigates and ships of the line, but the French immediately set about building armor-clads which no doubt could have made kindling-wood of the British ships of the line; and for a while, probably, had it become an issue between France and England, France might have become mistress of the seas. In the later period of our Mediterranean cruise, the British juniors were all talking of their first iron-clad, the *Warrior,* which had just been laid down and was to become the pioneer of the modern British navy.

Sailing from Gibraltar on November 13, 1859, the *Wabash* arrived at the Brooklyn Navy Yard on December 16. Two days later I was detached, with three months' leave of absence, which I spent at home in Vermont. Afterward I was in the *Powhatan* and the *Pawnee* in a cruise to Caribbean and Gulf ports, visiting Vera Cruz and getting my first experience of tropic seas and tropic countries. Many of the ships of that time were in command of Southern officers. Indeed, it was charged by those of Northern birth that the South had been favored in the distribution of commands. If so, it was due to the fact that the administrations had been Democratic, and Southern statesmen then were dominant in national affairs.

The captain of the *Pawnee* was Henry J. Harstene, a South Carolina man, who had had a very interesting career. He had once been in command of one of the Aspinwall steamers, an assignment that many naval officers found most welcome on account of the high pay. How completely times have changed! Consider a naval officer of to-day being detached to command a transatlantic liner! It was also a saying that it was Southern officers who received the Aspinwall steamers, while Northern officers had the less desirable billets of running to the coast of Africa. Harstene had won celebrity for finding Doctor Kane, the Arctic explorer, and he later took to England the British ship *Resolute,* which had been rescued from the Arctic Ocean by whalers, receiving the thanks of the British Government and many attentions. He was an eccentric as well as a very energetic man, and intensely Southern in his sympathies.

At a banquet given in Vera Cruz he declared that if South Carolina seceded he would take the *Pawnee* into *Charleston* harbor and deliver her over to the authorities of the State government. Our first lieutenant, or executive officer, Marcy, a most capable man, was the son of the former secretary of state. When we asked him what would happen if the captain started to make good his threat, he said quietly that he did not think that a captain of the navy might disobey the orders of his government to take his ship to the destination named in the orders — and this destination was not *Charleston.*

On the homeward cruise we heard of an overdue merchant-ship which had last been sighted on the South Atlantic coast. So we kept close to the coastline watching for her, but without success. When we were off *Charleston* I happened to be the officer of the deck. Our eccentric captain came on deck, clad, as he usually was, in a crazy-quilt blouse which he insisted was most comfortable. Its appearance bore out his statement that it was made of remnants of his wife's silk dresses, which probably partly accounted for his sentimental attachment to it.

"Take in the top-gallant sails!" he commanded.

I had them taken in.

"Now, set them again!" he commanded.

I had them set. All the while he had been watching me in a wild, abstracted fashion.

"Now, call all hands and take them in properly!" he commanded.

They had been taken in in a ship-shape manner the first time. But it was my business to obey. The summons of all hands brought Marcy and some of the other officers on deck. I have always thought that when Harstene gave the first order it was in his mind to turn our bow toward *Charleston*, and the taking in of the top-gallant sails was in preparation for this. But when he saw the ship's whole crew before him, he realized his folly, for he let the *Pawnee* keep her course.

Leaving the navy at the outbreak of the Civil War, he returned to South Carolina, and later died there; but I have often wondered how Marcy would have dealt with the situation if he had actually started the *Pawnee* into *Charleston* harbor. I am certain that she would not have gone very far. Although there were so many Southern officers in command of ships when the war began, there was not one who did not give in his resignation in a dignified manner, without attempting to turn his ship over to the Confederates.

Returning to the Naval Academy in January, 1861, I took my final examination, which brought me, at the age of twenty-three, through the grades of passed midshipman and master to that of lieutenant, in April. I was now a full-fledged and commissioned naval officer. It seems that I had not altogether wasted my time in festivities ashore in Europe, for in this final examination I was advanced to number three in my class. Of the two men above me, Reed and Howell, Reed was retired as a captain, and Howell, who afterward became a rear-

Lieutenant-Commander Dewey at the Age of Twenty-Nine

admiral, was mentioned in 1897 for the command of the Asiatic Squadron, which I received, while he was given the European Squadron. As I had finished my first year as thirty-third, I was able to report to my father that I had continually improved; and I might say, in view of his warning at the time of my appointment, that I had done "the rest" reasonably well.

Chapter Four - Beginning of the Civil War

After the Napoleonic wars an exhausted world knew a long period of peace, which, until the beginning of the Civil War, had been broken only by our war with Mexico in 1846, the Crimean War in 1854, and the Franco-Austrian War in 1859. This period had seen the development of steam. It had ushered in the great age of inventive genius and industrial organization in which we now live.

As Mexico had no navy our war with her had given us no naval experience of value except that of the mobility of steam-vessels on a blockade and in co-operation with the landing of troops. In place of sails, dependent on the variability of the winds, had come a motive power equally dependable in a ten-knot breeze or a calm. Our older officers had to admit that for expeditiousness in carrying, messages, in getting in and out of harbors and landing troops, steam did have the advantage over sail, and that it was a valuable auxiliary, but they still maintained that the talk about iron-clads as fighting-ships belonged to the realm of theorists and dreamers.

Later came the action at Sinope in the Crimea, of which I have already spoken, when the progressives saw their prophecies fulfilled by the success of the French floating batteries which led to the construction of the first iron-clads in Europe. The naval lessons of the Franco-Austrian War were as insignificant as those of the Mexican; but at the decisive land battle of Solferino rifles in place of smoothbore cannon were used for the first time in battle. This innovation, as vital in arms as that of iron ship-building, was the first step toward the enormous range of modern guns. It remained for the Civil War to test iron-clads in action, as well as the rifled gun, and also the ram. In the case of the ram the innovation was only the renewal of a form of attack of the days of the Roman galleys when the mobility of the vessel had been dependent upon the sweat of slaves. But the ram was soon to become again obsolete. It is inconceivable that with the long-range guns of later days opposing ships can ever survive long enough to come to close quarters, except when one or the other has already surrendered.

There was a saying in the sixties that the men of 1840 in our navy would have been more at home in the ships of Drake's fleet or in those of Spain's Invincible Armada than in the iron-clads of the Civil War; and I think that it is also safe to say that the men brought up to service in such a vessel as the

Mississippi, in which I saw my first service in the Civil War, would be more at home in the Armada than in a ship of the Dreadnought class. The inauguration of steam made naval science one of continual change and development, which it still remains.

It was borne home to the students of Annapolis in my day, as I have already indicated, that the officers of the navy, in its senior grades, should be men of progressive minds and of energetic and rapid action. Otherwise they would be quite unequal to the prompt adaptation of everything which the progress of science and industry offered for their use. At the outbreak of the Civil War our navy had no staff, and nothing like an adequate organization.

Mr. Lincoln had chosen Mr. Gideon Welles as his secretary of the navy. We are familiar with Mr. Welles's character through his very voluminous diary, which has lately been published. It has always been amazing to me how Mr. Welles was able to do so much writing and conduct the Navy Department in the midst of a great war.

He was certainly a man of prodigious industry. His lack of technical knowledge would have been a great handicap, if it had not been for the selection of an assistant secretary of the navy whose training made him an excellent substitute for a chief of staff. Gustavus V. Fox had served in the navy, but had resigned and become a most successful man of business. We cannot overestimate the value of his intelligent service to the country on meagre pay in sacrifice of private interests, for which he received hardly his fair due of honor. To him we owe the conception of the New Orleans campaign and, in part, the building of the *Monitor,* which took the mastery of Hampton Roads away from the *Merrimac.*

Upon taking up the reins of office he found a naval personnel with no retiring age limit; and a state of demoralization. Under President Buchanan, the most ordinary preparations had b6en neglected in face of an inevitable conflict. Our ships were scattered over the seas. Some were on the coast of Africa, some in the Far East, and some in South American waters. The excuse for this was the prevailing naval custom of the time which made the navy a disseminated force to protect our citizens in case of trouble in distant lands, and also to protect our foreign commerce, which then was wide-spread and now, unfortunately, has become almost obsolete. Now the battle-ship fleets of all nations are concentrated in home waters, and the cable keeps governments in touch with any danger-spots, which may be reached promptly with fast cruisers.

At the head of the officers' list at the beginning of 1861, were seventy-eight captains. A few of them, including Farragut, then quite unknown to the public, were men of energy who were in touch with the tendency of their time. But the great majority were unfitted for active service afloat. According to the existing law there was no supplanting them with younger men. The commanders, who were next in rank to the captains, were themselves fifty-eight or sixty years of age. Upper Lieutenants were usually past forty, some being as old as fifty. David D. Porter, who was later to become an admiral, was only a lieutenant. Thornton, the executive officer of the *Hartford*, the flag-ship of the East India Squadron at that time, later to become the famous flagship of Farragut in the Gulf, had been in the service thirty-four years.

Such a system was killing to ambition and enterprise. It made mere routine men to face a crisis in which energy and initiative were needed. No subordinate was expected to undertake any responsibility on his own account. So used were the junior officers — these "boys" of forty and fifty to the old captains — to being subordinate machines that their one care was to escape official censure by any action on their own account. Promotion had become so clogged that, as the secretary of the navy had already put it in 1855, the system was "neither more nor less than elevating the incompetent and then ordering the unpromoted competent to do their work."

If the men of forty and fifty were boys to those fine old veterans of the War of 1812, who had been rendered by age incapable of active command, then we young men out of Annapolis ranked as children. The first requirement, as Mr. Fox so well knew, was a complete and drastic reorganization of personnel, but not until December, 1861, was a law passed retiring all officers at the age of sixty-two, or after forty-five years of service. By this law, disregarding seniority, the President might put any captain or commander he chose in charge of a squadron with the rank of flag-officer.

The next year the grades of rear-admiral and commodore were established and the President had his authority for selection of the fit further strengthened. In this way the younger men, by virtue of their progressive training and ideas and the inevitable initiative, which youth develops in time of war, came to accept readily responsibilities which would have frightened men of fifty a few years previously. With many new ships going into commission, we were very short-handed, which accounts for the fact that I was to become executive of the *Mississippi* at the age of twenty-four.

Aside from the loss in numbers by retirement at the very beginning of the struggle, there was the loss due to the resignations of the officers who saw fit to follow the flags of their States and enter the Confederate service. One can only say that the latter responded to the call of duty in a period when the constitutional right to secession was sincerely held; and that many brilliant men, who must have risen to high place had they remained loyal, knew defeat and the deprivation of honor and pleasure of service in their profession in after years. They took the risk and they lost.

But not all Southern officers held the secession view. Loyalty was stronger relatively in the navy than in the army, for the reason that the naval officer felt an affection for the flag born of the sentiment of our splendid record in the War of 1812, and a realization born of his foreign cruises, that our strength before the other nations of the world, who selfishly wished to see our growing power divided, was in unity. Besides, naval life separates one from State and political associations.

It was inevitable, however, that Southern officers should feel that they would be held under suspicion by the National Government at a period when feeling ran so high. This was a contributing factor in the decision of many who hesitated long before they went over to the Confederacy. Flag-Officer Stribling, commander of the East India Squadron, was relieved simply because he was a South Carolina man, though he did not enter the service of the Confederacy after he returned home. Farragut, born in Tennessee, was one of the Southern officers who not only remained loyal, but of whose loyalty from the first there was never any question by the authorities. In his outright fashion in speaking to his Southern comrades, he left no doubt of his position, and he also warned them that they were going to have a "devil of a time" of it before they were through with their secession enterprise. It is only fair to add that they also gave us a "devil of a time."

Quite different factors entered into the war afloat and the war on shore. The South had soldiers, and it could find rifles for them. But it had few ships, and it lacked the resources with which to build more. Such a thing as offensive tactics at sea, except by the commerce-destroyers of the *Alabama* class, and in its harbors, except by river iron-clads, was out of the question. The offensive must be entirely on our side; the defensive was the enemy's, and splendidly and desperately he conducted it.

Our first duty was the blockade of all that immense coast-line from Hampton Roads southward to Key West and westward to the boundaries of Mexico. As the South was not a manufacturing country, it was dependent for funds on the export of cotton and on Europe for manufactured material. We had to close its ports and we had to prevent the running of the blockade wherever possible. Moreover, a blockade which was not effective did not hold in international law. Never before had any navy, and never since has any navy, attempted anything like such an immense task. That of the Japanese off Port Arthur was comparatively insignificant in the extent of coast-line which had to be guarded. At the close of the war the United States, in carrying on the war and blockade, had six hundred ships in commission.

In the strategy of the campaign on land the navy played an important offensive part which is unique in naval history. President Lincoln wished the Mississippi to flow "unvexed" to the sea. Once the great river was in the possession of the Federal Government, we had cut the Confederacy in two and separated its armies from the rich sources of supplies to the westward. In order to accomplish this feat, which was not finished until Vicksburg and Port Hudson were taken, a number of gun-boats built for the purpose were to work their way down the river, while we of the main fighting force of the Gulf Squadron were to begin our part in working up the river, running Forts Jackson and St. Philip and laying New Orleans under our guns. After my pleasant midshipman cruise, seeing the sights of the Mediterranean, I was to witness a style of warfare as picturesque as it was hazardous and exacting in its hardships.

Cruising in the open sea on the lookout for an enemy whom you are to meet in a decisive battle is simple, indeed, compared to the experience that was to try our nerves on the Mississippi. Here was a sufficient outlet for the abundant spirits of any young lieutenant or midshipman. It was war for us for four years, a war which brought us so frequently under fire, and required such constant vigilance, that war appeared to be almost a normal state of affairs to us.

The leaders on the other side were men bred to the same traditions as we were. Officers fought officers with whom they had gone to school, and with whom they had served and had messed. The recollection of old comradeship, while softening the amenities of a civil conflict, also touched us the more deeply with the sense of its horrors and waste, and brought to its conduct something of the spirit of professional rivalry. Unlike the officers of volunteer infantry who marched South to meet strangers against whom a strong sectional feeling had been aroused, we knew our adversaries well. We were very fond of them personally. To us they had neither horns nor tails. We felt that they were fine fellows who were in the wrong, and we knew that they entertained the same feeling toward us. We did not mean that they should beat us. They did not mean that we should beat them. This accounted for the fearful stubbornness with which we fought; and future generations, who may wish that all the energy spent had not been against brothers but in a common cause against a foreign foe, can at least rejoice in the heritage of the skill and courage displayed in a struggle which has no equal in magnitude or determination, unless in the Napoleonic wars.

On May 10, 1861, I reported for duty on board the old side-wheeler *Mississippi* (known as a steam frigate), on which I served until she was set on fire by the batteries of Port Hudson in March, 1863, when she perished on the river for which she was christened. It was the wonder of her funnels, spouting smoke to make her wheels move, and the sight of her guns that so impressed the Japanese, when Commodore Perry appeared off Tokio with her

as his flag-ship, that they concluded the treaty which opened up Japan to Western progress. From her, Mississippi Bay, in the neighborhood of Yokohama, takes its name.

She was now assigned to the blockade of the Gulf, and her captain was T. O. Selfridge, who was in

The U. S. Steam Frigate "Mississippi"

command of a steam man-of-war for the first time. As yet the blockade was hardly maintained in a rigid fashion. The old captains were so fearful of the loss of their ships that they were inclined to take few risks. A quasi-engagement near the mouths of the Mississippi took place, which was hardly more gratifying to the navy than Bull Run was to the army. The steam sloop *Richmond*, two sailing sloops, and a small side-wheel steamer, having entered the river, were surprised at anchor at the head of the passage just before daybreak by a ram, later known as the *Manassas*, which had been originally a Boston tug-boat. She rammed the *Richmond* and drove the Federal ships into retreat. This incident, known as "Pope's Run," from the name of the Federal commander, was pretty exasperating to the pride of service of the more energetic-minded officers of the navy.

The *Mississippi* saw only the dreary monotony of blockading without any fighting until Flag-Officer David G. Farragut arrived off Ship Island in February, 1862, to begin the campaign which was to lay New Orleans under our guns. From the day that he took command the atmosphere in the neighborhood of Ship Island, which was our important naval base for the Gulf, seemed to be surcharged with his energy. When Mr. Fox had proposed the attack on New Orleans, the most wealthy and populous city of the Confederacy, Mr.

Lincoln had said: "Go ahead, but avoid a disaster"; by which he meant, no doubt, that in case of failure he did not want to see a loss which would be a serious blow to Northern prestige.

After a canvass of all the captains in the navy, Farragut, on the recommendation of Mr. Fox and of Porter, had been chosen for this enterprise, which was to make his reputation. Though there is truth in the saying, "Young men for war, and old men for counsel," it does not always hold. Farragut was not one of the captains whose initiative had been weakened by age. The only criticism ever offered of him was that possibly he had too much of it. But that proved a very winning fault for him. He was sixty; which I, at least, ought not to consider too old, as I myself was sixty, or within two years of statutory retiring age, at the outbreak of the Spanish War.

Captain Melancthon Smith, Commander of the "Mississippi"

In the late seventies, when there seemed no hope of our ever having a modern navy, and many officers were talking of voluntary retirement, I always answered: "Not until the law makes me. While you are on the active list there is a chance for action."

Farragut has always been my ideal of the naval officer, urbane, decisive, indomitable. Whenever I have been in a difficult situation, or in the midst of such a confusion of details that the simple and right thing to do seemed hazy, I have often asked myself, "What would Farragut do?" In the course of the preparations for Manila Bay I often asked myself this question, and I confess that I was thinking of him the night that we entered the Bay, and with the conviction that I was doing precisely what he would have done. Valuable as the training of Annapolis was, it was poor schooling beside that of serving under Farragut in time of war.

Commander Melancthon Smith succeeded Captain Selfridge in command of the *Mississippi,* before the advance on New Orleans. By this time the six officers who were senior to me had all gone to other ships. With their departure I ranked next to the captain and became executive officer.

I was very young for the post, but fortunately looked rather old for my years. Indeed, I remember being asked one day, when there was a question about seniority for a court-martial, whether or not I was older than another lieutenant, who was in fact my senior by ten years. When Farragut explained to Captain Smith that there was complaint on the part of some officers on the navy list about my holding a position higher than theirs, the captain said:

"Dewey is doing all right. I don't want a stranger here."

Farragut, who was fond of the captain, answered:

"Then we will let him stay."

For many trying months I was about as close to Smith officially as it is possible for one man to be to another, and I learned to know and enjoy all his qualities. His was a pronounced character, absolutely fearless, with something of Farragut's grim determination in the midst of battle. He smoked continually, lighting one cigar with the butt of another, whether shells were bursting around him or he was lounging on deck.

In action he became most energetic; but in the periods between action he was inclined to leave all detail to his executive. His hobby, except in the matter of cigars, was temperance. I recollect that he saw me take a glass of champagne that was offered to me when I was in the house of a Union officer after the troops had taken New Orleans. He was puffing at a cigar as usual.

"Dewey, do you drink champagne?" he asked.

I had not tasted any for months, and very hard months they had been.

"Yes, I do when it is as good as this. I don't very often get a chance, these days," I answered.

"If I had known that," he said, very soberly, "I do not think that I should have had so much confidence in you."

However, he made a report after the loss of our ship that indicated that he still thought pretty well of me; and on his death after the war, when he had reached the rank of rear-admiral, he left me his epaulets and cocked hat.

He was also quite as religious as Farragut, who had unswerving belief in Providence as he had faith in the righteousness of the Union cause. One of the stories that went the rounds about Farragut was that once after he had said grace at dinner in his cabin he followed his amen with an outburst of "It's hot as hell here!" The time was midsummer on the Mississippi.

In the course of the preparations for taking New Orleans, when every man Jack of us was hard at it from sunrise to sunset, there was, naturally, some profanity. The men swore over their exasperating task, and I have no doubt that, as the director of their efforts, I may have sworn. One day, when we had a particularly trying job on hand, the captain appeared on deck from his cabin, where he had been overhearing the flow of sailor language. He looked as if he had borne about all he could. He told me to have all the crew lay aft. I ordered them aft. Then he said:

"Hereafter, any officer caught swearing will be put under suspension, and any man caught swearing will be put in double irons."

Having delivered this ultimatum he returned to his cabin. There was an end of swearing on the *Mississippi* from that minute. Profanity in the navy, particularly on the part of officers, was a relic of the days of rations of grog and boarding with the cutlass. An oath by an officer in giving a command, however exasperated he is, has ceased to be a means of expressing emphasis. The crew of the *Mississippi* found that they could work just as well without swearing.

And how we did work! Many of the junior officers were volunteers from the mercantile marine, not yet familiar with naval customs, and many of the men were practically raw recruits yet untrained. In fact, a leavening of experienced naval officers had more or less to act as teachers for the greatly increased personnel in the midst of active war conditions.

The *Pensacola* and our ship, the *Mississippi,* were the heaviest draught vessels that had attempted to go up the river. On account of our heavy gunpower it was most important that we should take part in the forthcoming battle of New Orleans. Farragut already had the rest of the fleet in the river waiting for us to get over the bar of the Southwest Pass when we came in from the blockade. We lightened ship by removing most of our spars and rigging and by emptying our bunkers. With our boats we took a day's supply of coal from the collier each day. Under a full head of steam, and assisted by the use of anchors and by tow-lines from the steamers of the mortar flotilla, both the *Mississippi* and the *Pensacola* worked their way through a foot of mud over the bar.

But the forty-gun frigate *Colorado* had to remain outside. Her crew was largely distributed among other ships. Her captain, Theodorus Bailey, a most gallant old officer, did not want to miss being in the forthcoming engagement. Farragut told him that he might go on board any ship he chose and such ship should lead in the attack, a suggestion which, of course, had to reckon with a welcome from the commanding officer of the ship chosen. No naval captain wants another man who ranks him on board, particularly during an action.

Captain Smith expressed himself very candidly to this effect when Captain Bailey concluded that he should like to go on board the *Mississippi,* and Farragut decided to put Captain Bailey as a divisional commander on board the *Cayuga,* one of the gunboats which was to lead the first division. Thus Captain Bailey had a better assignment than he anticipated, while all the captains of the larger vessels were equally pleased at the arrangement.

Between us and New Orleans were the two strong forts, St. Philip and Jackson, facing each other at a strategic point across a bend in the river where the channel was narrow; and above them was an obstruction of chain-booms and anchored hulks, which we must pass through. Once we had cleared a way through the obstruction we had to face the Confederate River Defense Squadron.

David D. Porter, now advanced to the rank of commander, had brought from the North a mortar flotilla of which great things were expected. It was thought that the mortars might reduce the forts by their heavy bombardment, or at least silence their guns while the fleet made its passage. There were twenty of the mortar schooners, each mounting a thirteen-inch mortar. Porter put them in position close to the wooded bank of the river, quite hidden from the forts, and disguised them by securing tree branches to their masts.

On the 18th, the day after we were over the bar, he opened fire. By carefully weighing the powder and measuring the angle excellent practice was made. All night long, at regular intervals of about ten minutes, a mortar shell would rise, its loop in the air outlined by the burning fuse, and drop into the forts. It must have been pretty hard for the gunners of the forts to get any sleep. We, with the fleet, were too busy to sleep much, but we were soon so accustomed to the noise, and so dog-tired when we had a chance to rest, that we could have slept in an inferno.

Every day gained was vital to Farragut. One day might make the difference of having to face either one or both of the new Confederate iron-clads being rushed to completion with feverish haste. As so frequently happened, his celerity served him well.

After crossing the bar the vessels had to be prepared for the river work before them. They were trimmed by the head, so that if they grounded it Would be forward. In the swift current of the river, if we grounded aft the ship would at once turn with her head downstream. Where feasible, guns were mounted on the poops and forecastle, and howitzers in the tops, with iron bulwarks to protect the gun crews. Farragut believed in plenty of armament. From him we have that *multum in parvo* of tactics: "The best protection against an enemy's fire is a well-directed fire of your own." But heavy gun-power in relation to tonnage was a principle with our navy from its inception.

It was an oddly assorted fleet that had been mobilized for the battle of New Orleans. A year had now elapsed since Sumter had been fired upon, and most of that time had been spent in getting ready for war, rather than in making war. As both sides were equally unprepared, the nation scarcely realized the effect of unpreparedness. How bitterly we would have realized it against a foe ready in all respects for conflict! It was not a matter of building a navy according to any deliberate and well-conceived plan, but of providing such material as we could in haste with the resources of the times, having in mind that we were in the midst of a revolution in naval warfare, when any enterprising development like the *Monitor* or the ram might upset all calculations.

First, Farragut had the big screw sloops *Hartford, Pensacola, Richmond,* and *Brooklyn;* then the side-wheeler *Mississippi;* the screw corvettes *Oneida, Veruna,* and *Iroquois;* nine screw gun-boats of five hundred tons, which were known as the "ninety-day gun-boats," because, with characteristic American enterprise in a crisis, they had been turned out by our ship-yards in ninety days. In addition was the mortar flotilla, not to mention ferry-boats and many other craft that did service of one sort or another. Farragut was always on the move, overseeing everything in person, breathing an air of confidence and imparting a spirit of efficiency. In those days he went from ship to ship, rowed by sailors, but later he had a steam tender.

Admiral David G. Farragut

There was hardly a night that the flag-ship did not signal to send boats to tow fire-rafts. These fire-rafts were one of the pleasantries of the enemy to try our nerves. In connection with the luminous flight of the mortar shells, they offered us quite all the spectacular display that we were able to appreciate. A fire-raft floating down with the current at five knots an hour, flaming high with its tar and resin, would illuminate the river from bank to bank; and if it could have rested alongside a ship for even a few minutes it must inevitably have set the ship on fire. Launches used to throw grapnels into the rafts, and other boats, forming line, would tow them to the shore, where they would burn themselves out.

On the night of the 20th of April occurred one of those brilliant exploits of daring courage so common in the Civil War that they became merely incidents of its progress. Any one of them in a smaller war, when public attention is not diverted over a vast scene of activity, would have won permanent fame. Lieutenant Caldwell, commanding one of the ninety-day gun-boats, the *Itasca,* and Lieutenant Crosby, commanding another, the *Pinola,* undertook the duty of cutting the obstruction across the river above the forts. Until there was a way through this, the whole fleet would be held helpless under the, fire of the forts; while turning for retreat in the swift current would have meant confusion.

During a heavy bombardment from the mortars they slipped upstream under cover of the bank. At times so rapid were Porter's gunners in their work that there were nine shells in the air at once. His object, of course, was to keep down the fire of the forts as much as possible in case the *Itasca* and the *Pinola* were discovered. They were discovered, but not until they had reached the obstruction.

As they had taken out their masts it was difficult for the gunners in the uncertain light to distinguish the gun-boats from the anchored hulks that had been used in making the obstruction complete. Laboring under fire, the gun-boats succeeded in a task which took them hours, and which would have been suicidal had the forts possessed a modern searchlight. It was concluded in dramatic fashion. After Caldwell, in the course of his and Crosby's manoeuvring, had got above the obstruction, with a full head of steam and the current to assist him, he rammed a stretch of chain, which snapped and left a space broad enough for any vessel of the, fleet to pass through.

Chapter Five - The Battle of New Orleans

About midnight on April 23 came the signal for which we were all waiting, two red lights at the peak of the flag-ship. It meant that the fleet was to get under way. We were ready and eager for the test after the long strain of preparation, in which all manner of ingenious suggestions had been applied in order that the fleet might get by the forts with as little damage as possible. Our hulls had been daubed with river mud in order to make them less visible in the darkness. Captain Alden, of the *Richmond,* had the idea, which worked out excellently, of having the decks around the guns whitewashed so that the implements required in the working of the guns could be easily identified by the gunners as they picked them up for use.

And with what insistent care we had drilled the guns' crews in order to insure rapidity of loading and firing! To protect vital parts of the ships from the impact of projectiles, chain cables were secured to the ship's sides. As the *Mississippi* was a sidewheeler we stowed our cables in the coal bunkers, between the wheels and the boilers and machinery.

Though we hoped that the fire of the mortars might keep down the fire of the forts, it was evident from all these precautions that Farragut was not over sanguine on this score. Before the fleet started, Lieutenant Caldwell, early in the evening, made another trip up the river to make sure that the way was clear, and this time a cutter actually rowed through the opening and sounded with a lead line.

The *Mississippi's* position in the advance was directly astern of the *Pensacola* in the first division under Captain Bailey, while Farragut with the *Hartford* led the second division. Our orders were to keep in column, maintaining distance from the ship ahead. It was evident that the ship in the lead would have the advantage, perhaps, of getting well by the forts before she was discovered, while the ships following would be subject to any delays caused by her. Captain Smith, of the *Mississippi,* had opposed trying to make the passage in the night. His idea was to go ahead full speed by day, fighting our way. Thus there would be no danger of running aground and we would know just what we were doing.

Varuna · Pensacola · Flagship Hartford in collision with fire raft
Gunboat Winona · Cayuga · Richmond · Mississippi destroying Hollin's Ram
Fort Jackson · Brooklyn · Kineo · Fort St. Phillip

BATTLE OF NEW ORLEANS, APRIL 24, 1862

"I cannot see in the night," he declared, with characteristic brevity. "I am going to leave that to you, Dewey. You have younger eyes."

He took charge of the battery, while I took up my post on the hurricane deck from which we handled the ship. For a man of twenty-four I was having my share of responsibility. I was also to have my baptism of fire. But I had little time to consider the psychology of an experience which is the source of much wonder and speculation to the uninitiated. When it comes, you are utterly preoccupied with your work; you are doing what you have been taught is your duty to do as a trained unit on a man-of-war. Only after the danger is over is it time to reflect. The wait before action is the period of self-consciousness, which ends with the coming of the first shot from the enemy or the command to "Fire!" from your own side.

Adapting our speed to that of the *Pensacola*, which was without lights, as all the vessels were, we steamed ahead, while the booming of the howitzers and the swish of their shells through the air made music for our progress.

Just as the *Pensacola* drew abreast of the forts the enemy discovered her and opened fire. We were so near the forts that we could hear the commands

35

of the officers. The *Pensacola* stopped and fired both broadsides which at first seemed to demoralize the enemy.

A second time the *Pensacola* stopped and discharged broadsides; and it was soon evident from the fact that the forts kept on firing that, although the mortars might reduce the fire from the forts, they could by no means silence them; nor could the *Pensacola*, which had the heaviest armament of any of our ships, silence them except for a brief interval during the effect of her broadsides. Therefore, all the ships, in order to get by, must run the gauntlet of a heavy fire.

It was most puzzling to me why the *Pensacola* had stopped, in view of the orders to steam past without delay. Either she could not resist pausing to engage the forts, or else there was something wrong with her engines. The latter, I believe, was the real reason. At all events, she did stop twice, which meant that we also had to stop. The *Mississippi* herself was already under fire and returning it, and while my attention was centred in trying to keep astern of the *Pensacola*, I received warning of an attack from another quarter.

Farragut had assigned to us Mr. Waud, an artist for an illustrated weekly. When he had asked for the best position from which to witness the spectacle Captain Smith advised the foretop, where we had a twenty-four-pound howitzer, Waud was an observant as well as a gallant man, and from the foretop he could see everything that was taking place even better than we could from the hurricane deck.

"Here is a queer-looking customer on our port bow," he called to me.

Looking in the direction which he indicated I saw what appeared like the back of an enormous turtle painted lead color, which I identified as the ram *Manassas*, which had driven the Federal ships from the mouth of the river the previous autumn, in the action called "Pope's Run." She was rebuilt entirely for the purpose of ramming, and if she were able to deliver a full blow in a vital spot she was capable of disabling any ship in the fleet.

The darkness and the confusion perfectly favored the role for which she was designed. By prompt action we might put a dangerous opponent out of commission before she had done any damage. There was no time in which to ask the advice of the captain, who was busy with the battery below. I called to starboard the helm and turned the *Mississippi's* bow toward the *Manassas*, with the intention of running her down, being confident that our superior tonnage must sink her if we struck her fairly.

But A. F. Warley, her commander, a former officer of our navy, was too quick for us. His last service had been in the *Mississippi* in a round-the-world cruise. He appreciated her immobility in comparison with the mobility of his own little craft and sheered off to avoid us. But, then, sheering in, he managed to strike us a glancing blow just abaft the port paddle-wheel.

The effect of the shock was that of running aground. The *Mississippi* trembled and listed and then righted herself. When I saw the big hole that the ram had left in our side I called, "Sound the pumps!" to the carpenter, an experienced old seaman, who was on the main deck near me.

"I have already, sir," he answered, "and there is no water in the wells."

He had acted promptly and instinctively in his line of duty. If there were no water I knew that there was nothing to worry about. It was the sturdy construction of the *Mississippi* that had saved us from serious damage. As she was one of our earliest steam men-of-war, her builders had taken extreme care lest the fear expressed in some quarters that her engines, making about ten revolutions a minute, would shake her to pieces, should be justified. She was filled in solid between the frames. The impact of the ram, which would have sunk any other ship in the fleet, had taken out a section of solid timber seven feet long, four feet broad, and four-inches deep. About fifty copper bolts had been cut as clean as if they were hair under a razor's edge. I remember seeing their bright, gleaming ends when I looked down from the hurricane deck in my first glimpse of that hole in our side.

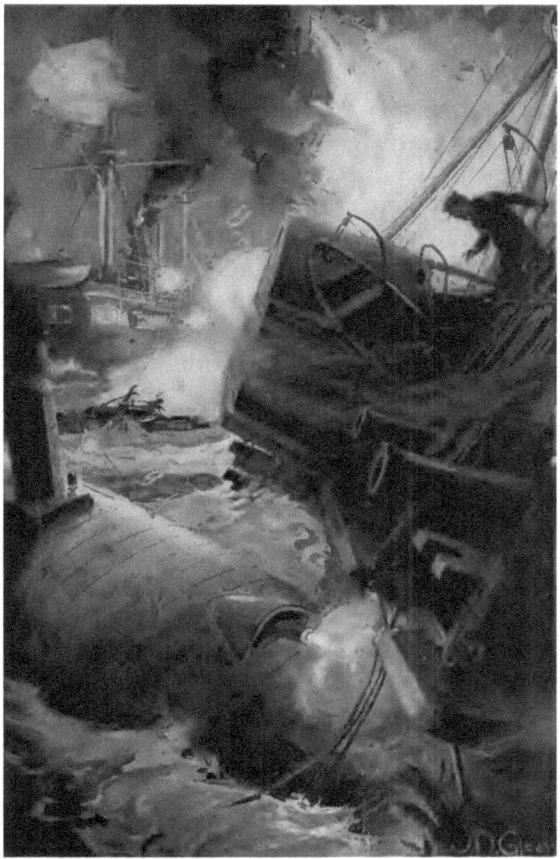

'I remember seeing their bright gleaming ends when I looked down from the hurricane deck in my first glimpse of the hole in our side"

If Warley, who knew just where the *Mississippi* was vulnerable, had been able to strike forward of the paddle-wheel, as he evidently was planning to do when we caught sight of the *Manassas* and went for her, he would have disabled one of our leading ships. This would have been a feather in his cap. But he gave a very lively account of himself, however, before the night was over, and the *Mississippi* had another chance at him.

The formation of the ships in our rear was pretty well broken up. Every ship was making its own way in the melee out of danger. Particularly was this true of the second division, under the lead of the *Hartford* with Farragut on board. When she came abreast of the forts the enemy had steadied down. The prefatory period of bombardment by Porter's flotilla had hardened them to mortar fire; and now they were hardened to broadsides and had the range of the passing ships. So they stuck to their guns calmly and made the most of their own fire. The *Hartford* and *Brooklyn* received a terrific cannonade.

Meanwhile the *Manassas*, like some assassin in the night, had proceeded down through the fleet, greeted by fire from our ships whenever she was recognized, and watching a chance for a murderous thrust. She succeeded in putting a hole in the *Brooklyn*, which might have been most serious were it not for the anchor chains on the *Brooklyn's* side which resisted the blow.

Throughout the passage of the forts fire-rafts were coming down-stream to add to the picturesqueness of the lurid scene and the difficulty of keeping our course. One of these rafts nearly brought the career of Farragut's flag-ship to a close. It was pushed by a little thirty-five-ton tug called the *Mosher*, manned by a dozen men under the command of a man named Sherman. To him belongs the credit of one of the most desperate strokes of heroism I have ever known. It is an example of how the South, with its limited resources, was able to maintain its gallant struggle for four years against great odds.

His tug had no guns and no armor. In the face of certain destruction from the guns of the *Hartford*, he pushed the raft against the *Hartford's* side. The *Mosher's* captain and crew all lost their lives, as far as is known, but they had the satisfaction of seeing flames darting up the *Hartford's* rigging and bursting through the ports, which, thanks to the discipline of her crew, were quenched. But though he had lost his flag-ship, Farragut would have gone past the forts with what remained of his fleet. We may be sure of that.

In passing the forts the *Mississippi* had fired grape and five-second shell from alternate guns. I was surprised to see how well the forts stood our own pounding and also how well we stood theirs. Though the *Mississippi* had been hit a number of times, our loss had been trifling — two killed and a few wounded. To judge by the noise, and the flashes of the mortars in air, and the guns from the forts, and the busy fleet, it seemed as if the destruction done must be far worse than it was.

I remember, however, as we passed out of range of the forts, thinking that some of the ships certainly would not get by. Three failed, these being in the rear of the second division. Of course we were all new to war. Neither our aim nor the Confederates' was as accurate as it was later; for example, at Port Hudson. In time we learned to pay attention less to the quantity of fire and more to the extent of its effect.

From all we had heard we were expecting a hard fight once we were beyond the obstructions above the forts. The Confederates had taken pains not to minimize the reports of the formidability of their River Defence Squadron. But, as so often happens, the enemy in reality was not anything like so powerful as rumor had made him. The big iron-clad *Mississippi* had not been completed in time to leave her dock in New Orleans, while her sister ship, the *Louisiana*, unable to move under her own steam, had been anchored above the obstructions to play the part of a floating battery.

The business of taking care of the other vessels of the Confederate River Defence Squadron fell to the other vessels of our fleet. The *Mississippi* had an individual score to settle. Dawn was breaking and we were just making out the ships around us, off the quarantine station, when we sighted that persistent ram *Manassas* coming up astern in her effort to attack the fleet a second time. The work of the battery being over, Captain Smith was on the hurricane deck with me. So deeply was he imbued with the spirit of ante-bellum days, when officers might be censured for acting on their own initiative without waiting for an order from a superior, that he felt that he must first ask permission before attacking the ram. He steamed alongside a gun-boat which he had mistaken at first sight for the *Cayuga,* the flagship of the flag-officer of our division, Captain Bailey.

"I want permission to run down the ram!" he called to the gun-boat.

Just as we saw our error, while every minute was valuable, the *Hartford,* smoke-blackened from the fire which the fire-craft had caused, and looking a veritable battle-stained and triumphant veteran of war, came steaming by. Farragut was in her rigging, his face eager with victory in the morning light and his eyes snapping.

"Run down the ram!" he called.

I shall never forget that glimpse of him. He was a very urbane man. But it was plain that if we did not run the *Manassas* down, and promptly, he would not think well of us. I never saw Captain Smith happier than he was over this opportunity. He was a born fighter.

"Can you turn the ship?" he asked me.

"Yes, sir," I answered.

I did not know whether I could turn her or not, but I knew that either I was going to do so or else run her aground. Indeed, the *Mississippi* had not yet made a turn in the narrow part of the river, and it was a question if she could turn under her own steam without assistance. But with so strong an incentive at the first trial we succeeded beautifully.

When Warley saw us coming he did not attempt to ram. He realized that the momentum of his three hundred and eighty-four tons was no match for our sixteen hundred and ninety-two tons when we were coming straight for him. As the *Mississippi* bore down on him, he dodged our blow and drove the nose of the *Manassas* into the bank. We fired two broadsides that wrecked her. Her crew began crawling ashore over her bows, and Captain Smith immediately sent a boat in charge of an officer to board and report her condition. He returned with Warley's signal-book and diary, to say that the outboard delivery pipes had been cut, and that the *Manassas* was sinking by the stern.

Captain Smith disliked to give up the idea of saving her. But, meanwhile, the gunners in the forts had found that the *Mississippi* was in range, and they began to pour in an increasingly heavy fire. As one weary gun's crew after another was called to their stations, and their welcome of our return to the scene of the night's activities grew hotter, it was out of the question for the *Mississippi* to remain a stationary target. There was nothing to do but to send the boat back in a hurry to set the *Manassas* on fire, and for the *Mississippi* to join the fleet at the quarantine station.

A little later the weight of the water flowing into the *Manassas's* stern raised her bow so that she floated free and drifted down the stream. As she appeared around the bend the mortar flotilla, which was not yet entirely certain of the result of the night's work, had a few moments akin to panic, and some of the unprotected auxiliaries of the fleet made ready for flight. When her condition was recognized an effort was made to secure her, but before anything could be accomplished she exploded and sank.

The *Mississippi,* proceeding upstream, found the fleet anchored seven miles above the forts at quarantine, and, as we steamed among the vessels, all the crews broke into hearty cheers for us over the news that we had brought. It was then that we saw our *Varuna,* a screw corvette of thirteen hundred tons, sunk to her top-gallant forecastle. But she was the fleet's only loss. She had been the second ship in line astern of the *Mississippi* in the first division. Being very speedy she had gone ahead of us, passing the forts in less than fifteen minutes, and found herself in the van of the whole fleet, engaging the Confederate River Defence Squadron. For a while she was without support. She fought with a gallantry worthy of her impetuosity, until she was finally rammed by the *Stonewall Jackson,* while the *Cayuga* and the *Oneida* coming up finished the work which she had begun by utterly routing the enemy. We saw its results in the burning wrecks of the Defence Squadron along the banks of the river. A broadside of canister had decided part of a Confederate regiment in camp along the levee to surrender. From the time that the two red lights had given the signal from the flag-ship to get under way until we were at quarantine only five hours had elapsed.

The fleet steamed from the quarantine station to a point about fifteen miles below New Orleans, where it anchored for the night. Weary as we were, there was very little sleep for any one, as fire-rafts and burning ships were drifting past us all night.

So far as we knew, the rest of the journey up to New Orleans would be without obstacles and in the nature of a parade. The next morning we were under way early, with everybody eager for a first sight of the city whose location we knew by the smoke rising from the Confederate storehouses and shipping which had been set on fire. Our purser, an elderly man whose place in battle was below looking after the wounded, was standing beside me on the hurricane deck, when suddenly batteries opened fire from both banks of the river at the ships ahead.

"Oh, that rash man Farragut!" he exclaimed. "Here we are at it again!"

But the opposition from the batteries *Chalmette* and *McGehee* was not formidable. Breaches for fourteen guns had been made in the levee walls, which was to become a favorite method of expeditiously emplacing a battery for a few salvos at a passing ship in the Mississippi River campaign. We suffered little damage ourselves, while we smothered *Chalmette* and *McGehee* with our broadsides. Soon we were abreast of the panic-stricken city, where we found that the Confederates had destroyed everything which they thought would be of military assistance to us, including the formidable iron-clad *Mississippi,* which was on the ways. Our guns not only commanded the streets, but also the narrow strip of land which was the city's only outlet except through the swamps.

The taking of New Orleans was the sensational achievement of the war thus far. With the flash of the splendid news through the North, Farragut became the hero of the hour. Succeeding victories could only brighten the fame that he had won. If he had not been a conspicuous captain before the War, probably it was because he had not the gift of self-advertisement which often wins attention in time of peace.

How many bubble reputations of that sort were burst in the first stages of the Civil War! But happily Mr. Fox knew Farragut professionally, and therefore his merits, and he was given important work to do immediately. Under another commander the story of New Orleans might have been different. Success always makes success seem easy. Many a commander could have found excuses for not trying to run the forts or for delay, which would have meant that both of the new Confederate ironclads would have been ready for battle when the passage was finally made. Like Grant, Farragut always went ahead. Instead of worrying about the strength of the enemy, he made the enemy worry about his own strength.

The Confederates had felt that New Orleans was secure. It did not seem to them that Yankee enterprise would be equal to a stroke over-sea at such a distance from our Northern ports. Surrounded by low land, the most populous city of the Confederacy was protected from land attack; but not from occupation by troops under escort of a naval force making a dash up the river.

As soon as it was evident that New Orleans was ours for the occupation, Farragut sent the *Mississippi* and the *Iroquois* back down the river to reinforce the force which he had left at quarantine. Neither the forts nor the iron-clad *Louisiana* had yet surrendered. But the position of both was untenable. We were in their rear and they were effectually cut off from the rest of the Confederacy. Indeed, a part of the weary garrison of the forts practically mutinied against holding out any further.

On the 28th the final terms of surrender were made, through Porter, in command of the mortar flotilla below the forts, which had not, of course, followed the fleet. I had the pleasure of stretching my legs ashore and of inspecting the results of the mortar fire on the forts, I was not deeply impressed by the damage that had been done. The shells had cut the levee bank in places and seepage had filled the bottom of the forts with mud. When a shell sank in this it made a great splutter without much destructive effect. Yet there is no doubt of the moral value of the mortar fire in assisting the passage of the fleet.

Among the Confederate ships was the *McRae,* which had been mercilessly engaged by the *Iroquois.* Her casualties in the exchange of broadsides at close quarters had been very heavy. Among the mortally wounded was her commander, Thomas K. Huger, whose case parallels that of Warley, of the *Manassas*. His last service in the United States Navy had been in the ship which he unsuccessfully engaged. Charles W. Read succeeded to the command of the *McRae*.

Read had been appointed to Annapolis from Mississippi, and was at the Naval Academy part of the time that I was, being in the class of i860. Now, I met him under circumstances that could appeal only to the chivalry of the victorious side.

"Savey" Read, as he was known to his fellow midshipmen, came on board the *Mississippi* to get permission to take his dying captain and the other wounded of the *McRae* to New Orleans. Later during the war he captured one of our vessels, and set forth on a career up and down our coast worthy of the days of Drake. Whenever he took a vessel that he liked better than the one with which he made the capture, he would transfer his flag to her. Appearing suddenly in the harbor of Portland, Maine, which was about the last place in which any one would have expected to see him, he was able to cut out one of our revenue-cutters, but was taken before he could get away with his prize.

As a prisoner of war he had to be quiet for a while; but eventually he was exchanged. Just before the close of the war he reappeared on the Red River. There he loaded the ram *Webb* with cotton and succeeded in passing our ships at New Orleans; but about fifty miles below the city he met the *Richmond*. Though it seems possible that he might have got by her, he ran the *Webb* ashore and set her on fire. He was on his way to Havana, and if he had arrived there with his cargo, such was the high price of cotton at the time, he would have made a small fortune with which to make a fresh start in life. I understand that he closed his career as a pilot of the Southwest Pass in the Mississippi delta.

Chapter Six - In New Orleans

We were invaders and in our own land. I was to have plenty of time in which to appreciate the bitterness toward the Northerner on the part of the people of a Southern city which was noted for its hospitality to strangers. For the *Mississippi* was stationed off New Orleans as a guard-ship for nearly a year. She was thought to be of too heavy draught to proceed up the river with the other ships in the spring of 1862, when Farragut made his first run past Vicksburg. Remaining behind with her was the *Pensacola*.

Moreover, it was important that some naval force should keep the streets under its guns and be ready to assist the army. General Benjamin F. Butler's army of occupation was none too numerous to look after a population that was doing everything possible to hamper it, while no doubt the adult males who were still at home — most of them were up the river with the Confederate army — would have risen at the first opportunity. In fact, they often declared that they would yet drive the Yankees into the river.

One of the forgings of the *Mississippi's* paddlewheel had been broken. We could not repair it and must have a new one to take its place. When we sought to have this made we found that the only place with facilities was the foundry and ship-works that had been constructing the Confederate iron-clads *Louisiana* and *Mississippi.* The owner positively refused to serve a Yankee ship in this fashion. We had to admire his loyalty to his cause; but war is war and we needed the forging. So General Butler was informed of the refusal. He acted with customary promptness by putting the recalcitrant foundryman under arrest, and was about to send him to Fort Jackson, when his wife came on board the *Mississippi* to see Captain Smith. She said that her husband's health was very poor, and confinement in Fort Jackson, which was in an insalubrious location, must mean his death. He had changed his mind and would make the forging now if he were released. She had been timid about going to General Butler — whom New Orleans regarded as a veritable monster — but wouldn't Captain Smith intercede with the general?

Captain Smith said that he had no interest in having her husband imprisoned, and he would much rather have him making the forging than on his way to Fort Jackson. He sent me to see the general, an eccentric, resourceful, determined character, hardly inclined to suavity, who had about the most thankless task that could fall to a general officer. He was in no danger of allowing sentiment to interfere with his rigorous sense of duty. He meant to make sure that there was no uprising against him and that his soldiers were respected.

I found him in full uniform at a desk, with his sword on and two loaded revolvers lying in front of him as a precaution against assassination, of which he was in some danger from the rougher elements of the population. He agreed with the view of Captain Smith; and while he was having a note written for the prisoner's release I remember that he pointed to a chest in the room and said: "That contains all of Judah P. Benjamin's private papers."

Benjamin was then secretary of state of the Confederacy. He afterward became queen's counsel, with an immense practice as a barrister, in England.

I was able to deliver the note for the foundryman's release just as the boat with him on board, bound for Fort Jackson, was casting off from the wharf.

On occasion the general could manifest a good deal of acerbity of temper. Some hitches occurred between the land and the sea forces, as usually happens when the two sister but distinct services, reporting to separate commands, are aiming to work in harmony.

One of the general's cares was sanitation. He was guarding against an epidemic of yellow-fever with a rigid quarantine. The *Tennessee,* one of the men-of-war, under command of Captain Philip Johnson, came up the river, and, contrary to the general's regulations, ran past quarantine. In fact, the ship had been off the yellow-fever-infected port of Galveston on the blockade, but had never allowed any of her crew ashore. And her reason for not stopping was a good one. She was leaking badly, and the only way that she could stay afloat was by keeping her circulating pumps at work. If she stopped her engines the pumps would stop. When Butler heard of this infraction of his rules he sent for Captain Johnson, and, despite Johnson's explanation, broke into one of those abusive tirades of which he was known to be a master.

"I have a great mind to put you in the parish prison," Butler announced in the presence of a number of his officers.

"Oh, no, you won't," Johnson answered. "And, besides, you must not talk to me that way. If your own officers will permit it, I won't."

As a lawyer Butler saw the point and waived the argument on this score, but sent word to Commodore Henry W. Morris, of the *Pensacola*, the senior naval officer present, that the regulations must be obeyed and the *Tennessee* must return and ride out her quarantine. Commodore Morris could be as urbane as Farragut. He was agreeable to the general's ultimatum, but he said that inasmuch as there had been exchanges of visits between the *Tennessee* and the other vessels of the navy lying in the river their crews must also have been infected, and therefore they would all go to quarantine. This would leave the general's force of occupation without the moral support of the guns of the navy commanding the streets. Though he affected controversially not to have a very high opinion of the navy, he had not so poor an opinion of it that he wanted to see us depart. So he allowed the crippled *Tennessee* to remain. She did not develop any cases of yellow-fever.

Butler was so extraordinary a character that perhaps another anecdote which refers to him may be worth repeating. When the *Mississippi* returned down the river after Farragut had anchored his fleet off New Orleans, we found a French gun-boat at quarantine. She had been cruising along the coast, as many foreign gun-boats were doing, looking after the interests of their nations and gaining professional points about naval warfare which would be of service to their naval staffs at home. The French commander asked Captain Smith if there were any objection to his going to New Orleans, where, of course, there were a great many French subjects living. It was quite within his international rights that he should go, and Captain Smith consented. When Butler, who was disembarking his troops and preparing to occupy the city, heard of this, he took a contrary view.

"We don't want the Frenchman around. He might make trouble," he said.

Captain Smith sent me aboard the gun-boat to say that General Butler would rather that she waited a few days before proceeding up the river.

"General Butler? General Butler?" said the French commander. "Oh, yes! He is *l'avocat-general*. He says I shall stay? Voila, I will go!" So he went, leaving the "lawyer-general" pretty angry but helpless.

Our social life ashore while we were off New Orleans was limited mostly to the scowls of the people we passed. But there were a few Union families where we were welcome. The courage of their loyalty in the midst of what seemed to us universal disloyalty was very appealing. In most instances they were families who had recently come from the North and had not yet im-

44

bibed the sentiments of their surroundings. But the true Southern woman would as soon have invited Satan himself as a Union officer to her house. To the Creoles we were loathsome Yankees, and, in turn, we thought of them as "rebels." Confederate was a little-used word on the Federal side in those days.

As an example of our own feeling I recall an occurrence during the visit of a British gun-boat, the *Rinaldo*. She was commanded by Commander, later Vice-Admiral, Hewett. His sympathies, as were the sympathies of so many Englishmen, were with the Confederacy. As New Orleans was now again in the control of the United States, there was nothing to prevent his presence there. It was merely a visit to the port of a country with which England was at peace. He was popular with the New Orleans people, and went about a great deal in creole society, and, in return, gave entertainments on board the *Rinaldo*, at which the Confederate cause was acclaimed, and to which none of the Federal officers were invited. This was somewhat exasperating to the Federals. One day when there was a party on board the *Rinaldo* the band began to play the "Bonnie Blue Flag," which was a Confederate air. Captain Smith sent for me at once and told me to go on board the *Rinaldo* and tell Hewett that that air was not permitted in New Orleans. Hewett was pretty angry when he received the captain's message, but he had to recognize that this time we were in the right. The air was not played on board the *Rinaldo* again.

Later Hewett put his sympathy for the Confederate cause into action. Though an officer of the British navy, he became commander of one of the blockade-runners which were fitted out in England. When our government privately sent word, as I understand that it did, that any British naval officers who were taken serving on a blockade-runner would be returned to the British government in double irons Hewett resigned his command. Many years afterward, in 1886, I happened to meet him in the United Service Club, in London. We had a pleasant conversation without once alluding to the time when I had told him that he must revise his musical programme.

Being on board a man-of-war off New Orleans through the summer was like being in a floating oven. It was out of the question to sleep in our cabins. We slept on deck. I do not suppose that the character of the mosquitoes on the Mississippi has changed with the passage of time. There was a big kind popularly called "gallinippers," which seemed to find shoe-leather an effective means of sharpening their proboscides before they reached the vulnerable part of your ankle.

Our existence was pretty monotonous for naval officers in the midst of the great war. We envied the men on the other ships on the blockade or up the river with Farragut. They were at least on the move, though they saw little fighting. But we had one compensation. While the health of the officers and crews up the river had been bad, we had extemporized a distilling-plant on board the *Mississippi* which gave us pure water to drink, and our health had been excellent.

Chapter Seven - The Battle of Port Hudson

The passage of Forts Jackson and St. Philip had been lively enough for the fleet, but that of running the batteries of Port Hudson was to prove a far more serious undertaking. I have often said that in this action I lived about five years in one hour.

At the beginning of the spring of 1863 Grant's and Sherman's armies were pressing toward Vicksburg. The farther that the Confederates fell back the more concentrated became their forces and the more desperate their resistance. After Farragut had returned down the river in the fall they had become awakened to the weakness of the river's defences and the necessity of keeping open communications with the rich granary to the west of the Mississippi in northern Louisiana, Arkansas, and Texas.

Their natural strongholds were Vicksburg and Port Hudson, and these they fortified with all the guns that could possibly be spared from other points. They had not the facilities that the North had for making artillery. Otherwise, by the plentiful distribution of batteries on the banks of the river where it was narrow and the current swift, the problem for the Union fleet would have been much worse than it was. Efforts at blockade with single detached vessels had failed, owing to the activity of improvised rams and gunboats which the Confederates kept up the tributaries. Farragut's object in trying to take the fleet above Port Hudson was to shut Vicksburg off from supplies on the river side, while the army was shutting it off on the land side.

He needed every available ship for his purpose; and he now concluded that the *Mississippi* was not of too heavy draught to navigate in the river above New Orleans. She was never meant for such work, but we were delighted over the opportunity for any kind of action after the dreary monotony of surveying from our deck the wharves of New Orleans. As executive officer in charge of the general details of the ship, I had aimed to make the best of the recess and overcome the handicap of my youth by my zeal in training the crew of three hundred men, for whom I was responsible to the captain in the same way that the manager of a corporation is responsible to its president and board of directors. We had developed the discipline of a regular force, and certainly, if drill of the guns' crews counted for anything, we should be correspondingly efficient in battle.

On March 14, 1863, we had anchored off Profit's Island, which is seven miles below Port Hudson, a little town that went into history because it happened to mark a sharp bend in the river running west-southwest for a distance of a mile or more. Beginning at the bend was a line of bluffs on the east bank, varying from eighty to a hundred feet in height. On the opposite bank there was a dangerous shoal-point. On the bluffs were heavy guns that could bear the length of the bend and cover this point. They had a plunging fire on us, while we had to fire upward at them. There were also guns at the base of the bluffs. The time chosen for the passage was night, again much against the predilections of Captain Smith.

First and last, the old *Mississippi,* on account of her side-wheels, had been in a class by herself in Farragut's fleet. Now the other big ships, the *Hartford,* the *Monongahela,* and the *Richmond,* each were to have a gun-boat made fast to the port side, which was the opposite side from the batteries. The object of this pairing was the assistance of the gunboat in helping her heavy-draught companion off the bottom if she ran aground. Thus Farragut applied the principle of the twin screws' facility in making a short turn by backing with one screw and going ahead with the other. But the *Mississippi,* being a side-wheeler, had to make the passage without a consort. We had an experienced pilot at our service, as had every ship. He was in one of the cutters under the guns on the port side, where he would at the same time be safe — for his safety was most important — and near enough to call his directions to the man at the wheel. Thus a river pilot had become a factor in fighting a ship which had been built to fight in the open sea with plenty of room for manoeuvring.

Starting at 10 p. m., after the *Hartford,* which led, came the *Monongahela* and then the *Richmond,* with the *Mississippi* bringing up the rear. Possibly Farragut realized that the *Mississippi* would be the most likely of the four to run aground, and therefore assigned her to a position where she would not get in the way of any following ship if she did run aground. The *Hartford* was already past the first of the batteries before the enemy threw up a rocket as a signal that she was seen, and the whole crest of the bluff broke into flashes. Piles of cordwood soaked with pitch were lighted on the shore opposite the batteries in order to outline the ships to the Confederate gunners. One of my Washington friends, Chief-Justice White, was a boyish aide to the command-ing general of the Port Hudson defences. He tells me that the Confederates got the better of us that night, and I must say that I have to agree with him.

The air was heavy and misty. Almost immediately after we were engaged, a pall of smoke settled over the river and hung there, thickening with the progress of the cannonading. This was more dangerous than the enemy's fire, which was pounding us with good effect, while we could see nothing but the flashes of their guns as a target. The *Hartford*, however, had good luck as well as advantage of position. She was at least pushing ahead of her own smoke, while every other ship was taking the smoke of those in front of her. The *Mississippi* had the smoke of all three.

At the bend, the current caught the *Hartford* and swept her around with her head toward the batteries, her stem touching ground. But the *Albatross,* her gun-boat consort, helped her 5ff. Then, applying the twin-screw method, with the *Hartford* going ahead strong with her engines while the *Albatross* backed, the *Hartford* got her head pointed upstream again and steamed out of the range of the batteries with a loss of only one killed and two wounded.

The Confederate gunners had not depressed their guns enough for the *Hartford*, but they did not make this error as the other ships came in range.

When the *Richmond,* the second ship in line, was in front of the last battery, a shot tore into her engine-room. Such was its chance effect that it twisted the safety-valve lever, displacing the weight and quickly filling the engine-room, fire-room, and berth deck with steam. In short order the steam pressure fell so low that she could not go ahead under her own motive power. The *Genesee,* her gun-boat, was not able with her own power to make any headway for the two vessels against the strong current. There was nothing to do but for the pair to make an expeditious retreat downstream to safety.

The *Richmond's* gunners, working in furious haste, intent on delivering the heaviest possible fire, did not know that their ship had turned around. Therefore they were firing toward the bank opposite that from the batteries. Mistaking the flashes of the *Mississippi's* guns for the flashes of the enemy's, they fired at her. On our part we did not know in the obscurity of the smoke and darkness that our ships had been disabled. The *Richmond's* casualties included her executive officer. Lieutenant A. Boyd Cummings, who was mortally wounded.

As the *Monongahela* came along she found herself in the range of musketry from the low bank on the port side, which was silenced by her gun-boat, the *Kineo.* But the *Kineo* received a shot which jammed her rudder-post and rendered the rudder useless. As a result the *Monongahela* had to do all the steering. She ran aground, and the *Kineo*, carried on by her momentum as the *Monongahela* suddenly stopped, tore away all of her fasts by which she was bound to the *Monongahela* except one. Then the *Kineo* got a hawser to the *Monongahela*, and, laboring desperately, under fire, succeeded after twenty-five minutes' effort in getting the *Monongahela* free of the bottom.

Meanwhile, Captain McKinistry, of the *Monongahela,* had had the bridge shot away from under his feet, and had received such a fall in consequence that he was incapacitated. Lieutenant-Commander N. W. Thomas took command in his place. The *Kineo* drifted on downstream, while the *Monongahela* proceeded on her way until a heated crank-pin stopped her engines, when she had to drift back downstream under the fire of the batteries. She sustained a heavy loss in killed and wounded.

I refer to the experiences of the three ships which had preceded the *Mississippi* in order to show the hazardous nature of Farragut's undertaking. His flag-ship, the *Hartford*, and her consort, the gun-boat *Albatross*, were all of his command which he had with him the next morning, and it was many weeks before any of the other ships could join him.

The *Mississippi,* bringing up the rear, was soon enveloped in the pall of smoke. We went by the *Monongahela* when she was aground without, so far as I know, either seeing or being seen by her. Both Captain Smith and myself felt that our destiny that night was in the hands of the pilot. There was nothing to do but to fire back at the flashes on the bluffs and trust to his expert knowledge. It was a new experience for him, guiding a heavy-draught ocean-going ship in the midst of battle smoke, with the shells shrieking in his ears. By the time that the *Mississippi* came within range of the batteries they were making excellent practice. Our mortar flotilla posted below the bend was adding to the uproar. When there was a cry of "Torpedoes!" it might have been alarming had we not seen that bombs striking close to the ship had splashed the water upon the deck. None actually struck us. Some one else shouted, "They're firing chain-shot at us!" an error of observation due to the sight of two bombs which passed by in company, their lighted fuses giving the effect of being part of the same projectile.

We were going very slowly, feeling our way as we approached the shoal point. Finally, when the pilot thought that we were past it, he called out: "Starboard the helm! Full speed ahead!" As it turned out, we were anything but past the point. We starboarded the helm straight into it and struck just as we developed a powerful momentum. We were hard aground and listing, and backed with all the capacity of the engines immediately. In order to bring the ship on an even keel, we ran in the port battery, which, as it faced away from the bluffs, was not engaged. Every precaution to meet the emergency was taken promptly; and there was remarkably little confusion, thanks to the long drills which we had had off New Orleans, and to the fact that all but a few of the crew had already been under fire in passing Forts Jackson and St. Philip.

But no amount of training could altogether prepare men for such a situation as we were in. With our own guns barking, and the engines pounding, and the paddle-wheels making more noise than usual, because we were aground, it was difficult to make commands heard. In half an hour the engines never budged us, while steadfastly and even unconcernedly the engine-room force stuck to their duties. We were being more frequently hit; the toll of our dead and wounded was increasing. Naturally, too, gunners of the enemy, who could see the ship outlined by the bonfires on the bank on the opposite side of us from the batteries, had not failed to note that we were aground. The advantages of training on a stationary target allowed them to make the most of our distress, while the flashes of our own guns and the bursting of the enemy's shells only made the intervals of darkness the more baffling to the eyes. I remember hunting about the deck for Captain Smith and finding him lighting another cigar with a flint quite as coolly as if he were doing it when we lay anchored off New Orleans,

"Well, it doesn't look as if we could get her off," he said.

"No, it does not!" I had to tell him.

Then came the report that we were on fire forward in the store-room. Investigation proved that this was true. The store-room was filled with all sorts of inflammable material and was below the water-line, supposedly out of reach of any shot.

It was not until forty years afterward that I learned how the fire had started, and this from a gentleman whom I met at Palm Beach, Florida. He had served in what was called the "hot-shot" battery. This battery had a furnace in which they heated their round shot red-hot before firing them. When I asked him how they kept the shot from igniting the powder, he said: "We put wads of wet hay or hemp between the shot and the powder." Our bow in grounding had risen so that the storeroom was above the water-line, and one of these hot shot having a plunging trajectory had entered. While we were fighting the fire in the store-room. Captain Smith had given the order to throw the guns of the port battery overboard in the hope that this would lighten the ship enough to float her. But the order was never carried out. He had to face the heartbreaking fact, to any captain of his indomitable courage, of giving up his ship. He had opposed fighting in the night and in the night he had come to grief.

"Can we save the crew?" he asked me.

"Yes, sir!" I told him.

But there was no time to lose. Delay only meant still more wounded to move, with the danger of the fire in the store-room reaching the magazine before they were away. Not once had our starboard battery ceased firing. The gunners had kept to their work as if they were sure of victory, gaps caused by casualties among the guns' crews being filled in a fashion that was a credit to our morale; for it is in such a crisis as this that you may know whether all your labor in organization and drills has had a vital or a superficial effect.

And the battery must continue to fire up to the very minute of abandoning the ship, the gunners being the last of the enlisted men to go. Down on the spar-deck I found everybody full of fight. I remember as I passed along seeing Ensign Barker, now Rear-Admiral Albert S. Barker (retired), sighting a gun. To show what a small detail, even in a time of such tension as that was, may impress itself on the mind, I recollect that Barker was wearing eyeglasses. I had never seen him with them on before.

"What are we leaving her for?" Barker asked. He was thinking only of his part, without knowing that there was a fire forward. When I explained, he comprehended the situation. It was Barker who brought the *Oregon* out to Manila after the Spanish War and who took over the command of the Asiatic station on my departure for home.

The three boats on the starboard side toward the enemy's batteries had all been smashed by shells. The three on the port side were still seaworthy.

We got all of the wounded in the first boat, and started that down the river, with directions to go on board one of our ships. The second and the third, which had some of the slightly wounded, as well as members of the crew who were unhurt, were told to make a landing nearby on the bank and to send the boats back immediately. They were slow in returning. As soon as they were against the ship's side the crew began crowding and the officers had difficulty in keeping order. For the moment the bonds of discipline had been broken. The men were just human beings obeying the law of self-preservation.

I apprehended the reason why the boats had been slow in returning. There was disinclination on the part of the oarsmen who had reached safety to make the trip back. What if the next time the boats did not return at all? They were our only hope of safety. To swim in that swift river-current was impossible. To expect rescue in the midst of battle, when no one could be signalled in the darkness and pandemonium, was out of the question. It would be a choice of drowning or of burning for those who were caught on board the *Mississippi.*

I determined to make sure of the boats' return, and in the impulse, just as they were going to push off, I swung myself down by the boat-falls into one of the boats. Not until we were free of the ship did I have a second thought in realization of what I had done. I had left my ship in distress, when it is the rule that the last man to leave her should be the captain, and I as executive officer should be next to the last.

That was the most anxious moment of my career. What if a shot should sink the boat? What if a rifle bullet should get me? All the world would say that I had been guilty of about as craven an act as can be placed at the door of any officer. This would not be pleasant reading for my father up in Vermont. He would no longer think that I had done the "rest" reasonably well. If the ship should blow up while I was away and I should appear on the reports as saved, probably people would smile over my explanation.

We were under fire all the way to the shore, but nobody was hit. As we landed on the beach I said to the men in the boats:

"Now, all of you except four get to cover behind the levee. Those four will stay with me to go off to the ship."

They obeyed one part of my command with great alacrity. That is, all but one scrambled over the levee in a free-for-all rush. The one who remained standing was a big negro, the ship's cook. He evidently understood that I meant him to be one of the four.

"I'm ready to go with you, sir!" he said. And he was perfectly calm about it.

Each of the others had thought that the order was not personal. But when I called out, shaming them, in the name of their race, for allowing a negro to be the only one who was willing to return to save his shipmates, I did not lack volunteers.

Then in the dim light I discerned one man standing by the other boat, which had landed some distance up the beach.

I called: "Who is that standing by the cutter?"

The answer came: "It is I, sir, Chase" (one of the acting masters).

"Why don't you go off to the ship and get the rest of the officers and men?" I asked.

"I can't get the men to man the boat!" he said.

When I called out asking if they meant to desert their shipmates there was no reply. Then I told Chase to use his revolver and make them go, which he did. It is my firm belief that neither one of the boats would have ever returned to the ship if I had not gone ashore in one of them.

I was certainly as relieved to reach the ship as the men had been to reach shore. When I say that I lived five years in an hour, I should include about four and a half of the years in the few minutes that I was absent with the boats.

As soon as I was on deck Captain Smith came to me and said: "I have been looking all over for you. I didn't know but that you had been killed."

I explained hastily, and added that we had two empty boats alongside, which we might not have had except for my indiscretion.

"We must make sure that none is left aboard alive," said the captain.

Then we began a search whose harrowing memory will never fade from my mind. We went up and down the decks, examining prostrate figures to make sure that no spark of life remained in them, haste impelling us in the grim task on the one hand, and, on the other, the fear that some poor fellow who was still unconscious might know the horror of seeing the flames creep up on him as he lay powerless to move. Meanwhile, we kept calling aloud in the darkness that this was the last chancer to escape. As a result of the thorough search, we found one youngster, little more than a boy, who was so faint that he could scarcely speak. We pulled him out from under the body of a dead man, in the midst of a group of dead who had been killed by the bursting of a shell.

The next step was to make certain that the ship should not fall into the hands of the enemy. Captain Smith gave orders to fire the ship in two places in order to make absolutely sure of her destruction. This was our last service to that old vessel which had known so many cruises, and it was performed while the batteries on the bluff were continuing to improve their practice.

With Ensign O. A. Batcheller I went below to start a blaze in the wardroom, which is both the officers' sitting-room and mess-room and, in a sense, their home afloat, while the rest of the ship is their shop. I had a lantern with me, I remember, and when I got below I looked around at the bare oak table and chairs, wondering what there was that I could ignite. I did not want to delay the boat, and, under the circumstances, as long as we had to go, we did not care to remain in that inferno of shellfire any longer than necessary. I ran into my stateroom, and pulling the mattress off the berth hurried back with it to the wardroom. Then I ripped it open and put it under the dining-table.

When I had piled the chairs and any other combustibles around the table, I took the oil lamp out of the lantern and plunged it into the mattress, with the result that I had a blaze which required immediate evacuation of the wardroom by Batcheller and myself. My mattress was all that I had tried to remove from my state-room. But just as we were going Batcheller cried: "I'll save that, anyway!" and seized a uniform frock-coat before he ran up the ladder ahead of me.

In the last boat, besides the captain, were one of the engineers, Batcheller, myself, and four men. I waited on my juniors to precede me, and then the captain waited for me, so that he was the last man ever to press his foot on the *Mississippi's* deck. This order of our going was carried out as regularly in keeping with naval custom as if it had been some formal occasion in a peaceful port.

As soon as we were free of the ship's side the powerful current caught us and swung us downstream. At the same time, the fire we had started in the wardroom broke through the skylight in a great burst of flame, illuminating the whole after part of the ship. It must have revealed our boat clearly on the bosom of the river, and it was a signal to those on the bluffs along the banks to break into that rebel yell which I then heard in full chorus of victory for the first and only time in my life. It was not pleasant to the ear. The Confederates were gloating over what was the most triumphant of sights to them and the most distressing of sights to us. I remember thinking: "How they must hate us!"

Meanwhile, there was no cessation in the fire, and our boat was a target for the batteries. Not one of the officers and crew, except Ensign Batcheller, had saved any of his personal belongings. All the clothes we had were those in which we were clad. Captain Smith had on his sword, and also buckled to his belt a pair of fine revolvers. He still had a cigar in his mouth, and was as calm as ever. But suddenly he unbuckled his belt and threw both sword and revolvers overboard.

"Why did you do that?" I asked.

He was a man of few words, who made up his mind decisively, and his answers were always prompt.

"I'm not going to surrender them to any rebel," he said. This illustrated very well the strong feelings of the time, which now, happily, have no interest for us except in the psychology of history.

"We need not land, but go to one of our ships downstream," I answered.

At all events, I concluded to keep my sword. Every one in the boat, except Captain Smith and myself, was at the oars, rowing as energetically as if we were in a race. I had the tiller. We were moving so rapidly that we were not hit, and when we were safe around the bend and in sight of the *Richmond* of our fleet, which we were to board in safety, it was evident that the captain had been a little precipitate. A few days afterward, when he was still without a sword. Captain Smith gave my sword a glance and remarked:

"You would not have had that if you had followed your captain's example."

This was said without a smile, very much in the manner of a bishop. The captain would have made a most dignified bishop and of the church militant.

I recollect, too. Ensign Batcheller holding up the uniform coat he had saved, after we had reached the *Richmond,* as a token of the advantage he had over the rest of us. Ensign E. M. Shepard examined the coat and said:

"Thanks, very much, Batcheller, but that's my coat!"

So it was.

Besides setting her on fire in two places, as an additional precaution before abandoning her, we had cut the *Mississippi's* outboard delivery pipes. Thus she filled with water astern, just as the wreck of the ram *Manassas* had in the battle of New Orleans, and with the same result. Her bow was lifted sufficiently for her to float free of the bottom, and she swung around with the current. Her port guns were loaded, and now, as they faced the Confederate batteries, the heat reached the primers and she came downstream, a dying ship manned by dead men, firing on the enemy; and some of the shots, I am told, took effect.

As she drifted toward us a mass of flame, she had the whole river to herself, lighting its breadth and throwing the banks of the levee in relief. The *Richmond* slipped her chain in order to make sure of not being run down. Captain Smith and his officers were standing on the deck of the *Richmond* watching her, while I, with that rebel yell of triumph still echoing in my ears, was thinking of the splendid defiance of the last shots in her guns being sent at the enemy.

"She goes out magnificently, anyway!" I said to the captain, glad to find some compensating thought for our disaster in a moment when all of us were overwrought by what we had been through.

"I don't think so!" he returned sharply.

I saw that he had misunderstood the idea that led to my remark. I shall never forget the look on his face as he saw his ship of which he had been so proud drifting to her doom. Farther downstream she went aground and soon after exploded. Such was the end of that brave, sturdily built old sidewheeler.

It is hard to say whether or not Port Hudson can be considered as a setback for the navy. Farragut himself got through. The affair was in keeping with his character. Though the three other ships failed, the navy had appeared before the country as ready to take any risk. We had made amends for the disaster at Galveston some two months previously, when the *Westfield* had been destroyed and the *Harriet Lane* captured, which had been unfortunate in its effect. Considering the state of mind of the country, the need was for some deed of daring aggressiveness. However, the Navy Department determined to hold in its leonine old fighter a little, and he was told not to risk his ships where it could possibly be avoided.

In speaking of the loss of the *Mississippi,* Farragut said that he was sorry to lose a good vessel and so many brave men, but that you could not make an omelet without breaking eggs. When Captain Smith, who was as serious as Cromwell and withal extremely sensitive, heard this remark, he appeared hurt; for he said, in his sober fashion: "He calls us an omelet!" Far from any criticism ever being passed in any quarter on the abandonment of the *Mississippi,* the captain had letters of praise for his conduct from both Mr. Welles and Mr. Fox. "The noble ship has gone," wrote Mr. Fox, "but the navy and the country have gained an example. However, it was to be expected of him who in this war has done all things well."

In that disaster, as in every action, I myself had gained experience in the midst of danger and confusion when I was still young enough to profit by the lesson. No word of commendation I have received is more precious to me than that of Captain Smith's report, in which he said:

"I consider that I should be neglecting a most important duty should I omit to mention the coolness of my executive officer, Mr. George Dewey, and the steady, fearless, and gallant manner in which the officers and men of the *Mis-*

sissippi defended her, and the orderly and quiet manner in which she was abandoned."

Chapter Eight - Prize Commissioner

After the battle of Port Hudson I had a radical change of occupation and scene. My new duties called for the abilities of a judge and a merchant rather than those associated with my profession. As prize commissioner at New Orleans I had to adjudicate controversies concerning cargo captured on the blockade, and, when I had declared it legitimate prize, to sell it for the government. As most of the contraband was cotton, I became quite an expert in the fluctuations of the cotton market.

The auctioneer who acted as salesman for me, though born in Kentucky, was a pronounced Union man. When he first came to New Orleans he had sold a great many negroes as a matter of course in his business. Though this was not exactly agreeable work, he had not developed any keen sensitiveness about it. Slavery was an accepted institution to which everybody had become accustomed. However, a single revolting and illuminating experience made him an abolitionist.

One day he was asked to go to a hotel to look at some human "property" with a view to its sale to the highest bidder. The man who owned the "property" took him into a room where three girls were seated sewing. The girls, being octoroons and having the peculiarly white complexion of many octoroons, were, as the auctioneer declared, whiter than his own daughter.

"I told that fellow that he would have to get somebody else to sell those girls," he said.

He made up his mind that an institution that permitted such a thing ought to be wiped out. He was not against the South, but against slavery.

As I lived on shore rather than on shipboard, I came to see a great deal more of New Orleans than I had while I was serving on a ship alongside the wharves. The life of the city had now adapted itself to the Union occupation. Business went on quite as usual. Except for the absence of many of the men in the Confederate army, you would hardly have realized that a state of war existed.

With the appetite of youth, after navy rations and that stiff fight at Port Hudson, I was able to do justice to New Orleans cookery, which I found was worthy of its reputation. Never before had I known such good food and so cheap. We had not only the pompano and other delicious fish, but also that delectable upland plover, the "papabote."

My service as Prize Commissioner was relatively brief. Summer found me back on the river as executive officer of the sloop *Monongahela*, which was stationed below Port Hudson, under my old captain, Melancthon Smith, for a short time until he was ordered north, when Captain Abner Read took command. As the *Hartford* was above Port Hudson, Farragut made the *Monongahela* his flag-ship when he was looking after operations on the lower reaches of the river. He lived mostly on deck and naturally at such close quarters that I saw a great deal of him.

He was not given to "paper work" or red tape, by which I mean lengthy written detail in his conduct of operations. I remember the simplicity of his methods particularly in contrast with those of another admiral with less responsibility, who could not get along without a force of clerks. There was a saying that his principal place for filing papers was his own coat-pocket. His was the supreme gift of directness and simplicity in great affairs, so valuable in time of war. Generally he wrote his orders himself, perhaps with his knee or the ship's rail as a rest. I recall that one day when he was writing he looked up and said:

"Now, how in the devil do you spell Appalachicola? Some of these educated young fellows from Annapolis must know!"

A man who had such an important command could hardly have been more democratic. One night I had given orders for a thorough cleaning of the ship the next morning. I was awake very early, for it was stiflingly hot. Five o'clock came and I heard no sound of the holy-stones on the deck. So I went above to find out why my orders were not obeyed, and my frame of mind for the moment was entirely that of the disciplinarian. There was no activity at all on deck. I looked around for the officer of the deck. He was an old New England whaler, brown as a buccaneer, who had enlisted for the war from the merchant service. I recollect that he wore small gold rings in his ears, a custom with some of the old-fashioned merchant sailors who had travelled the world over. I found him seated up in the hammock netting where it was cool, with Farragut at his side.

"Why aren't you cleaning ship?" I asked.

"I think I am to blame," said Farragut, with his pleasant smile. "We two veterans have been swapping yarns about sailing-ship days."

The old whaler did not see how he could leave Farragut when Farragut wanted to talk, and inwardly, perhaps, he did not fail to enjoy his position as superior to the young executive officer's reprimands.

As a rule, no captain or executive officer likes having his ship the flag-ship of a commander-in-chief. But Farragut was so simple in his manners and so free from the exactions due to official rank, that he was most welcome, crowded as our quarters were. Being a companionable man, he liked company, even when he was under fire. I recall a certain afternoon when he announced that he was going in his little steam tender to have a look at the Port Hudson batteries. First he asked Captain Thornton A. Jenkins, his chief of staff, if he would not like to come along. The captain begged to be excused. Then he asked Captain Smith, who also begged to be excused. Neither saw any purpose in an interruption of his duties to make a trip in the heat in order to be shot at. But Farragut was not going alone. He clapped me on the shoulder and said: "Come along, youngster!" which was equivalent to a command to one of my rank. As I went over the side Captain Jenkins said to me:

"Did you ever know a man before who always had a bee buzzing in his ear?"

We went up into the range of the batteries and drew their fire. But as we steamed rapidly and in a zigzag course we were not hit. Meanwhile Farragut seemed to be having the best kind of a time. No doubt, he got the information that he wanted.

It was while serving on the *Monongahela* that I had the closest call in my career. We were steaming up the river, escorting a small gun-boat with ammunition for Banks's army. As I have previously mentioned, all that a field-battery had to do in order to have a little practice against a Union man-of-war was to cut embrasures for its guns in the levee and let drive. The levee furnished both an excellent screen and excellent protection. In fact, the gunners used these embrasures with much the effect of the modern disappearing gun. They ran the muzzle through the opening when they wanted to fire and then drew it back out of sight for loading, with neither themselves nor the gun at all exposed, while our shots would either be buried in the levee walls or whistle harmlessly overhead. But a man-of-war was a big target, and a single shot striking in a vital part might do great damage.

When a field-battery, hidden in the fashion I have described, unexpectedly opened on the *Monongahela* at close range in the vicinity of Donelsonville, Captain Jenkins, Farragut's chief of staff, who was aboard, thought that the only thing to do was to get out of range at full speed. This did seem the part of wisdom. Certainly our experience proved that it was for poor Read. He paid the penalty for taking a contrary view.

"I have never run from any rebel yet," Read declared, "and I'm not going to run now."

So he slowed the *Monongahela* down to engage the battery. He and Captain Jenkins and myself were standing near each other on the quarter-deck and we had fired only a few shots when there was a blinding flash in my eyes. I felt the stunning effect of the concussion of an exploding shell — which always raises the question of whether you will be alive or dead the next second. However, I realized that I was unhurt, and as the air cleared and I was once more standing solidly on my feet, with full possession of my faculties, I saw Read prostrate on the deck, his clothing badly torn and blood pouring from several places. Captain Jenkins was also down. It was clear that the command of the ship had devolved upon me, so I gave the order, "Full speed ahead!" The *Monongahela*, being very fast for a ship of her time, was soon out of range of the batteries.

Captain Read had been mortally wounded and died the next day, while Captain Jenkins had been wounded slightly, but in a curious way. The shell had exploded at a point in the ship's side where a rack of cutlasses was located and had hurled fragments of cutlass in all directions. Although our station on the quarter-deck was some distance from the point of explosion, a cutlass blade (about half length) had struck Captain Jenkins's leg with such force as to knock him down. That nothing worse than a bruise resulted was due to the fact that the blade struck fairly with its flat surface. Had the edge been turned, serious injury would have been inflicted.

When we examined the spread of the shell by the places where the fragments had struck, it was inexplicable how I had ever escaped without a scratch. It almost made me believe in luck. For that matter, any one who has seen much fighting becomes a sort of fatalist. Evidently my time had not yet come.

With the taking of Vicksburg in July, Port Hudson fell in consequence. At last President Lincoln had his wish. The Mississippi "flowed unvexed to the sea." There was no longer the need of any large naval force on the river. I was transferred to the *Brooklyn,* Captain Emmons, which had been ordered North to report to Rear-Admiral Dahlgren, who was in charge of the blockade off *Charleston*, South Carolina.

Chapter Nine - On the James River

After eighteen months of service on sea-going ships navigating a river, it was a pleasure to be back in a sea-going ship's natural element; and I thoroughly enjoyed our cruise across the Gulf of Mexico with our sails spread. Captain Emmons, who had his nickname, as every officer of the navy had, was known as "Pop." He would never get my name right, always calling me "Mr. Dewar." We stopped in at Port Royal, and I recall, as we entered the harbor, that I was standing between him and the pilot when we sighted a vessel coming out.

"Starboard the helm!" said the pilot.

"Port the helm!" said Captain Emmons,

"Steady!" I said.

Captain Emmons turned on me.

"What do you mean, Mr. Dewar, by countermanding my orders?" he demanded.

"Well, sir, the pilot said starboard and you said port, so I wanted to avoid having the helmsman try to do both at once," I responded.

"Steady, then!" returned the captain. It transpired that this compromise in authority saved us from any danger of collision.

The prospect of taking part in Dahlgren's operations against *Charleston* was not altogether inviting to the officers of the Brooklyn. Farragut had fought his campaign on the lower Mississippi with wooden ships of the antebellum type and small gun-boats. There were some iron-clads on the upper Mississippi, but those built for use in harbors where they must stand some seaway were all on the Atlantic coast. It was out of the question to add armor to the wooden ships, as they had not the buoyancy to carry it. At *Charleston* the Confederates had their most powerful batteries. If the *Brooklyn* engaged them it would be pitting wooden sides and smooth-bore guns against the latest type of rifled gun. In fact, ours would be the only fighting-ship in Dahlgren's command that was not armored.

Upon our arrival at *Charleston*, while Captain Emmons went on board Dahlgren's flag-ship to report, we had time to look over his vessels and to realize how suicidal it would be for us to join in any attack on the defences of the harbor. We had an example in the monitors, which we saw for the first time, of how rapidly both the offensive and the defensive features of men-of-war had improved under the impulse of war conditions. Besides the division of monitors with their revolving turrets — modelled on that first experiment which had driven the Confederate *Merrimac (Virginia)* to cover — there was also the *New Ironsides,* that followed conventional ship construction and had armored sides. The combination of the two principles, an armored ship with revolving turrets, forms the principle of the battleship of to-day.

COMMODORE THATCHER   CAPTAIN EMMONS   REAR-ADMIRAL DAHLGREN

Having been executive officer of one ship that had been lost, I did not care to repeat the experience. We were all pleased when Captain Emmons came off to report that it was not the *Brooklyn* that Dahlgren wanted, but Captain Emmons to serve on his staff. So the *Brooklyn* proceeded to the New York Navy Yard to be overhauled before returning to Farragut's command in the Gulf, where she was to participate in the battle of Mobile Bay. Meanwhile, I had my first holiday from duty since the war had begun, which I spent at my home in Vermont.

Captain James Alden succeeded Captain Emmons in command of the *Brooklyn* and he wanted me to go with him as executive officer; so did Farragut. But strong objections on account of my youth were made to the Navy Department on behalf of officers who were my seniors and held less important assignments. As I was now nearer the influence of Washington than when I was directly under Farragut and his great personal prestige, the objections prevailed, and in one sense fortunately for me. It will be recalled that it was the *Brooklyn* that led the wooden ships in past the forts at Mobile, following the monitors. When the monitor Tecumseh was sunk by a torpedo and Captain Alden saw torpedoes ahead of the Brooklyn, he stopped his ship, throwing the column out of formation. Farragut, with his famous call of "Damn the torpedoes! Go ahead!" signalled to proceed and steamed past the *Brooklyn* in the *Hartford*, taking the lead away from her.

My next ship was hardly of the importance of the *Mississippi,* the *Monongahela,* or the *Brooklyn.* I was to put the *Agawam,* a third-rate, wooden, side-wheel steamer, into commission at Portsmouth, My friends explained to me that I had been given this task in organization and discipline because I had made a reputation as an executive officer equal to any emergency. However that may be, there can be no doubt that both the crew of the *Agawam* and the nature of the vessel and of the service expected of her gave me quite enough to do from the moment that I reported on board her, in November, 1863, until I was detached from her, a year later.

She was built particularly for river service and being a double-ender, with two rudders of the ferryboat type, she was as difficult in handling as in keeping ship-shape. During the spring and summer of 1864 I saw some pretty active and trying service on the James River, where we were operating in

The U. S. S. "Agawam"

support of General Butler's abortive expedition toward Richmond, while Grant was fighting the Wilderness campaign.

For about a month the *Agawam* was the flagship of Rear-Admiral S. P. Lee, commanding the North Atlantic Squadron, Lee was another one of the captains who, at the outbreak of the Civil War, was still in the prime of his powers. He was off the Cape of Good Hope in command of a ship bound for China when he heard that Sumter had been fired on. Without waiting on an order from Washington, he started home on his own responsibility, in the conviction that the services of his ship would be needed. He was a man of prodigious and conscientious industry.

Commander A. C. Rhind, in command of the *Agawam*, had earned a reputation for fearlessness in the war and fearlessness in controversy before the war. While in the Pacific Squadron years before, as I recall, he had been suspended by Boutwell, the commander of his ship. Afterward, when his case was on trial in Washington, he posted a notice outside the Navy Department to this effect: "Boutwell is a liar and a scoundrel." Though the Retiring Board dropped him from the navy, he was able to have himself reinstated, and to prove that, however eccentric he might be in time of peace, he could be of great service in battle.

The *Agawam's* most important action occupied her off and on for six days in pounding the Confederate batteries at Four Mile Creek to aid General Butler's attack. On the first day we engaged one battery of rifled guns which we could locate and two batteries of mortars and heavy guns which we could not locate; and we kept up a continuous fire for four hours, until our ammunition was exhausted. But we had pretty well silenced the enemy before we drew off, and on succeeding days we did not have to endure so heavy a fire. The *Agawam* was little damaged, though hit a number of times, and our only loss was from an exploding shell on the quarterdeck which killed two men and wounded six.

In one sense the fighting was the easiest part of the work. The hard part was the life aboard the stuffy double-ender in the midst of heat and mosquitoes, striving all the while to develop a kind of efficiency suited to the tasks for which such a clumsy craft was adapted.

But if the *Agawam* were not much to look at. Commander Rhind surely fought her as if she were a battle-ship. She exemplified the spirit which our naval force had developed by the summer of 1864. We were hardened and ready for any kind of service; and the survival of the fittest, through the test of the initiative required and the hardships suffered, had brought to the front a type of man who sought responsibilities instead of waiting for them to find him out.

When Rear-Admiral David D. Porter succeeded Rear-Admiral Lee in command of the North Atlantic Squadron in September, 1864, he sent for me to become executive officer of the Minnesota, one of the big steam-frigates of the same class as the *Wabash* in which I had made my midshipman cruise on the Mediterranean. But I was on board the *Minnesota* less than one day. Her captain voiced the old complaint about my youth, and Porter not being of the mind to assign him an executive whom he did not want, I returned to the *Agawam*.

But Porter had kept me in mind, and later he wrote to Assistant Secretary of the Navy Fox asking him to assign me to be executive officer of the *Colorado,* of the same class as the *Wabash*. From the outset of the war, Fox had had great confidence in Porter's judgment; and so, in spite of my youth — twenty-seven — I was to have a position which is equivalent in these days to being executive of a first-class battle-ship. Instead of vegetating on the *Agawam* on river blockade duty, I was to be in both actions against Fort Fisher, for which Porter was now making his preparations.

Porter, though only a lieutenant in '61, was most influential by right of his very active mind and energetic personality. He had been partly responsible for having the then unknown Farragut given command of the Gulf Squadron, which Porter himself could not have taken because of insufficiency of rank. It was thought, however, that Porter, on account of his command of the mortar flotilla, which was a new and spectacular addition to our forces, would receive most of the distinction for the battle of New Orleans. Farragut running past the forts in the darkness with his wooden ships became the hero of the operation; though it might be said that the glory was kept in the family, as Porter and Farragut were foster-brothers. It was intended that Farragut should take command at Fort Fisher, but his health, after the wearing campaign in Southern waters which had culminated at Mobile, would not permit. He gladly relinquished the honor in favor of Porter, thus, in a way, reciprocating the favor that Porter had done him three years previously.

Chapter Ten - The Battle of Fort Fisher

We were now coming to the final act of the terrific drama of civil conflict. With the length of the Mississippi in our possession, with every port on the Gulf of Mexico flying the national flag, our forces were closing in on the last remnants of the Confederacy, which had only two ports remaining that would admit of the approach of a vessel of over twelve feet draught, *Charleston* in South Carolina and Wilmington in North Carolina.

Charleston was not so difficult to blockade as Wilmington. While we had some twenty vessels on the blockade off *Charleston*, more than thirty had usually been watching off the two entrances to Wilmington. Even then the runners would frequently slip by under cover of fog or when a gale was blowing. The Confederates fully realized the strategic importance of the position, and commanding New Inlet, at the mouth of the Cape Fear River, was Fort Fisher, which they had sought to make impregnable with all the resources at their command. Once both *Charleston* and Wilmington were effectually closed, then, with Sherman's army swinging in northward and Grant's approaching Richmond, the enemy was literally sealed up and must face the spring of 1865 without hope of supplies.

The plan was to silence Fort Fisher by the fire of the fleet and then to take it by assault with troops which were brought by sea under General Butler. For the purpose Porter had the largest naval force yet assembled. Including every available fighting-ship, it was even more heterogeneous than that of Farragut at New Orleans. Big frigates of the *Colorado* type, iron-clads and monitors, double-enders, gun-boats, and merchant-vessels transformed into ships-of-war, and every one, according to the American custom, bristling with all the armament that it could possibly carry. The *Colorado,* which had an armament of forty smooth-bore guns before the war, now had one rifled 150-pounder, one ii-inch shell gun, and forty-six 9-inch shell guns.

Commodore H. K. Thatcher, in command of the *Colorado,* welcomed me on board heartily, notwithstanding my youth. He said that the ship was in a bad state and gave me full authority in the government of the crew of seven hundred men. My predecessor as executive officer had had a pretty wearing and unhappy time of it and was retired shortly after leaving the ship. There had been as many as a hundred men in irons chained between the guns along the gun-deck at one time. As officers passed along, the men would call out: "Look at the brass bound ---," "brass bound" referring to the officer's gold braid. My predecessor was what is known as a rather erratic martinet. He was harsh, yet he did not secure discipline. I was told that one of his favorite questions to a culprit had been: "How would you like to walk through hell barefoot?" One seaman was reported to have answered: "A dozen times to get out of this!"

Most of the junior officers, as they had been on the other ships on which I had served, were volunteers. Some were highly efficient, others, who had secured their commissions through political influence, were inferior in every way to many of the men over whom they were supposed to exercise command. A portion of the crew which had been recently shipped was a motley collection of flotsam of various nationalities. We were in the period of recruiting by draft and of "bounty jumper" substitutes. While too much cannot be said in praise of the heroism and devotion of the men who enlisted for the war out of patriotic motives, there is little danger of exaggerating the toughness and worthlessness of many who came in at the close of the conflict and, in a later time, helped to swell the pension fund. One glance by a recruiting officer of to-day would have been enough to have rejected at least one-third of the crew of the *Colorado,* just on their looks.

In passing, I think that I may say that our lowest types of men to-day are not so depraved, ignorant, and generally intractable as the corresponding type of the sixties. After all, the world does grow better.

I did not mean on a ship where I was responsible for discipline to have a hundred men in chains on the gun-deck or to have them calling out abusive epithets to their superiors. If the state of insubordination on board had been responsible for Porter's desire to have me become executive of the *Colorado,* then I felt myself bound to live up to his expectations. It had been my experience that only a minority of any crew were trouble-makers. A larger proportion was all on the side of discipline and decency. But one professional tough is capable of corrupting at least two other men who are easily led. It was a case of my being master, or the rough element being master.

When I called all hands my first morning on board, not all responded. It was explained that on account of the cold weather a number of the men would not get up. Certain of the junior officers seemed afraid of some members of their own crew. I went among the hammocks, and whenever I found one occupied I tipped the man out of it; and I aimed to do this in a way that left no doubt of the business-like intentions of the new regime. The men saw that I meant to be obeyed, and afterward when I called all hands all appeared on deck.

Gradually I was able to identify the worst characters. They were the ones I had to tame, and then those who were insubordinate out of a spirit of emulation would easily fall into line. The ringleader was a giant, red-headed Englishman by the name of Webster. Many of his mates were in bodily fear of this great brute. The prison being full, I had him put down in the hold in irons.

One day I heard a breaking of glass and the orderly reported to me that Webster had broken free of his irons, had driven the sentry out of the hold, and in a blind rage was breaking up stone bottles of soda and ale which were stored there. I sent the master at arms to arrest him, and the master at arms came back to report that Webster had sworn that he would kill the first man who tried to come down the ladder into the hold.

Such a situation was not to be endured. I took my revolver and started for the hold. When I came to the ladder Webster yelled up the threat which had made the others hesitate in view of his known ferocity. Of course, any one going down the ladder would expose his whole body to an attack before his head was below the deck level and he could see his adversary. But any temporizing with the fellow meant a bad effect on the whole ship's company.

"Webster, this is the executive officer, Mr. Dewey," I called to him. "I am coming down and, Webster, you may be sure of this, if you raise a finger against me I shall kill you."

I stepped down the ladder quickly, to see Webster standing with a stone ale bottle in his hand ready to throw. But he did not throw it and submitted to arrest peaceably.

This incident and a few others, while the junior officers were developing a new spirit under Commodore Thatcher's wise support and firm direction, soon brought a change over the ship. The ruffians were cowed and we were free of the obnoxious spectacle of men in irons on the gun-deck and of abuse in answer to an officer's commands.

The Confederates had counted much on the weather to delay any bombardment on Fort Fisher. December and January are the season of the heaviest blows off the coast. While preparing for the attack the ships must lie exposed to the seas sweeping in from the open ocean. A gale rose just as the fleet was mobilizing. It dragged many anchors and pretty well dispersed the vessels, increasing the discomforts of the soldiers aboard the transports by sea-sickness.

An act of gallantry of the same order as that of Lieutenants Crosby and Caldwell in cutting through the obstructions above Forts Jackson and St. Philip was to prepare the way for the actual bombardment and assault. An old vessel, the *Louisiana,* was filled with powder and disguised as a blockade-runner, with a view to running her in close to Fort Fisher in the night and deserting her after laying time fuses to the powder. It was thought that the force of the explosion of such an enormous amount of powder would damage the fort and dismount the guns. Commander Rhind, my old captain of the

Agawam, was in charge of the undertaking. He carried it out without being discovered by the enemy.

I recall how we who were on board the fleet at anchor some twenty-five miles from the fort waited through the night of December 23rd for the explosion. Shortly before two o'clock on the next morning we saw something like distant lightning on the horizon. After a time came a dull, thundering sound, and a couple of hours later a dense cloud of smoke swept over us, such as might have come from a volcanic eruption.

The effect of the enormous charge, which was necessarily at some distance from the fort, was negligible for our purposes. This experiment was magnificent and spectacular but not helpful, as both Porter and Butler were soon to learn. Many were of the opinion that it might have been effective if the *Louisiana* had been grounded instead of having been blown up while floating free of the bottom. As it was, the shock was lost in the water and the gunners in the fort were so little disturbed that they thought the sound was that of the boiler of some blockade-runner that had blown up.

At daylight our ill-assorted fleet stood in for New Inlet, which the forts commanded. We were attempting something in the way of formation which this fleet had never tried, but which would have been child's play to a fleet of the present time. An officer who may have been with our squadron entering Manila Bay, with the ships keeping their intervals precisely, or who is used to the manoeuvres of the North Atlantic fleet at the time of writing, can hardly realize the difficulties of securing anything like precision with the utterly inharmonious elements that Porter had under his command.

As we approached the Inlet it looked for a while as if our long column would be tied in a knot. However, it straightened out with surprising regularity, thanks to the experienced officers, each of whom knew how to handle the peculiarities of his own ship. Vessel after vessel in order, if not keeping its proper distance, came into the position assigned it, without any break in Porter's plan.

Shortly before 1 PM., the *New Ironsides*, which was at the head of the first division, opened fire; and at 1.30 the *Colorado,* second in the column of the heavy ships, or the second division, was engaged. Each vessel dropped anchor from bow and stern. Each one practically became a floating battery pouring shells into the fort. For over three hours the cannonade continued, that of the fort gradually weakening. When the flag-ship signalled at 5.30, "Prepare to retire for the night," it seemed to us that we had pretty effectually silenced Fisher. The *Colorado* had been struck a number of times, but not seriously. All the casualties in the fleet that day, with the exception of a boiler explosion on the *Mackinaw*, were due to the bursting of the 100-pounder Parrot rifled guns. These proved to be about as dangerous to us as to the enemy and were not used again.

Meanwhile, the transports had been delayed in getting up. But that night all arrived and the land attack was planned for the following day. Having found that the depth of water permitted, the *Colorado, Minnesota,* and *Wa-*

bash, heavy-draught ships, were the next morning able to approach closer to the fort. We fired at slow intervals, as if we were at target practice, and we could see shell after shell taking effect. It seemed as if our fire must reduce these earthworks to so many sand dunes. With such a long line of ships firing and at such a long face of works; with the air in a continual thunder and screech, there was no time to observe anything except the work of your own ship and the signals from the flag-ship.

At times the *Colorado* would be the target for a number of guns, and again we would seem to have silenced the batteries facing us. But there was never a moment when our men were not doing their work steadily and without a thought on the part of any one but that we had the fire of the forts well under control. We had one rifled gun disabled, and were receiving only desultory attention from the enemy when, under signal from the flag-ship, the other ships began drawing off.

The *Minnesota* and the *Colorado* remained anchored before the forts while the rest of the fleet was passing out of range. Suddenly the batteries concentrated on us. Our capstan was shot away; a 10-inch solid shot penetrated the starboard side, carrying away the lock and screw of No. 4 gun, killing one man and wounding five men, and carrying away the axle and starboard truck of No. 5 gun on the port side.

It was a time for quick thinking on the bridge. We had been told to discontinue action, but not to withdraw; and it was out of the question to endure that grilling fire in which we were being repeatedly hit. For an instant the alternative of slipping anchors and steaming away was considered by Commodore Thatcher, but that meant retreat without orders and possibly having our decision misconstrued, while we should be heavily pounded in the very act of retiring. We had silenced those guns that were barking at us once and we could do it again, the commodore concluded. As senior officer present he signalled the *Minnesota* to fire for her own protection, and repeated to the flag-ship the reason why we were opening fire contrary to orders. I ran along the gun-deck, where I found the men chafing in their inaction or astounded and apprehensive over the damage that was being wrought, and I kept calling: "Fire! Fire as fast as you can! That is the way to stop their fire!"

Our gun crews obeyed with the avidity of desperation. Occupation with their work gave them no time to consider the effect of the enemy's shells, to which our guns blazed in answer with telling accuracy. The batteries found out that we were anything but disabled, and they were silent when the signal from the flag-ship came, this time not to discontinue but to retire from action. These few minutes of splendid and effective gunnery developed a fine spirit in the whole ship. We. steamed out of range with the satisfaction of the victor amid the cheers of the fleet.

All day we had been watching in vain for signs of the approach of the army's assaulting force over the sand dunes. When we received orders that night to proceed to our base at Beaufort we knew that Fort Fisher was not to be ours this time. Butler had decided that the fire of the fleet had not done the fort enough damage to make the assault practicable; and after all the powder we had burned he returned with his troops on board his transports.

It is not for me to go into the details of an old controversy; but the fact remains that three weeks later another assault did succeed after the defences of Fort Fisher had been considerably strengthened. The upshot was not an altogether felicitous ending of Butler's military career, and its lesson would seem to be that the thing to do when your country expects you to attack is to attack.

While Porter was continuing the blockade he sent any vessels not needed for this purpose to Beaufort for ammunition, and asked for further instructions. Their character at that stage of the war was inevitable. Gentle and patient as President Lincoln was, he

U. S. S. Colorado

had indomitable firmness on occasion. Only four days after Butler had withdrawn with his transports. Porter had a message from the secretary of the navy that Lieutenant-General Grant would send immediately "a competent force, properly commanded," to undertake the assault in which Butler had failed.

"Properly commanded" meant the choice of Major-General A. H. Terry. While we mobilized at Beaufort and waited for his coming we labored in heavy weather getting coal and ammunition on board and a second time going through the details of making ready for bombardment. We were practically at anchor in the open sea, with the breakers rolling in from thousands of miles. Some of the heavy transports rode out a gale in the company of the men-of-war. But no accident occurred and no appreciable delay in the preparations.

The fact that the Confederates had boasted of a victory after Butler's withdrawal — though they had not sunk a single vessel and had inflicted but few casualties and little damage, while our troops had not attempted an assault — aroused in both our army and navy the determination to wipe out such an impression promptly. On the 12th of January we sailed from our base at Beaufort, forty-eight men-of-war in all, escorting the numerous army transports. That night we anchored within twelve miles of the fort. The next day we proceeded to take up our old positions. As the smaller ships were ahead, they received a vigorous fire until the heavier ships came up, when their powerful armament soon drove the Confederate gunners into their bomb-proofs. Meanwhile Terry's troops had been put ashore. This time there was no question of discretion on the part of the army commander. Fort Fisher was to be taken at any cost.

As darkness fell, the fleet was pouring out ammunition without stint. A breeze rising lifted the pall of smoke, revealing the fort clearly, lighted by the flashes of our shells. At 9 a. m. the next morning, the 14th, the signal came from the flag-ship, which meant that all was ready to carry out the plan that had been arranged between Porter and Terry. While the troops assaulted on the land side, a force of sixteen hundred sailors and marines were to assault the sea face of the fort. Every ship sent its quota. As executive officer, I should have been in command of the Colorado's force, but, despite my plea, Commodore Thatcher would not let me go. Being the senior officer present after Porter, if anything should happen to Porter the command of the fleet would fall to him and, in consequence, the command of the ship to me. In view of such an eventuality I was ordered to remain on board, much to my disgust.

The *Colorado's* part during the day was the same as that at the previous bombardment. We joined the other ships in pounding the batteries as hard as we could with all our guns. How terrific that bombardment was may be realized when I say that in the two days Porter's fleet discharged against Fort Fisher over eighteen thousand shells.

This time we did not have to watch in vain for signs of the assaulting force. We could see very clearly the naval detachment which had landed under the face of the fort. The seamen were to make the assault, while the marines covered their advance by musketry from the trenches which they had thrown up. For weapons the seamen had only cutlasses and revolvers, which evidently were chosen with the idea that storming the face of the strongest work in the Civil War was the same sort of operation as boarding a frigate in 1812. Such an attempt was sheer, murderous madness. But the seamen had been told to go and they went.

In face of a furious musketry fire which they had no way of answering they rushed to within fifty yards of the parapet. Three times they closed up their shattered ranks and attempted another charge. but could gain little more ground. How Flag Captain Breeze, who was in command, leading his men and waving his sword, escaped death, is one of those marvels that almost make one accept the superstition that some men do lead a charmed life.

Our losses in the assault in officers alone were four killed and fourteen wounded, which is proof enough of how unhesitatingly they exposed themselves, following Breeze's example. The falling figures of the killed and wounded and the desperate rallies of the living were as clear as stage pantomime to their shipmates on board the fleet, who witnessed a piece of splendid folly of the same order as the charge of the Light Brigade, in which, however, it was not a case of one wild ride but of repeated attempts at the impossible. We may be proud of the heroism, if not of the wisdom, of the naval landing force's assault on Fort Fisher, which, no doubt, did serve some purpose in holding the enemy's attention while the army pressed in from the rear.

We had glimpses of the blue figures of the soldiers as they progressed in taking the outer defences, finally storming their way into the works themselves with a gallantry and precision in the face of heavy losses which would not be gainsaid. Soon after nightfall the last shot in resistance was fired from the fort. The fleet sent up rockets celebrating the victory won by an attack which must stand high in history, both for its skill and its courage. Indeed, the manner in which Major-General Terry had conducted the whole operation was significant of the efficiency of the officers and men of the veteran army which was the instrument with which Grant won peace at last.

What Appomattox was for the Federal army, Fort Fisher was for the Federal navy. Professionally the war had meant nearly four years' training for me as an executive officer. Had I had my choice of experience, it could not have been better in its training for command. I knew the business of being the responsible executive of a large crew on a big ship, with my work subject to the direction of an older head.

Soon after Fort Fisher Commodore Thatcher was relieved from the *Colorado* and promoted to acting rear-admiral to relieve Farragut in command of the Gulf Squadron. He wished me to go with him as his chief of staff, but I was only about to receive my promotion as lieutenant-commander, and the Navy Department again found my youth an obstacle. And my youth in the eyes of Captain R. H. Wyman, who took Thatcher's place, also made me inacceptable to him as executive. In six months after I left the *Colorado,* however, she had lost a hundred men by desertion. A sort of left-handed promotion took me to the *Kearsarge,* the victor over the *Alabama,* as executive, and I was on board her on that happy day for the Union cause when we dressed ship in honor of the surrender of Lee to Grant.

Chapter Eleven - Service After the War

With the war over, the officers and men of the navy were entitled to a holiday. The European Squadron was re-established. We crossed the Atlantic with the prestige of veteran ships and a veteran personnel which had revolutionized naval warfare. Our presence in European waters once we spoke for a united country again — after all the vicissitudes of the four years during which the blockade had developed hostility both in England and France — could not help having an international significance. If not regarded with affection, we were regarded with respect and interest. Our officers were given leave of absence which enabled them to see the capitals; and in many other ways the service was most agreeable.

After being with the *Kearsarge* for nearly a year I became executive officer of the *Canandaigua.* Then Rear-Admiral Goldsborough, commanding the European Squadron, who as captain had been superintendent the first year that I was at Annapolis, took me as his flag-lieutenant, giving me my first staff experience. When the executive officer of the *Colorado* in which I had served at Fort Fisher, was detached, the admiral, who had always had a fondness for me, I think, on account of the fight in the messroom, said:

"Now is your chance! Take the *Colorado* and make a man-of-war of her."

So I had my old ship from which I had been detached because of my youth at the instance of Commodore Thatcher's successor, after I had seen her through a battle. There had been friction between her captain and her executive, and discipline was at a low ebb. However, it was soon restored. Thus, from 1862 to 1867, I had been executive officer of no less than nine ships.

Among the officers on the *Colorado* was Lieutenant-Commander William T. Sampson, afterward commander of the North Atlantic Squadron in the Spanish War, with whom I formed a life-long friendship. Nature had been kind to Sampson. Not only had he a most brilliant mind and the qualities of a practical and efficient officer on board ship, but he was, in those days of his youth, one of the handsomest men I have ever seen, with a bearing at once modest and dignified. Already he was a marked man among his fellow-officers, who, in a profession which is so strictly technical, are the best judges of a *confrère's* abilities. As a mess companion he was an inspiration, and many were the professional discussions we had, now agreeing and now disagreeing with equal earnestness. As young men we were looking ahead to the future developments of naval science which had been given such an impetus from '61 to '65, while we still enjoyed the traditions of the old sailing-ship days, and frequently, in passage from port to port, had the *Colorado* under full sail, while our engines were silent.

Altogether I was in European waters over two years. About a week before the *Colorado* was to start for home, when the whole squadron was in the harbor of Cherbourg, the *Franklin* came in, bearing the four-starred flag of Admiral Farragut, whose forthcoming cruise in European waters was to be a triumphal progress. His was now the great naval name of the world.

He was sixty-six years old. He seemed as lively as in the days on the Mississippi, and we thought that he would live to hale old age to enjoy the honors he had so deservedly won. When he came on board the Colorado with his staff, he was received with all the pomp of his rank, including airs by our band of thirty-two pieces, which had no equal in the navy. He went all over the ship, inspecting every detail, and made no concealment of his delight over what he saw. Before going, he turned to Captain Pennock, his brother-in-law, who was captain of the *Franklin*, and said:

"Pennock, I want the *Franklin* to be just like this."

European hospitality was harder on his health than the Mississippi campaign, and after that tour of many ports with continual social functions, when he returned home everybody remarked that he was rapidly failing. His last cruise was from Norfolk to Portsmouth. Though he was in his cabin and scarcely able to rise, when a man-of-war passed and saluted his flag he felt it his duty to put on his uniform and go on deck. That was the last time that his flag was ever saluted at sea. He died in the commandant's house at Portsmouth. Not long before his death my father-in-law and I called on him. It was a shock to see how pale and thin he had become. Yet, ill as he was, he retained his old-time cheerful manner, which had ever endeared him to his subordinates. Many years afterward I had the pleasure of unveiling a bronze tablet to his memory in the house where he died.

In September, 1867, soon after the *Colorado* was back in the Brooklyn Navy Yard, I was detached and ordered to the Naval Academy in charge of the fourth class of midshipmen and in general charge of the ships stationed there. This was my first assignment to shore duty, excepting the short period as prize commissioner in New Orleans, for nine years, or since 1858, when I started on my midshipman cruise on the *Wabash*.

A month after receiving my orders I was married in Portsmouth, N. H., to Susan Boardman Goodwin, daughter of ex-Governor Goodwin, of New Hampshire; and so I took my bride to Annapolis, where I spent three happy years. There were a great many other young officers and their brides at that station. David D. Porter, then vice-admiral, was superintendent, and he was as fond of spirit in social functions as in war. There was so much gayety that one cynical officer referred to the institution as "Porter's Dancing Academy." However, Porter's great reputation left him free of any imputation of having the frivolous side of his nature overdeveloped at the expense of any other. Few men whom I have known had such a buoyantly irrepressible, active temperament as he. His mind seemed equally resourceful in a battle or at a reception.

During my first year the midshipmen lived on board the training-ships stationed at Annapolis, which included the brave old *Constitution*. Their quarters were stuffy, and, on account of poor ventilation, were no place for growing boys who needed plenty of fresh air. The next year, however, they lived in the new building, which was much better for them, while they still might drill as seamen on board ship and know life in ship's quarters on cruises.

Porter was succeeded during the last year of my stay at Annapolis by Rear-Admiral John L, Worden, who made me his aide in addition to my other duties. Neither Porter nor Worden was a graduate of Annapolis. As the Academy had been established only twenty-two years, no graduate as yet had enough rank to be superintendent.

Worden was a positive character, in keeping with the determined way that he fought, not only the *Monitor* in the famous action against the *Merrimac*, but also the other ships intrusted to his command during the war. In common with many of the older officers, he was not yet convinced that the academic schooling of Annapolis was a wiser system in giving future officers a groundwork than the old-fashioned system of apprenticeship on board ship while actually cruising. I recollect that one day, when I was at work at a desk in his office, he had a midshipman up for some infraction of discipline, and he broke out:

"Where you ought to be, young man, is not ashore in a landsman's school, but right on board ship, where you would learn the business of being a seaman in the same hard school that I learned it."

At this, well knowing the admiral's views on the score, which were often repeated, the midshipman grinned slightly, perhaps unconsciously.

"Don't you grin at me or I will throw you out of the window!" Worden blazed.

The midshipman's face went very stiff and sober at such a "dressing down" from the autocrat of Annapolis and one of the great heroes of the war. For some reason I myself could not resist a smile at the situation, and the admiral caught me at it, too. For a minute I did not know but he might try to throw me out of the window. However, he controlled his temper and said nothing.

Upon leaving the Naval Academy I had my first regular command, though on various occasions I had been acting commander of a vessel in the regular commander's absence. I was given the *Narragansett*, a third-class sloop. I had spent three months on board her in New York harbor without orders to go to sea when I was transferred to the *Supply,* one of three naval vessels that had been detailed to take supplies contributed by the American public to the relief of the French who had suffered privations in the siege of Paris. She was an antiquated storeship of a little over five hundred tons burden.

As we had to cross the Atlantic under sail, the relief we carried was not very expeditious, to say the least. When we arrived at Havre we found the wharves piled with supplies which were neglected, as at that time Paris was in the throes of the Commune. A telegram from the committee in charge of delivering the stores instructed me to take them to London, where they could be sold and the proceeds distributed to better advantage than if I landed them. So I took the *Supply* up the Thames to the London docks, where I turned my cargo over to the committee, consisting of the American minister, Mr. Junius S. Morgan, Mr. Charles Marshall, the banker, and Mr. Charles Lanier. I spent a delightful month in London with my friend Francis Blake, a banker, who had formerly been in the navy.

Upon my return I was at the Boston Navy Yard for a few months, and then was sent to the naval torpedo station at Newport. Here, on December 23, 1872, my son, George Goodwin Dewey, was born. The death of his mother occurred five days later, and in the following February I was detached from a station which was ever to have sad associations for me.

While at Newport I had received my promotion as commander, and now, in the spring of 1873, 1 was given the *Narragansett* again. She was in Panama Bay, where I joined her, and with her I spent over two years surveying the peninsula of Lower California and the coast of Mexico as far as Cape Corrientes. The charts which we made are still in use.

We were in the Gulf of California when the newspapers arrived with word of the *Virginius* affair. Resentment against Spain was so strong in the United States that war seemed inevitable. Going into the wardroom, I found the officers sitting about in various attitudes of despondency. Among them was Ensign, now Rear-Admiral, Badger, who remembers the conversation very well. I asked them why they were so blue. They said that there was to be war with Spain and, marooned thousands of miles from home, they would be entirely out of it.

"On the contrary, we shall be very much in it," I said. "If war with Spain is declared, the *Narragansett* will take Manila."

I had always been interested in the Philippine Islands and had read whatever books I could find relating to them, and my familiarity with the subject immediately suggested them as a logical point of attack. If the inevitable conflict with Spain had come then, it is possible that I should have enjoyed the same privilege that was to be mine twenty-five years later.

The *Narragansett* frequently took refuge in the hurricane anchorage at La Paz, usually for the purpose of working up our charts and refitting ship. On these occasions I often visited the silver mines located at Triunfo in the interior, about forty miles from La Paz. These mines were owned and managed by Americans, who also filled all the subordinate positions requiring expert knowledge. The heavy labor was done by Mexicans, some five or six hundred being employed. Mr. Brook, the manager, was most hospitable. I was made to feel very much at home at his residence at the mines, and enjoyed many delightful rides from that point as a base, in company with him and his ten-year-old son.

While the *Narragansett* was lying in La Paz harbor, delayed by bad weather beyond her expected sailing date, a messenger from the mines brought on board a note from Mr. Brook. The note was obviously written in great haste and stated that the Mexicans at the mines had risen against the Americans and were besieging them in their compound and threatening to massacre the entire colony. Appeals for relief had been sent to the governor at La Paz, but without result. Mr. Brook was writing to me, he said, in the faint hope that my ship might still be in port. He begged me to take some action promptly if his note reached me, as he could not hope to hold out much longer.

The governor of the district, whose head-quarters were at La Paz, was a brigadier-general in the Mexican army, and a rather domineering character, I had inferred from my previous associations with him. He had under his immediate command In La Paz about one hundred regular Mexican troops. The *Narragansett*'s landing force was very small. I realized that there would be little promise of any result other than catastrophe if I should endeavor to despatch such a small body through forty miles of hostile country, leaving between themselves and their base a force of the enemy so greatly superior in numbers as the Mexican guard in La Paz. It was obvious that other tactics were demanded.

I sent for my executive officer. Lieutenant George C. Reiter, now a rear-admiral on the retired list, and directed him to call at once upon the governor in company with our consul, and convey to him my request that he despatch troops immediately to the relief of the beleaguered American colony at the mines. He was to state further to the governor that, in the event of failure to act promptly and effectively in compliance with my request, I should take possession of the city and the custom-house and should retain possession at least pending instructions from my government. With the mail facilities at that time, certainly two months would elapse before such instructions could reach me from Washington, a fact well known to his Excellency. Mr. Reiter lost no time in getting ashore, nor did my message to the governor lose any of its force in transmission.

The governor expressed astonishment and some petulance. He exclaimed:

"Why does your government send irresponsible boys in command of its ships to foreign ports? "

At the time I was thirty-six years old, and therefore not exactly a boy.

Mr. Reiter assured him that I meant literally every word that I had said. The governor, looking from his window, observed that the *Narragansett* had just completed a shift of anchorage to a location commanding the main street of the city, his own official residence, and the custom-house. He sent word, and kept it, that the troops would be despatched immediately and that I need have no further apprehensions.

Some months later I received from the Navy Department a clipping from a New York newspaper' with head-lines announcing, "The right man in the right place," and text which narrated in laudatory terms the foregoing incident. The clipping was pasted on a sheet of official note-paper and followed by a written line: "The Department still awaits your report on this subject." In reply I informed the department exactly what had happened and stated that I had not considered it of sufficient importance to be made the subject of a report. I awaited the department's comment with some anxiety. When it came, however, it was to the effect that my action was fully approved.

Two years in the Gulf of California means practical isolation; and surveying in that hot climate, as we used to keep at it from dawn to dark, was hard work. It was with the pleasant anticipation of seeing my little son and the home country that I received my orders detaching me from the *Narragansett* in the spring of 1875.

Chapter Twelve - Building the New Navy

In the long period of inertia for our navy after the Civil War, while the country took no interest in its defences and our ships did little cruising, officers saw relatively a great deal of shore duty. Nearly every officer of this time was, sooner or later, connected in one capacity or another with the light-house service.

After two years as light-house inspector for the second district, with headquarters at Boston, in April, 1878, I was made naval secretary of the light-house board. This was my first tour of duty with residence in Washington. Major Peter C. Hains, of the engineer corps, was the army secretary, while the other members were two army and two naval officers, and three civilians, including Professor Henry, secretary of the Smithsonian Institution, a scientist of high repute in his day, to whom many gave the priority of credit for the invention of the magnetic telegraph.

Among the questions that came up for settlement was the substitution of mineral for lard oil in the lamps. Professor Henry favored lard oil, which cost about seventy-five cents a gallon, while mineral oil cost eight cents. Major Hains and myself were for the innovation, which was accepted after we had convinced the professor by practical demonstration that mineral oil was the cheaper and really the better illuminant. We saw electric lights used in the large sea-coast light-houses for the first time; the introduction of gas-lighted buoys, which were already in use in Europe; and we changed the system of paying the employees (which had been a source of dissatisfaction) from that of orders on the collectors of customs to the simple one of direct payment by the inspectors.

This position of naval secretary I held for the usual term of four years, beginning in the administration of President Hayes, and extending through the brief administration of President Garfield and the first year of President Arthur's. I found myself in Washington social life, with its round of dinners and receptions, which were a new and enjoyable experience to me, if exhausting physically. Among statesmen Blaine and Conkling were at the height of their careers; Grant's candidacy for a third term developed and failed; and Admiral Porter and General Sherman, whom I frequently met, were still living.

With the passage of time I had lost none of a Vermonter's fondness for good horse-flesh, and riding was my favorite exercise. On my afternoon constitutionals I often came up with a fine-looking, white-bearded old gentleman, who always wore a German cap. Sometimes as I overtook him I would draw rein and we would pass the time of day. Then, as I liked to go faster than he did, I would draw ahead of him, always receiving the politest bow in exchange for my own.

He struck me as a most delightful person — and I conceived a real liking for him. One day I asked the watchman at the gate of the Soldiers' Home who this old gentleman was. He answered, "His name is Bancroft, and he is from Berlin." From this I knew that he was the historian and former secretary of the navy, and that he must have developed a fondness for German caps when he was our minister to Germany.

The next time that I met him when I was riding I introduced myself and said:

"As an officer of the navy, who owes so much to the Naval Academy that you established, I want to thank you."

I could see that he liked the compliment with its reference to a service which many of that generation had forgotten, and so we became good friends. I enjoyed many anecdotes from him when I slowed the pace of my horse to that of his in our afternoon rides.

I was at a dinner later when both he and General Sherman were present. Menus were passed around with a request for autographs. General Sherman wrote his and underneath a word which Mr. Bancroft could not make out.

"What is it?" Mr. Bancroft asked.

"General," answered Sherman.

Mr. Bancroft, who had already written his autograph, asked for the menu back and under his name he added, "Octogenarian." He lived to be very old, and in his latter days his mind was feeble. He had to give up riding and was a familiar figure in the streets of Washington leaning on the arm of his German man-servant.

One day when I was walking with Admiral Porter and we passed Bancroft I heard the valet say to him: "Lift your hat. That is Admiral Porter." For it was a custom in Washington to lift the hat to the admiral. Mr. Bancroft obeyed the valet's military direction, and Porter said to me: "Here he is told to lift his hat to me when I used to salute him as a superior." Porter had lifted his own hat in a manner that showed that the old feeling of a junior officer in the presence of a former secretary of the navy had not passed.

In October, 1882, I was ordered to the command of the *Juniata*, which was to proceed to the China station by way of the Mediterranean, the assignment being most welcome on account of my health. The *Juniata* was a second-rate sloop, built in 1861. When I had gone to Europe with the *Wabash* on my midshipman cruise it had been in one of the finest frigates of my time. At the same station, in 1866, I joined a sister ship of the *Wabash*, the *Colorado*, with the prestige that our navy had won in the Civil War. Now I was going in a relic of a past epoch of naval warfare, which you would have expected to see flying the flag of some tenth-rate power. She was as out of date as the stagecoach. Her round bottom made her roll heavily with even a light swell, and an English sea-captain at Fayal declared that he had seen her keel out of water.

Naval science had gone ahead rapidly and we had stood still. While Europe was building armored battle-ships and fast cruisers, we were making no additions to our navy. We had no sea-going commerce to protect. With the coming of steel hulls and steam this had all passed to England and France, and that rising sea-power, the German Empire. Therefore, no one had any direct interest in the navy. Our antiquated men-of-war had become the laughing-stock of the nations. Their only possible utility was as something that would float for officers and men to cruise in in time of peace and be murdered in by a few broadsides in time of war. We had appropriations only for running expenses and repairs, none for building new ships. Italy, Spain, and Holland were each stronger on the sea than the United States.

A sea-voyage did not bring me the improvement in health for which I had hoped; rather the contrary. When our antique *Juniata* entered the harbor of Gibraltar I was too ill to be on the bridge. Mr. Sprague, our consul, brought off a British physician for consultation with our ship's surgeon, and they made a thorough examination of me. A number of times he pressed his hand very forcibly against my liver, asking, "Does that hurt you?" and each time, though I had an excruciating twinge, I managed to keep a straight face and reply, "No."

It was a foolish self-deceit on my part, but I was not minded to have any medical decision put me ashore and keep me from going to the Far East where I had not as yet served. I thought I could wear down my indisposition, as many another man has thought under similar circumstances.

When we arrived at Malta, however, I was taken ashore to the British Naval Hospital, with a complication of typhoid fever and abscess of the liver. I owe my life to the skill and care of the head surgeon, Dr. James Nicholas Dick, a genial, warmhearted, capable Irishman. For some time I had a tube in my side, and

Captain Dewey at the Age of Forty-Six

every day, rather than trust any junior surgeon or nurse, he himself attended to the abscess. He is still living, and is now Inspector General Sir James Nicholas Dick, of the Directors General of the Medical Department, retired, and Honorary Surgeon to the King.

After I was out of the hospital and the *Juniata* had proceeded on her way under a new commander. I was given sick-leave. Travelling from one resort to another in search of health, finally, in February, 1884, I brought up at Santa Barbara, California, which will ever have the most grateful associations in my memory, for there I fully recovered, and to my delight, might again apply for assignment to duty.

Now, at the age of forty-seven, I received my promotion from commander to captain, a grade which, thanks to the slowness of advancement, I was to hold for twelve years, or until a year before I went out to the command of the Asiatic Squadron, when I was made a commodore. I was given command of the *Dolphin*, which was not yet in commission. Later, owing to the disputes which arose over this, the first of our new ships, and the delay in getting her to sea, I was offered the command of the *Pensacola*, which I gladly accepted.

Of her I could say what the officer who had charge of towing the dry-dock to the Philippines said, when he was in my office in the General Board after his return and was looking at a picture of the Dewey riding a heavy sea: "I think I should know her if I ever saw her again!" The *Pensacola* had been the companion of the Mississippi in the laborious business of getting her over the bar for the battle of New Orleans, and she had been anchored in the river off New Orleans ahead of us during our long stay there in '62. At the close of the war she was already obsolete as a fighting naval unit, in comparison with the *New Ironsides* or the monitors. Twenty years later, when the armored ships built in Europe five years previously were already out of date, and those built ten years previously were being put in reserve, she went abroad bearing the flag of Rear-Admiral *Franklin*,

She was interesting because of her antiquity; but for the sake of picturesq uenes

Captain Dewey on the Bridge of the "Pensacola"

s as a survival, which was her only claim to attention, it would have been better if she had been a relic of the War of 1812, which, for practical purposes, she might just as well have been. But there were statesmen who averred that if the *Pensacola* had fought well in the Civil War, she also would fight well enough in the '80's. The best face we could present to foreign officers was to say that we were starting a new navy, while we kept the *Pensacola* and vessels of her class shipshape and tried to learn modern gunnery by target practice with her obsolete guns. There was not a fourth-rate British cruiser of modern build that could not easily have kept out of range of her battery, torn her to pieces, and set her on fire.

When I was on the Colorado as executive officer in '65 I was very young for my position. Now I was old for a captain who had just been promoted from commander, and at an age when many English officers receive the grade of rear-admiral, which I was not to have until I was sixty-one. In those days naval officers had reason for regretting their choice of a profession in which they had to see the officers of other nations enjoying the use of material for keeping up with professional progress which they themselves wholly lacked. We knew that any one of the powers might require us to submit to humiliating exactions because we were incapable of defence by sea. The more earnest the effort of an officer to keep up with progress despite his handicaps, the more sensitive he was to them. It was easy then for an officer to drift along in his grade, losing interest and remaining in the navy only because he was too old to change his occupation.

Yet the spirit of the Revolution, of 1812, and of Farragut and Annapolis did not die. It remained to develop the efficiency of the new navy, which was to have its trial in the Spanish War. We had a fine-spirited crew on board the *Pensacola*, and I often wondered how they were able to keep up their interest in such an old tub. When I visited the Mediterranean again it was on the *Olympia*, homeward bound from the Orient, and it was a source of much satisfaction to be returning from a victory won with ships of our new navy, in view of the wounds to my sense of professional pride as captain of the *Pensacola* fourteen years previously.

As we had no commerce or interests to protect in Europe, and were unable to protect them if we had, the presence of our squadron in European waters was perfunctory. It used to be a saying among the officers that we went from port to port to meet our wives, who were travelling ashore, and to get letters from sweethearts. One could easily have reasoned that the Navy Department, knowing that we could be of no service as an instrument of warfare, meant us to enjoy a pleasantly conducted European holiday.

In the summer of 1885 we avoided the heat of the Mediterranean by going to northern waters, where our ports of call included Stockholm and Copenhagen. At Stockholm, King Oscar of Sweden came on board. He had been a naval officer when called to the throne, and had the true sailor's fondness for the service. While taking a glass of wine and a piece of hardtack in the cabin and looking out on the gun-deck, he remarked to those about him: "This is the kind of kingdom for a man to have. I would rather command a man-of-war than be king of any country in the world." And turning to Commander Bridgeman, of the *Kearsarge*, he said: "Would not you, captain?" Bridgeman answered, with a smile: "I have only tried the man-of-war, your Majesty."

With the coming of winter we were back south, touching at whatever Mediterranean ports pleased the squadron commander, from Tangier to Alexandria and Villefranche to the Piraeus. At the Piraeus we were visited by King George of Greece. The evening before the *Pensacola* left the Piraeus I dined with the royal family, the only guest, and on leaving after dinner the King accompanied me to the outer door and said: "The next time you come I hope you will be admiral." It was a source of much regret that I could not go to Greece with the *Olympia* on my way from Manila when I was an admiral, but it meant two weeks' quarantine, and I was therefore obliged to forego the pleasure. We spent all the summer of '87 in the Mediterranean, and in August

Rear-Admiral *Franklin* reached the retiring age. His flag was hauled down and that of Rear-Admiral James A. Greer was hoisted in its place.

At Malta we saluted a flag comparatively a newcomer to the Mediterranean, and, indeed, to the Atlantic — the Japanese, flying from the Japanese cruiser *Naniwa*, under command of Captain I to, who was later the victorious commander-in-chief in the naval battle of the Yalu in the Chino-Japanese War. It was the *Naniwa* under Captain Togo, later the victor of Tsushima Straits, which, by sinking the transport *Kowshing* at the outset of the Chino-Japanese War, precipitated an international incident.

During this European cruise I had the opportunity of studying the character of other navies and of judging of their relative efficiency, whether British, French, Spanish, or Italian. Though service in European waters is delightful, I had developed the strong conviction that the maintenance of a European squadron by the United States was poor naval policy.

About the year 1890, when I was chief of the bureau of equipment of the Navy Department, I was lunching one day with Secretary of the Navy Tracy. In the course of our conversation he said: "Dewey, if you were secretary of the navy, what would you do with our ships in time of peace?" Having already given this subject considerable thought, I replied: "I would bring all the ships home from the European station, the South Atlantic station, and the South Pacific station, then divide them into two parts; one part I would keep on the North Atlantic station, and the other in the Pacific. Of those in the Pacific, I would keep the larger part on the Pacific coast and the remainder in Asiatic waters."

The secretary said, "Why?"

"Well," I replied, "to begin with, we have no defence for our coasts except the navy [the coasts were not defended then by the army as they now are]; and in the second place, our officers and men would have an opportunity to become acquainted with our own coasts, which they are not able to do now; and above all, we would be spending the country's money at home and giving our people a chance to see something of the navy, which they can't do when it is scattered over all the world. We don't need to keep ships constantly on foreign stations — we have no interests there for them to protect, and there is really nothing for them to do. But if anything occurs which makes it necessary for ships to visit foreign countries, let us send a squadron of four ships instead of one, for whatever is to be done can be accomplished by four better than by one."

This was a view that might not be welcome to officers or to their wives, who liked to see Europe, or to admirals who enjoyed the official honors that await a squadron upon entering a foreign harbor. But it was certainly in the interest of efficiency. If there must be junketing, let it be where our own people, who pay for the navy, rather than foreigners, might see the ships. Much junketing of any kind is a distraction that interferes with application and routine, and therefore with efficiency.

One reason, perhaps, why so little was seen of our ships in home ports for twenty years after the Civil War, was that the sight of them might arouse the people's demand for a naval policy which did not represent a mere waste of money in keeping the relics in commission. The people might have insisted on better ships, and Congress had other uses for its funds, in the midst of increasing pension expenditures, than spending it on such a luxury as building men-of-war, which brought no return in patronage. I often wondered, during the '70's and '80's, on whose shoulders outraged public opinion would have placed the responsibility if there had been war and consequent national disaster. There was only one alternative for the naval captain of a wooden ship in an engagement with an armor-clad, and that was to go down with his ship. Then, at least, no one could say that he had not done all that could be expected of him.

Secretary Tracy did not act on my advice, for it was a little ahead of his time. But when I returned from Manila I had the pleasure of again expressing my views about the value of concentration, which was soon thereafter put into practice, not only at home but by foreign governments as well. If we send battle-ships to Europe to-day, it is only for a brief visit of courtesy. Naval experts have ceased to think in terms of single ships; they think in squadrons and fleets.

The return trip across the Atlantic with the *Pensacola* was my last experience on board a ship that carried sail, and my last sea-service until I was to hoist my commodore's broad pennant. The next eight years were spent in work which, to my mind, was the best sort of preparation for the duty that was to devolve upon me with the outbreak of the Spanish War.

Having witnessed one abrupt transition in the navy in the Civil War, I was to witness another — this time to armored steel vessels with powerful engines and guns in turrets. We had allowed Europe to have fifteen years the start of us, and at last were trying to catch up with her, while our officers had been only observers from the outside. rather than participants in the evolution. Those of us who had not lost heart and who had kept in touch with progress by study and observation took up our tasks with avidity, while those who had been discouraged and content to drift, thinking that we should never have anything better than the *Pensacolas* and *Juniatas*, found themselves timid about responsibilities requiring technical knowledge in place of old-fashioned gunnery and seamanship.

I now had sufficient rank to become a bureau chief, and was made chief of the bureau of equipment on July 20, 1889, succeeding my life-long friend the later Rear-Admiral W. S. Schley, at a time when we were busy with the equipment of the ships of our new navy, which was now entering upon a forward stage with our first battle-ships being planned. There was nothing showy about the four years' service that followed. The detail was not exacting, but vitally engrossing and important. In common with every other ambitious officer of the navy, I was feeling the pulse of the new spirit and problems. If, professionally, we had to smile a little when our public exulted over the sending of the White Squadron abroad in order to show our new navy to Europe, we knew that this squadron was only a pioneer of something better to come. For these small unarmored cruisers were not built to fight with armored ships.

However, we needed cruisers in order to have a fleet, and these were an excellent beginning, considering how little we had to work with at first, either in appropriations or in ship-yards. Neither the pride of our public nor of our officers would have listened to the suggestion of going to the great ship-yards of Europe for our pioneer men-of-war. We must build them and arm them ourselves. It was better to make a modest start in a thorough manner than a too ambitious start with bad results. After the squadron of cruisers a squadron of armored fighting-ships was bound to come.

When my four years were up as chief of the bureau of equipment I served for a year as a member of the light-house board, and in October, 1895, was made president of the board of inspection and survey. This was a very important duty. All the new vessels which were then nearing completion were subject to the board's inspection and approval. Ours

The U. S. battleship "Texas"

was the responsibility that the construction from stem to stern was sound and that the builders kept the letter of the specifications. By this time the country had become interested in its navy. Any failure of our new battle-ships to come up to the mark was bound to excite public suspicion, if not to develop a scandal. With the board rested the final word of acceptance of any ship after she was finished.

Thus it was that I presided at the trials of the *Texas, Maine, Iowa, Indiana,* and *Massachusetts* — all the battle-ships except the *Oregon* which were to demolish the Spanish squadron at Santiago — and also the armored cruiser *Brooklyn* and, among the unarmored cruisers, the *Nashville, Wilmington,* and *Helena,* and a number of torpedo-boats. I knew the ships, how they were built, and what was to be expected of them, and I felt that if I had not kept up with the progress of my profession it was not for want of application or opportunity.

On May 23, 1896, I had received my promotion from captain to commodore, but I remained for another year as president of the board of inspection and survey, while my rank entitled me to the command of a squadron as soon as there was a vacancy.

Chapter Thirteen - In Command of the Asiatic Squadron

It had been a rule with me never to try to bring political influence to bear on the Navy Department in my favor and never to join any group of officers in a common effort for bettering their position perhaps at the expense of other officers, not to say at the expense of the efficiency of the service. When the question of a successor to Acting Rear-Admiral McNair in command of the Asiatic Squadron arose, in the summer and fall of 1897, I knew that Commodore John A. Howell and myself were being considered for the position.

The most influential officer in the distribution of assignments was Rear-Admiral A. S. Crowninshield, chief of the bureau of navigation, and a pronounced bureaucrat, with whose temperament and methods I had little more sympathy than had the majority of the officers of the navy at that time. He would hardly recommend me to any command; and his advice had great weight with John D. Long, who was then secretary of the navy.

Theodore Roosevelt was assistant secretary of the navy. He was impatient of red tape, and had a singular understanding both of the importance of preparedness for war and of striking quick blows in rapid succession once war was begun. With the enthusiastic candor which characterizes him, he declared that I ought to have the Asiatic Squadron. He asked me if I had any political influence. I expressed a natural disinclination to use it. He agreed with the correctness of my view as an officer, but this was a situation where it must be used in self-defence. One letter from an influential source in favor of Howell had already been received by the department.

"I want you to go," Mr. Roosevelt declared. "You are the man who will be equal to the emergency if one arises. Do you know any senators?"

My heart was set on having the Asiatic Squadron. It seemed to me that we were inevitably drifting into a war with Spain. In command of an efficient force in the Far East, with a free hand to act in consequence of being so far away from Washington, I could strike promptly and successfully at the Spanish force in the Philippines.

"Senator Proctor is from my State," I said to Mr. Roosevelt. "He is an old friend of the family, and my father was of service to him when he was a young man."

"You could not have a better sponsor," Mr. Roosevelt exclaimed. "Lose no time in having him speak a word for you."

I went immediately to see Senator Proctor, who was delighted that I had mentioned the matter to him. That very day he called on President McKinley and received the promise of the appointment before he left the White House.

When I next met Crowninshield he told me that, although I was to have the appointment — a fact which did not seem to please him any too well — Secretary Long was indignant because I had used political influence to obtain it. I went in at once to see Mr. Long, and said to him:

"Mr. Secretary, I understand that you are displeased with me for having used influence to secure command of the Asiatic Squadron. I did so because it was the only way of off-setting influence that was being exerted on another officer's behalf."

The U. S. S. *Charleston*

"You are in error, commodore," said Mr. Long. "No influence has been brought to bear on behalf of any one else."

Only a few hours later, however, Mr. Long sent me a note in which he said that he had just found that a letter had been received at the department which he had seen for the first time. It had arrived while he was absent from the office and while Mr. Roosevelt was acting secretary, and had only just been brought to his attention.

An order issued on October 21, 1897, detached me from duty as president of the board of inspection and survey on November 30, with directions that I should take passage to Japan in a Pacific Mail steamer sailing from San Francisco on December 7, and report to Acting Rear-Admiral McNair on board the flag-ship *Olympia* as his relief.

In the month that I had remaining in Washington I studied all the charts and descriptions of the Philippine Islands that I could procure and put aside many books about the Far East to read in the course of my journey across the continent and the Pacific. At that time, not one man in ten in Washington thought that we should ever come to the actual crisis of war with Spain.

Whether there was likelihood of war or not, it was my duty to make sure that the squadron was properly prepared for any emergency and that not a single precaution was left to chance. Inquiry about the quantity of ammunition in the squadron developed the fact that there was not even a peace allowance. Although a further supply had been ordered, no one had seemed to think it necessary to facilitate its shipment, thanks largely to the red tape of official conservatism.

Naturally it was my business to request that it should be forwarded immediately. The department informed me that the trans-Pacific steamers would not receive it, that no merchant-vessel could be found to take it, and that it would have to await the sailing of the U. S. S. *Charleston*, then under repair and not likely to be in commission for six months. Vigorously supported by Mr. Roosevelt, I finally succeeded in having an order issued that the *Concord*, then fitting out at the Mare Island Navy Yard for service on the Asiatic station, should transport as much of the supply as her limited carrying capacity would permit.

When I reached San Francisco there was time before sailing to visit the Mare Island Navy Yard in order to see in person that the ammunition was being put on board the *Concord* and to impress upon the commandant of the yard the absolute necessity of loading her with every pound that could possibly be carried. I pointed out that by touching at Honolulu *en route* for supplies much valuable stowage room that must otherwise be devoted to provisions and stores could be given up to ammunition, while certain stores which ordinarily would be shipped from San Francisco might just as well be procured on arrival in Japan. Commander Asa Walker of the *Concord,* actively entered into the spirit of my wishes.

In consequence a small vessel of only seventeen hundred tons displacement was able to carry about one-half of the total supply, or nearly thirty-five tons. The remainder (some thirty-seven tons) was shipped by the old sloop-of-war *Mohican to Honolulu, and there transferred to the cruiser* Baltimore, when, with the accelerating rush of events, it was decided, the following March, to send her to reinforce the Asiatic Squadron. As a matter of fact, she reached Hong Kong only forty-eight hours before our vessels left that port in obedience to the Queen's proclamation of neutrality, and the ammunition was transferred to the other vessels of the squadron in Mirs Bay on the day of the declaration of war.

Even with the total amount thus sent, the whole supply on hand when the ships went into action in Manila Bay was inferior to the storage capacity of their magazines and shellrooms, being, according to the calculation of the officers of

Admiral Dewey and his dog, "Bob," on the Deck of the "Olympia"

the squadron, only about sixty per cent of the full capacity. Authoritative statements have been made to the effect that the squadron was amply supplied with ammunition. It was not even fully supplied, let alone having any reserve.

Therefore, considering that I was operating seven thousand miles from the nearest United States navy yard, and considering the possibility of a prolonged engagement with the Spanish squadron, such apprehensions as I had when we left Mirs Bay were not confined entirely to the hazards of action. It is not for me to criticise the department, but only to state a fact and to repeat that there can be no neglect so inexcusable as that which sends any modern squadron into battle not only without its magazines and shell-rooms filled, but without a large reserve of ammunition within reach. However, even if we had had less ammunition, we should have gone into Manila Bay; for such were our orders and such was the only thing to do.

When I was assigned to the command the number of flag-officers allowed by law was six rear-admirals and ten commodores; but in order to give our fleet commanders in foreign waters a position commensurate with the dignity of the country they represented, it had been for many years the unvarying custom that every commodore ordered as commander-in-chief of the Asiatic Squadron should hold the acting rank of rear-admiral from the moment that his flag was hoisted. So long, indeed, had this practice been followed that it had come to be regarded as almost a right. It was a surprising innovation when Secretary Long informed me that in my case I was to hoist the broad pennant of a commodore and not the flag of a rear-admiral.

No one could have known better than Rear-Admiral Crowninshield, Secretary Long's chief adviser, how subordinate this would make my position in all intercourse with the squadron commanders and officials of other nations, and particularly in case any necessity for combined international action should arise.

Admiral Dewey and the officers of the "Olympia"

This was one of those little pin-pricking slights which are bound to be personally unpleasant to any officer of long service. But, as one of my friends pointed out, by way of a sentimental compensation, the only one of my predecessors who had won great name by his action in the Far East also held the rank of commodore. This was Matthew C. Perry, the masterful diplomatist who opened up Japan to civilization by mingling suavity with forcefulness in such a manner that he is to-day almost as much acclaimed in Japan as if he were a national hero. After all, if Manila were won it did not much matter whether it were won under a commodore's or a Rear-Admiral's emblem.

In the harbor of Nagasaki, Japan, on January 3, 1898, I took over the command from Acting Rear-Admiral F. B. McNair, and hoisted my broad pennant on the *Olympia*. My staff was Lieutenant T. F. Brumby as flag-lieutenant and Ensign H. H. Caldwell as flag-secretary, with Ensign F. B. Upham as aide. Brumby and Caldwell had accompanied me from home, and both remained with me constantly until my return to America. The squadron at that time was hardly a formidable force for war purposes, consisting of the cruiser *Olympia* (flagship), the *Boston* (a small cruiser), the *Petrel* (gunboat), and the antiquated *Monocacy,* a paddle-wheel steamer of the Civil War period, fit only for river service. But the crews were mostly long-service men and their spirit was fine.

A long official letter transmitting the files and records of the command to its new commander-in-chief was interesting, in that it contained no hint of the pregnant events then impending. The uneasy state of affairs in Korea, some anti-missionary riots in China, the seizure of Kiau Chau Bay by the Germans one month earlier, the attitude of the Japanese, and some minor international matters were mentioned; but in no manner was there any forecast given of the work in which the squadron would soon be so vitally interested.

The only reference to the Philippines was a short paragraph, to the effect that "for some time the newspapers have contained accounts of a rebellion in progress in the Philippines"; but that "no official information has been received in relation thereto, and no information of any sort that shows American interests to be affected."

In fact, at that time the Philippines were to us a *terra incognita.* No ship of our service had been there for years. When, after my appointment as commander of the Asiatic Squadron, I sought information on the subject in Washington, I found that the latest official report relative to the Philippines on file in the office of naval intelligence bore the date of 1876.

Mr, Charles B. Harris, recently appointed from Indiana, an energetic and delightful man, was consul at Nagasaki. I recollect that Mrs. Harris, who was a strong advocate of peace and much interested in missions, asked me why we needed to maintain expensive men-of-war and their officers and men. I laughingly told her that sometimes missionaries found their lives in danger and asked for protection; again, our country had been known to go to war in the past and might in the future, in which event our squadron was supposed to represent us against the enemy on the seas. After the battle, in answer to Mr. Harris's letter of congratulation, I said that I trusted that Mrs. Harris now knew why we maintained a navy, to which he cleverly replied that not only did she know, but so did more than eighty million other Americans.

A custom of each new commander-in-chief of our Asiatic Squadron to ask for an audience with the Emperor of Japan had latterly fallen into neglect. The Japanese, in view of the part that Commodore Perry had played, had remarked an omission which so proud and so sensitive a court would be the last to overlook. It seemed to me important to observe this and every other amenity which in any degree would tend to retain the good-will of a friendly nation. Therefore, I requested the audience without delay and proceeded to Yokohama, where I expected the *Concord* at an early date with her precious cargo of ammunition.

Accompanied by my personal and fleet staff I was received first by the Emperor and afterward by the Empress. These receptions, which were very cordial, had little of an oriental character. If we except the surroundings, the decorations of the palace, and the costumes and occasional genuflections of the servants, the scene might as well have been laid at the court of Berlin, St. Petersburg, or any European capital as in that of Tokio. His Majesty was in military dress in the midst of a brilliant suite of aids, court chamberlains, and other court functionaries in occidental uniforms, while the Empress was in a Parisian costume and attended by a single maid of honor, who served as interpreter.

Both their Majesties spoke in Japanese. But while the Emperor's interpreter translated his remarks in an ordinary tone of voice, the Empress's interpreter never addressed her above a whisper. What a contrast was my reception to that of the other American commodore who had cast anchor in the Gulf of Yeddo forty-four years previously! One commodore was regarded with an apprehensive consternation, only rivalled in degree by the cataclysmic changes in beliefs, customs, and policy of which he was the precursor; while the other was welcomed with all the amenities of modern times. The one, after vexatious delays, was allowed to meet the representatives of an invisible and impotent Mikado; while the other was openly received by a constitutional monarch. The one landed in a country secluded in insular oriental isolation, while the other debarked in a thriving port open to the commerce of the world, from which he travelled to Tokio by rail. Of all the changes which the world has seen in the last century, none has been so phenomenal as that so splendidly accomplished by Japan since the memorable visit of Commodore Perry.

This audience with the Emperor established pleasant relations with the court and many Japanese officials, while the good-will of the Japanese government was shown by the discretion and courtesy of the Japanese Navy, which was always represented by one or more vessels in Manila Bay during the tedious and trying days of the blockade in the interval between the annihilation of the Spanish squadron and the occupation of the city by our troops.

The *Concord* arrived in Yokohama on February 9. On the loth she transferred her ammunition, and on the nth the *Olympia* sailed for Hong Kong, to which port the *Petrel* had already been ordered. My decision to take the squadron to Hong Kong was entirely on my own initiative, without any hint whatsoever from the department that hostilities might be expected. It was evident that in case of emergency Hong Kong was the most advantageous position from which to move to the attack.

The news of the *Maine* disaster, which occurred February 15 (February 16 in the eastern hemisphere), was known in Hong, Kong when the *Olympia* arrived there on February 17. But official notification did not reach the flagship until the following day. Its wording shows how carefully our government was moving in a moment of such intense excitement:

"Dewey, Hong Kong:

"Maine destroyed at Havana February 15th by accident. The President' directs all colors to be half masted until further orders. Inform vessels under your command by telegraph.

"Long."

Though President McKinley was still confident that war could be averted, active naval measures had already begun, so far as navy-yard work upon ships and initial inquiries with regard to the purchase of war material were concerned. But the first real step was taken on February 25, when telegraphic instructions were sent to the Asiatic, European, and South Atlantic Squadrons to rendezvous at certain convenient points where, should war break out, they would be most available.

The message to the Asiatic Squadron bore the signature of that assistant secretary who had seized the opportunity, while acting secretary, to hasten preparations for a conflict which was inevitable. As Mr. Roosevelt reasoned, precautions would cost little in time of peace and would be invaluable in case of war. His cablegram was as follows:

"Washington, *February* 25, '98.

"Dewey, Hong Kong:

"Order the squadron except the *Monocacy* to Hong Kong. Keep full of coal. In the event of declaration of war Spain, your duty will be to see that the Spanish ' Squadron does not leave the Asiatic coast, and then offensive operations in Philippine Islands. Keep *Olympia* until further orders.

"Roosevelt."

(The reference to keeping the *Olympia* until further orders was due to the fact that I had been notified that she would soon be recalled to the United States.)

I despatched a cablegram to expedite the arrival of the *Boston* and the *Concord* and one to the United States consul at Manila, in which I asked him for information concerning the fortifications, submarine mines, and general defences of Manila Bay, and to keep a close watch upon the movements of the Spanish squadron. Meanwhile, with my staff, I went into exhaustive consideration of the grave question of a supply of coal, provisions, and other necessaries for a squadron seven thousand miles distant from any home base, which would result from a proclamation of neutrality by the various governments. Although no instructions to such effect had been received from the department, discreet negotiations for the purchase of supply steamers with full cargoes of coal were initiated.

The *Boston* and the *Concord* soon arrived, as did also the *Raleigh,* sent as a reinforcement from the Mediterranean; while the antiquated *Monocacy* was laid up at Shanghai and a part of her officers and crew were transferred to the ships at Hong Kong. These vessels were now carefully overhauled and docked, kept constantly full of coal and provisions, their men thoroughly drilled, machinery put in prime condition ready for moving at a moment's notice, and preparations to land superfluous material and woodwork perfected, while I aimed to take every care in the inspection of ships and crews and to use all the knowledge of my experience to improve the efficiency of the whole for battle.

The U. S. cruiser "Boston"

Aside from the crisis of our relations with Spain, it was a critical period in international relations in the Far East. Germany, in forwarding her ambitions for colonial expansion, had just taken Kiau Chau as a punitive measure for the killing of missionaries, thus bringing the province of Shantung under the sphere of her influence. England, which had occupied Wei-hai-wei, was looking askance at Russia, who was fortifying herself at Port Arthur. The dismemberment of China seemed imminent to many observers. Hong Kong harbor was crowded with men-of-war; there was a feeling of restlessness and uncertainty in the air.

A feature of the imperial German policy at this time was the Kaiser's sending of his brother Prince Henry of Prussia to the Far East, flying his flag as a rear-admiral and second in command of the German squadron. The prince arrived at Hong Kong on March 8. He was then under forty years of age, vigorous, a charming companion, and a thorough sailor who had really worked up through all the grades from midshipman to rear-admiral. Although brought up in the strict forms of court etiquette, he was delighted to cut adrift from conventionalism whenever circumstances would permit.

Soon after the arrival of the German squadron a curious international question arose. Some of the German seamen came on board the *Olympia* to pay a friendly visit to members of our crew. Among them was a seaman of the cruiser *Gefion*, who was recognized by the officer of the deck and by others of our personnel as a deserter from one of our own ships. As he wore the German uniform and belonged to the crew of a German man-of-war, he could not well be arrested. But when the fact that he was a deserter had been

90

proved indisputably he was ordered to leave the ship. A correspondence with the German rear-admiral ensued, in which our demand for the surrender of the deserter was met by the assertion that he was a German subject and a seaman in the German Navy, and in neither capacity would he be given up.

Owing to the presence of a European royal prince, which was rare in the Far East, there was much entertaining by the officials of the British crown colony of Hong Kong and much interchange of hospitalities among the ships. Among the numerous dinners was one given by Prince Henry on board of his flag-ship, the *Deutschland,* when the acting governor, Major-General W. Black, the commandant of the British naval station at Hong Kong, the commodore of the American squadron, and the captains of several British, American, and Russian men-of-war were the principal guests.

As is customary on such occasions, toward the end of the dinner Prince Henry proposed, in succession, the health of the heads of the various nationalities represented, the toasts being drunk standing and the *Deutschland's* band at the same moment playing the appropriate national air. The usual procedure is that, after a toast to his own sovereign, the host proposes, in turn, the health of the ruler or chief magistrate of each country represented at the table, these toasts being given in the order of rank of the senior officer present.

In this case the first toast was naturally one to the health of the German Emperor, then one to the Queen of England; and though the next should have been to the President of the United States because we had a squadron commander present, Prince Henry made it to the Czar of Russia, represented by a captain, and placed the President of the United States at the end of the list. With the toast to the President the band played "Hail, Columbia."

For many years in our service confusion existed as to the identity of the national air of the United States. This was due to the assignment by navy regulations of one air, "The Star-Spangled Banner," to be played at morning colors, and another, "Hail, Columbia," at evening colors. Characteristic instances of the embarrassment, in the exchange of international courtesies, which naturally resulted from this circumstance had frequently come to my notice. Now, as the guests were reseating themselves after this toast, I reminded the prince that "Hail, Columbia," was not our national air.

"What is it?" his Highness asked.

"The Star-Spangled Banner," I told him; and added that I should be happy to send him a copy. I despatched one the same night, and it was played by the *Deutschland's* band at colors the very next morning.

It was my good fortune some years later to be instrumental in permanently eliminating all confusion to officers on this subject. Through a personal appeal to President Roosevelt I had an order, dated April 22, 1904, issued by the then acting secretary of the navy, Charles H. Darling, directing that thereafter "The Star-Spangled Banner" should be played at both, morning and evening colors, and should be regarded, for the purposes of the navy, as the national air. Subsequently it was adopted both in the army and the navy regulations.

The relegation of the President by Prince Henry to the last toast was not a thing to be considered as a personal matter, but as one affecting the nation and its head, whom I represented, and also as expressive of an attitude not altogether uncommon at that time with some European powers. This attitude I felt I could not overlook. Therefore the American officers were conspicuous by their absence thereafter at entertainments given at Hong Kong in Prince Henry's honor, until at one of them the prince remarked that no Americans were present, and asked his hostess the cause.

"It is one that your Royal Highness should be aware of," she replied. When he pleaded ignorance she told him the reason why I had taken offence.

The next morning, unattended and in citizen's clothes, he came on board the *Olympia* to call, and with fine candor expressed his regret for an error in which there had been no intentional slight and which was due to his lack of experience in such matters. After that we saw a great deal of each other, and neither of us hesitated to express our convictions freely in our talks. Upon one occasion, in discussing the possible outcome of our complications with Spain, Prince Henry remarked that he did not believe that the powers would ever allow the United States to annex Cuba.

"We do not wish to annex Cuba, your Highness," I answered, "but we cannot suffer the horrible condition of affairs which exists at present in that island at our very doors to continue, and we are bound to put a stop to it."

"And what are you after? What does your country want?" the prince asked jokingly on another occasion, in referring to the general scramble for a foothold in the Far East.

"Oh, we need only a bay," I said jokingly in return, having in mind that this was all the Germans said that they wanted at Kiau Chau. It did not then occur to me that we should be taking Manila Bay permanently.

Chapter Fourteen - Final Preparations for War

Mr. O. F. Williams, our consul at Manila, diligently responded to my request for information, and remained at his post in spite of threats and warnings that his life was in danger. Indeed, he did not obey when he had been three times cabled by his government to leave, and when he had been notified by the Governor-General of the Philippines that his safety could no longer be assured, as a mob or an assassin might kill him at any hour. Only upon receiving a peremptory request from me did he finally withdraw from his post and start for Hong Kong on April 23rd.

The information which we had received from him, while naturally not technical, was highly valuable. Through him we learned of the mounting of six new guns on Corregidor, at the entrance to Manila Bay, of the number of men-of-war and other vessels in the bay, of feverish activity upon the fortifications, and the state of the struggle of the Spanish with the insurgents. His copious cables and letters included all the extravagant rumors rife in the streets of the city. There was a persistent one of the imminent attack by the American squadron, another of the coalition of all Europe against the United States, and still another that our government was beseeching the Pope to intercede and save us from destruction by the army and navy of Spain, and this last was deemed so authentic that it was ordered to be publicly proclaimed in all the Philippine churches.

In the midst of such canards, which received credence on all sides, the poor consul was at times much bewildered. However, we found that we had underestimated the resources of the defence. The number of vessels at Cavite was incorrect, and no report had been made of the twenty-odd small gunboats in Philippine waters which by initiative and daring might have been utilized to make the entering of Manila Bay a hazardous undertaking. Moreover, there had been no proper enumeration of the shore batteries with their seventeen heavy rifled guns at the mouth of the bay and forty other guns mounted in the Manila and Cavite fortifications.

On March 11, in cabling to Washington a request that the two vital essentials, ammunition and coal, should be sent from San Francisco, I had stated that all the good coal in the market had been purchased by other governments, and it was important to provide for a fresh supply. In answer, Secretary Long authorized me to contract for the delivery of five thousand tons direct from England, if necessary; but it was not until I made another inquiry by cable, on March 21, that I received any news as to a further supply of ammunition. Now I learned officially for the first time that the *Baltimore* would reinforce my squadron, bringing the ammunition which was at Honolulu; and on April 3 came the definite word that she had left Honolulu for Hong Kong. The *Baltimore* was a most welcome addition to my force, though without her I had been quite ready to enter Manila Bay.

Meanwhile, the coal which had been contracted for was on its way from Cardiff in the steamer *Nanshan*. On April 4 I sent a cable to the department suggesting that the *Nanshan* should be purchased before the outbreak of hostilities. This idea had occurred to the department at the same time, and its cable on the subject crossed my own. It also authorized the purchase of another supply vessel and placed at my service the revenue-cutter *McCulloch*, which, fortunately, happened to be at Singapore, en route to San Francisco. By this time our government was losing its confidence in maintaining peace, for in his cable of April 5 Secretary Long had said: "War may be declared. Condition very critical."

Much credit is due to Pay-Inspector D. A. Smith, who had charge of securing supplies and arranging the contracts for coal. His energy, tact, and business qualifications not only provided for the present exigencies, but made ample preparation for future supplies which might be obtained in spite of the international limitation on purchases once war was begun. Assistance which would be dependent entirely on the friendship and attitude of the British government was not sufficient surety for a squadron seven thousand miles from home. In Chinese ports we might have a freedom that we could not have in the crown colony of Hong Kong, which was under the rule of a great, responsible European nation, which would immediately be held accountable by Spain if any leniency in enforcing the laws of neutrality should favor the United States.

Accordingly, the commander of the old *Monocacy*, stationed at Shanghai, was set secretly to work. Through the medium of an efficient Chinese comprador this officer soon perfected arrangements for an immediate or a future supply of coal or provisions, independent of international complications. An isolated locality for receiving these supplies, and for making temporary repairs, if necessary, to any ship of the squadron injured in battle, was selected. In a critical article on the Spanish War so able a strategist as Admiral Luce said:

"The defeat of the American Squadron at Manila Bay, May 1st, 1898, would have been a disaster the extent of which it would be difficult to compute. Failure to gain a decisive victory even would have been almost as bad as actual defeat, for the American commander had actually no base to fall back upon, no point d'appui. The risks taken were enormous but fully justified by the event."

His conclusion was only natural, from the information he had at hand, because I had not communicated to the department our arrangements, which were quite obvious precautions to us who were on the spot. We appreciated that so loosely organized a national entity as the Chinese Empire could not enforce the neutrality laws.

In this connection I received rather a surprising cable on April 2 from Secretary Long. He reminded me of the well-known international law, that after the outbreak of hostilities further supplies and coal could not be obtained at the neutral ports, except to enable me to proceed home. He concluded as follows: "Only the Japanese ports are available as storehouse. Should advise storehouse at Nagasaki, Japan, for the base of supplies or supply steamer to accompany the squadron."

If any nation in the world would be scrupulous in the enforcement of every detail of neutrality it would be Japan. It hardly seemed possible that we could have made some secret diplomatic arrangement with her of which I had not been fully advised. Indeed, such an arrangement was a little too good to be true to any one who knew the Far East.

In order to be sure of my ground, I sent this cable to the American minister to Japan: "Am informed, in case of war with Spain, Japanese ports can be used by this squadron as base for supplies and coal. Is this correct?" Minister Buck sent the following in return: "Ports cannot be used as base for supplies and coal. Ships homeward bound could get them. Japan would concede nothing beyond strict neutrality."

If I had acted on the secretary's advice, not only should we have given a sensitive nation offence, but our squadron might have suffered a good deal of inconvenience. Having Minister Buck's cable, I knew that we were right in thinking that there was no dependence for a base except on Chinese ports. In answer to the first inquiry made of the commanding officer of the *Monocacy* at Shanghai he said that he could obtain the supplies, but that there would be international complications in time of war. I told him that international complications, where the China of that day was concerned, were a secondary consideration and to go ahead.

In accordance with the department's consent I bought the steamer *Zafiro* as a supply ship, but I did not comply with the department's suggestion to man and arm the *Zafiro* and the *Nanshan*. This would have given them the status of American naval vessels and therefore made them subject to the restrictions of neutrality laws, not to mention that they could have been made of no real value as fighting units. We registered them as American merchant-steamers, and by clearing them for Guam, then almost a mythical country, we had a free hand in sending them to English, Japanese, or Chinese ports to get any supplies we might need on the way to Guam. Their English crews, including the officers, with the spirit of true seamen, agreed not only to stand by their ships, but welcomed the prospect of an adventurous cruise. In order to have some one aboard who understood naval tactics and signals, an officer and four men from the squadron were detailed for each vessel.

Now, with all preparations complete, we awaited the arrival of the *Baltimore*. Had the morale of the squadron for the next two weeks not been of the highest standard, it might have been affected by the reiterated statements of the Hong Kong papers that the strength of the forts at Manila and the extent of the mine fields at the entrance to the bay in connection with the strength of the Spanish naval forces made Manila quite impregnable. The prevailing impression among even the military class in the colony was that our squadron was going to certain destruction.

In the Hong Kong Club it was not possible to get bets, even at heavy odds, that our expedition would be a success, and this in spite of a friendly predilection among the British in our favor. I was told, after our officers had been entertained at dinner by a British regiment, that the universal remark among our hosts was to this effect: "A fine set of fellows, but unhappily we shall never see them again."

Every day of our last week at Hong Kong brought some new development. On the 17th the *McCulloch* arrived; on the 19th the ships were painted war color; on the 21st Washington cabled that war had not yet been declared, but might be at any moment; on the 22nd we were delighted by the sight of the Baltimore steaming into the harbor; and on the 23 d I received a letter from the acting Governor of Hong Kong, Major-General Black, enclosing an official promulgation of the war neutrality "proclamation, and requesting that our squadron should leave the harbor not later than 4 PM., April 25.

We had arranged to have a dock empty and ready to receive the *Baltimore* immediately she arrived, and the vitally important work of cleaning and painting her under-water body was accomplished before the expiration of the time limit set by the governor. As a passenger on an incoming Pacific Mail steamer came Commander B. P. Lamberton, who had been detailed by the department to command the *Boston.* But Captain Frank Wildes, of the *Boston,* was not the sort to give up his command on the eve of an engagement without a protest.

The matter was easily arranged to the satisfaction of both by having Lamberton take up his duties on the flag-ship as my chief of staff. Thus I secured the aid of a most active and accomplished officer at a time when there was positive need of his services; but not until later did I realize how much I owed to the sympathetic companionship of Lamberton's sunny, hopeful, and tactful disposition.

For other reasons Lamberton's arrival was most fortunate. Both of the senior officers of the flag-ship *Olympia* were so out of health as to be barely fit for routine duty, while neither was equal to undergoing the fatigue of an active campaign. The executive officer was therefore invalided home and his place taken by Lieutenant C. P. Rees, of the *Monocacy.* Ill as he was, it was not in my heart to refuse the request of gallant Captain Gridley to remain in command. In a month after the victory he, too, was invalided home and died in Japan on the way.

Since April 15 repeated cables to Consul Williams at Manila advised him to come to Hong Kong. But it was not until the 23d that the British consul at Manila wired me that Williams had safely started on the *Esmeralda.* It was this news that led me to cable to Washington that I should go to Mirs Bay to await his arrival. On the 24th the Boston, *Concord, Petrel, McCulloch,* the collier *Nanshan,* and the supply ship *Zafiro* left Hong Kong for this anchorage, which was some thirty miles away. The next day, Monday, April 25, the *Olympia, Raleigh,* and *Baltimore* followed. The *Raleigh* was crawling under one engine in consequence of a break-down in a circulating pump. This was repaired that night at the Kowloon dock-yard, opposite Hong Kong, and was promptly on board the ship the next morning.

The ammunition brought by the *Baltimore* was distributed among the ships, which were thoroughly cleared for action. The crews were exercised again at sub-calibre target practice and battle quarters, and the squadron finally put upon a war footing with regard to armed watches, suppression of nightlights, and other details. Meanwhile, we kept up communication with Hong Kong by means of a tug chartered for the purpose, and Flag-Secretary Caldwell remained in the city until the squadron left Mirs Bay to keep in telegraphic touch with Washington. Meanwhile, Mr. J. L. Stickney, a graduate of Annapolis, who had resigned from the service to enter journalism, had appeared and asked permission to come on board for the battle. As the *Olympia* was short-handed for junior officers I decided to make him my volunteer aide, while Caldwell was assigned to the guns.

At 12.15 PM., on the 25th, came this cable from Secretary Long:

"War has commenced between the United States and Spain. Proceed at once to Philippine Islands. Commence operations particularly against the Spanish fleet. You must capture vessels or destroy. Use utmost endeavor."

We were ready to obey. But Consul Williams, who had so persistently delayed in spite of my requests, had not yet arrived, and, knowing that he was due within two days, I determined to wait for him, in the hope that he might bring some later information concerning the defences. On the morning of the 27th the little tug *Fame* was sighted in the distance, with him on board and bringing important news, as we shall see later. The commanding officers of the squadron were directed to assemble on the flag-ship for a general conference in relation to the latest details which he had brought. Meanwhile, signal was given to prepare for getting under way, fires were spread, and at 2 p. m., after the consul had gone on board the *Baltimore* and the captains returned to their ships, the squadron was in motion. We proceeded in two columns, the fighting ships forming one column, and the auxiliary vessels another twelve hundred yards in the rear; and with a smooth sea and favoring sky we set our course for the entrance to Manila Bay, six hundred miles away.

Chapter Fifteen - The Battle of Manila Bay

Manila Bay is a spacious body of water opening out from a narrow entrance between high headlands and expanding toward a low-lying country until it has a navigable breadth of over twenty miles. On either side of the inlet are high volcanic peaks densely covered with tropical foliage, while in the passage itself lie several islands. The principal islands, Corregidor and Caballo, divide this entrance into two channels, known as Boca Grande, the great mouth, and Boca Chica, the little mouth.

Boca Chica has a width of two miles, while Boca Grande would have double this if it were not for the small island of El Fraile. This, being some distance off the main-land, practically reduces the breadth of Boca Grande to about three miles. Corregidor and Caballo are high and rocky, effectually commanding both entrances, while El Fraile, though smaller, is large enough to be well fortified and to aid in the defence of the broader channel.

No doubt the position is a strong one for defensive batteries, but the Spaniards, in keeping with their weakness for procrastination, had delayed fortifying the three islands until war appeared inevitable. Then they succeeded in mounting sufficient guns to have given our squadron a very unpleasant quarter of an hour before it met the Spanish squadron, provided the gunners had been enterprising and watchful.

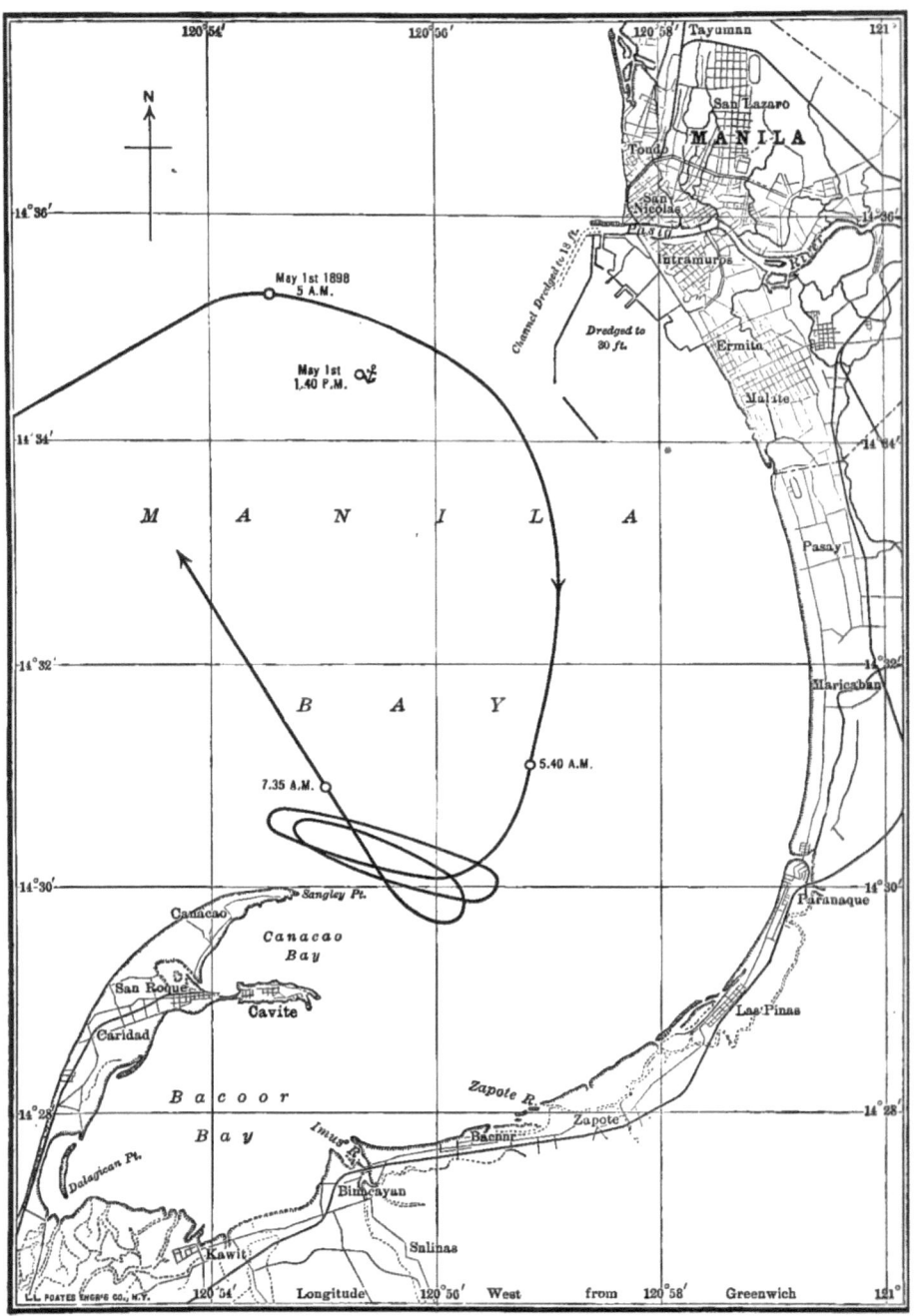

Track of Commodore Dewey's Squadron During the Battle of Manila Bay

Examination of these batteries after their surrender on May 2 showed that there were three 5.9-inch breech-loading rifles on Caballo Island, three 4.7-

inch breech-loading rifles on El Fraile rock, and three 6.3-inch muzzle-loading rifles at Punta Restinga, commanding the Boca Grande entrance, which our squadron was to use; three 8-inch muzzle-loading rifles on Corregidor, three 7-inch muzzle-loading rifles at Punta Gorda, and two 6.3-inch breechloading rifles at Punta Lasisi, commanding the Boca Chica entrance. The complement manning these batteries, as given by the official papers found in the commandant's office at Cavite Arsenal, was thirteen officers and two hundred and forty-six men. While the muzzle-loaders were relatively unimportant, the six modern rifles commanding the Boca Grande, at a range of a mile and a half, if accurately served, could deliver a telling fire.

A cable received from our consul-general at Singapore the day before we left Mirs Bay stated that the Boca Grande channel had been mined. His information was from the steamer *Isla de Panay,* which had just arrived at Singapore from Manila. This agreed with the accounts of Consul Williams, and with those of merchant-captains from Manila who had recently arrived in Hong Kong.

This subject of mines had been fully discussed in the conferences of myself and staff and the captains of our ships. We decided that submarine mines in Boca Grande might safely be considered a negligible quantity. First, the depth of water rendered the planting of submarine mines in Boca Grande, except by experts of much experience, a matter of great difficulty; secondly, either contact or electrical mines would deteriorate so rapidly in tropical waters as to become ineffective in a short time after being placed; and, thirdly, all agreed that the many reports of warnings to vessels, of notices that the passage was dangerous, of compulsory pilotage, and of spectacular zigzag courses appeared suspiciously like a cry of "wolf," intended to have its due effect upon a presumptuous enemy.

It was a similar course of reasoning, I recalled, that opened the Suez Canal during the Arabi Pasha rebellion. Hundreds of merchant-steamers had been blocked at the entrance to the canal in the fear of mines said to have been planted by the Egyptians, when an Italian man-of-war under the command of a torpedo expert (late Vice-Admiral Morin, minister of marine) appeared. He said that the Egyptians had hardly skill enough to lay mines properly, and if these had been laid as long as reported they were probably innocuous. So he steamed through the canal in spite of warning, and thus raised a blockade that had lasted for weeks.

The city of Manila lies upon the eastern side of Manila Bay, some twenty-five miles from the entrance, with the headland of Sangley Point and the naval station of Cavite five miles nearer. At all these places there were shore batteries, which added materially to the problem that our squadron had to solve. The batteries on the water-front of the city had thirty-nine heavy guns, four 9.4, four 5.5, two 5.9, two 4.7 breech-loading rifles; nine 8.3 muzzle loading mortars; eighteen 6.3 muzzle-loading rifles; and eight breech-loading Krupp field-pieces. At Sangley Point was a battery with two 5.9 breechloading rifles and at Canacao one 4.7 breech-loading rifle. These three guns and three of the Manila batteries fired on our ships during the engagement. It will be noted that four guns of the Manila batteries being over 9-inch were larger calibre than any on board our ships.

Before reaching the entrance to Manila Bay there is another bay which might be made an invaluable aid to the protection of the capital and its harbor from naval attack. This is Subig Bay, situated thirty miles to the northward of Corregidor and directly upon the flank of any enemy threatening Manila. With this strategic point effectively occupied, no hostile commander-in-chief would think of passing it and leaving it as a menace to his lines of communication. But with it unoccupied the way was clear.

The Pasig River, Manila

The Spaniards had inaugurated a small naval reservation at Olongapo, the port of Subig, and at various times appointed boards of officers to report upon the strategic advantages of the situation. So emphatic were the recommendations of these boards in favor of Subig as a naval station in place of Cavite that the change might have been made except for the strong social and official opposition, which preferred life in the capital to comparative exile in a provincial port. Therefore, the fortification of the bay had been neglected; and although at the last moment there was a nervous attempt to improvise defences, so little was done that when, on April 26, the Spanish admiral finally realized that Subig Bay was the strongest point for the defence of his fleet and of Manila, and accordingly sailed from Cavite for Subig, he found, upon arrival, that comparatively nothing had been accomplished and that the position was untenable.

Only twenty-four hours before the arrival of our scouts he got under way and steamed back to Cavite. In his official report he writes feelingly of his disgust that no guns had been mounted and that the entrance had not been mined. He was in error about the mines, however. A Spanish officer assured

100

the executive officer of the *Concord* that eighty mines had been planted in the entrance to Subig Bay.

Some fifteen others which the Spaniards had neglected to plant were found later by our officers in the Spanish storehouse at the Subig Bay naval station. In order to get their powder the insurgents had pulled up many of the eighty that had been planted.

So far as our squadron is concerned, no doubt if we had entered Subig Bay we should have found the mines there as negligible a quantity as those which had undoubtedly been planted in Manila Bay and its entrance. [1] I simply mention their existence to show the state of misinformation in the Spanish admiral's mind about his own resources. He naively adds, in continuing his report, that under the circumstances his vessels could not only have been destroyed if found in Subig Bay, but that, owing to the great depth of water, they would have been unable to save their crews in case of being sunk. What a singular lack of morale and what a strange conclusion for a naval officer!

A comparison of the relative strength of the two squadrons about to be engaged may easily be made by consulting Appendix A, which, however, does not mention some twenty-five small gun-boats not brought into action, but which might have been transformed into torpedo-launches for night attack or defence of the entrance to the bay. In action we had six ships to the Spaniards' seven, but we were superior in class of vessel and in armaments.

We had fifty-three guns above the 4-inch calibre and the Spaniards thirty-one; fifty-six guns under 4-inch to the Spaniards' forty-four; eight torpedo tubes to the Spaniards' thirteen; officers and men, 1,456 to the Spaniards' 1,447. It will be seen that, in keeping with American naval precedent, we were much more heavily armed in ratio to our personnel than the enemy. Neither side had any armored ships and both fought with brown powder. The fact that we were not armored made the heavy guns of the Spanish batteries, if they were brought to bear on us, a serious consideration.

As for the batteries noted in the *Olympia's* official log as having fired on us during the battle and verified after the surrender, they were two 6.3-inch muzzle-loaders and three 9.4-inch from the Manila batteries; two 5.9-inch from the Sangley Point battery; and one 4.7-inch from the Canacao battery. All except the two muzzle-loaders mentioned were modern breech-loading rifles.

As we cruised southward after leaving Mirs Bay, the weather was such that we could continue the preparation of crews and ships for action by drilling the men again in battle drills and their stations in case of fire, and for repairing injuries to the ships by shell-fire, while we built barricades of canvas and iron to shield the gun crews, protected the sides and ammunition hoists with lengths of heavy sheet chain faked up and down over a buffer of awnings, and threw overboard much extra wood-work which, while essential to comfort in time of peace, might become ignited in an engagement. Had the Spaniards disposed of their wood-work their ships would have burned less fiercely both at Manila and at Santiago. At night all lights were extinguished except one on the taffrail to denote position, and even this was so carefully screened as to be visible only from directly astern. The presence of the squadron on the waters was denoted alone by the dark forms of the ships and the breaking of phosphorescence at their bows and in the wake of their propellers.

Now, Consul Williams, when he came on board just before our departure from Mirs Bay, had brought news which was anything but encouraging. It upset my preconceived ideas, as I had counted upon fighting in Manila Bay. Just as the consul was leaving Manila he had learned of the sailing of the Spanish squadron for Subig Bay. Thus Admiral Montojo at the last moment seemed to have realized the strategic advantage of Subig over Manila, which we had hoped he would fail to do. When we sighted land near Cape Bolinao early on the morning of May 30, the *Boston* and *Concord* were signalled to proceed at full speed to reconnoitre Subig Bay.

Later, some of our officers declared that they heard the sound of heavy guns firing in the direction which the *Boston* and *Concord* had taken. Though I could not hear any firing myself, I sent the *Baltimore* to support the two scouts if necessary, and to await the rest of the squadron at the entrance to the bay.

As the day broke the coast of *Luzón*, which had been indefinitely seen on the horizon, appeared clearly in outline. We kept at a distance of three or four miles as we cruised slowly, keeping our speed to that of our slowest vessel, the collier *Nanshan*. In the hope of obtaining news we overhauled some of the fishing-boats in our path, but they knew nothing of the movements of the Spanish squadron. At 3.30 in the afternoon the three ships which had been sent ahead as scouts were sighted at the entrance to the bay. I waited very anxiously for their signal. When it came, saying that no enemy had been found, I was deeply relieved. I remember that I said to Lamberton, "Now we have them."

The distance from Subig Bay to Corregidor was only thirty miles. As we had decided to run past the batteries at the entrance to Manila Bay under cover of darkness, we slowed down and finally stopped. All the commanding officers were signalled to come on board the flag-ship. When they were in my cabin, and Wildes, of the *Boston,* and Walker, of' the *Concord*, had corroborated in person the import of their signals that there were no Spanish vessels in the vicinity, I said:

"We shall enter Manila Bay to-night and you will follow the motions and movements of the flagship, which will lead."

There was no discussion and no written order and no further particulars as to preparation. For every preparation that had occurred to us in our councils had already been made. I knew that I could depend upon my captains and that they understood my purposes. My position in relation to my captains and to all my officers and crews was happy, indeed, by contrast with that of the unfortunate Montojo, who tells in his official report of how, upon arriving at Subig Bay on the night of April 25 with six of his ships, he found that none of his orders for the defence of the bay had been executed. [2] The four 5.9-inch guns which should have been mounted a month previously were lying on the shore; yet in landing-drill our men have often mounted guns of equal calibre on shore in twenty-four hours. Aside from the planting of the mines which have been mentioned and the sinking of three old hulks at the eastern entrance of the bay, nothing had been done.

Soon after his arrival at Subig on the 28th Admiral Montojo received the following cable from the Spanish consul at Hong Kong:

"The enemy's squadron sailed at 2 p. m. from Mirs Bay, and according to reliable accounts they sailed for Subig to destroy our squadron and then will go to Manila."

A council of war was held, and the captains of the Spanish ships unanimously voted to return to Manila rather than, as their own consul had expressed it, be destroyed where they were. So on the morning of the 29th the Spanish squadron steamed back to Cavite. The attitude of the commanding officers must have been the attitude of the personnel. Any force in such a state of mind is already half beaten. The morale of his squadron, as revealed by Montojo's report after the battle, bore out my reasoning before the war had begun, that everywhere the Spaniards would stand upon the defensive. This must mean defeat in the end, and the more aggressive and prompt our action the smaller would be our losses and the sooner peace would come.

When my captains, after receiving their final orders on board the flag-ship, had returned to their own ships, the squadron resumed its course to Corregidor. As the gloom of night gradually shut out the details of the coast, the squadron steamed quietly on toward the entrance of Manila Bay with all lights masked and the gun crews at the guns. By degrees the high land on either side loomed up out of the darkness, while the flag-ship headed for Boca Grande, which was the wider but comparatively little used channel. A light shower passed over about eleven o'clock and heavy, cumulus clouds drifting across the sky from time to time obscured the new moon. The landmarks and islands were, however, fairly visible, while compass bearings for regulating our course could readily be observed.

It was thirty-six years since, as executive officer of the *Mississippi,* I was first under fire in the passage of Forts Jackson and St. Philip under Farragut, and thirty-five years since, as executive officer, I had lost my ship in the attempted passage of the batteries of Port Hudson. Then, as now, we were dependent upon the screen of darkness to get by successfully, but then I was a subordinate and now the supreme responsibility was mine.

If the guns commanding the entrance were well served, there was danger of damage to my squadron before it engaged the enemy's squadron. If the Spaniards had shown enterprise in the use of the materials which they possessed, then we might have expected a heavy fire from the shore batteries. One who had military knowledge did not have to wait for the developments of the Russo-Japanese War to know how quickly modern guns of high velocity and low trajectory may be emplaced and how effective they may be, when fired from a stationary position, against so large a target as a ship. Had the batteries searchlights they could easily locate us, while we could locate them only by the flash of their guns.

When we were ten miles from Boca Grande we judged, as we saw signal lights flash, that we had already been sighted either by small vessels acting as scouts or by land lookouts. El Fraile was passed by the flag-ship at a distance of half a mile and was utilized as a point of departure for the course up the bay clear of the San Nicolas Shoals. When El Fraile bore due south (magnetic) the course was changed to northeast by north. We were not surprised to find the usual lights on Corregidor and Caballo Islands and the San Nicolas Shoals extinguished, as this was only a natural precaution on the part of the Spaniards.

There were no vessels, so far as we could see, cruising off the entrance, no dash of torpedo-launches which might have been expected, no sign of life beyond the signalling on shore until the rear of the column, steaming at full speed, was between Corregidor and El Fraile.

As we watched the walls of darkness for the first gun-flash, every moment of our progress brought its relief, and now we began to hope that we should get by without being fired on at all. But about ten minutes after midnight, when all except our rear ships had cleared it, the El Fraile battery opened with a shot that passed between the *Petrel* and the *Raleigh*. The *Boston, Concord*, *Raleigh*, and *McCulloch* returned the fire with a few shots. One 8-inch shell from the *Boston* seemed to be effective. After firing three times El Fraile was silent. There was no demonstration whatever from the Caballo battery, with its three 6-inch modern rifles, no explosion of mines, and no other resistance. We were safely within the bay. The next step was to locate the Spanish squadron and engage it.

Afterward we heard various explanations of why we were not given a warmer reception as we passed through. Some of the officers in the El Fraile battery said that their dilatoriness in opening fire was due to the fact that their men were ashore at Punta Lasisi and could not get off to their guns in time after they heard of the squadron's approach. An eye-witness on Corregidor informed me that our squadron was perfectly visible as it was passing through the entrance, but for some extraordinary reason the commanding officer gave no orders to the batteries to open fire.

Perhaps the enemy thought that he had done all that was necessary by cutting off the usual lights on Corregidor and Caballo Islands and San Nicolas Shoals for guiding mariners, and he expected that without pilots and without any knowledge of the waters we would not be guilty of such a foolhardy attempt as entering an unlighted channel at midnight.

Once through the entrance, as I deemed it wise to keep moving in order not to be taken by surprise when the ships had no headway, and as, at the same time, I did not wish to reach our destination before we had sufficient daylight to show us the position of the Spanish ships, the speed of the squadron was reduced to four knots, while we headed toward the city of Manila. In the meantime the men were allowed to snatch a little sleep at their guns; but at four o'clock coffee was served to them, and so eager were they that there was no need of any orders to insure readiness for the work to come.

Signal lights, rockets, and beacon lights along the shore, now that we were sure of grappling with the enemy, no longer concerned us. We waited for dawn and the first sight of the Spanish squadron, which I had rather expected would be at the anchorage off the city of Manila. This seemed naturally the strong position for Admiral Montojo to take up, as he would then have the powerful Manila battery, mounting the guns which have already been enumerated, to support him. But the admiral stated in his report that he had avoided this position on account of the resultant injury which the city might have received if the battle had been fought in close proximity to it. [3]

The *Nanshan* and *Zafiro*, as there was no reserve ammunition for either to carry, had been sent, with the *McCulloch*, into an unfrequented part of the bay in order that they should sustain no injury and that they might not hamper the movements of the fighting-ships. When we saw that there were only merchantmen at the Manila anchorage, the squadron, led by the flag-ship, gradually changed its course, swinging around on the arc of a large circle leading toward the city and making a kind of countermarch, as it were, until headed in the direction of Cavite. This brought the ships within two or three miles of shore, with a distance of four hundred yards between ships, in the following order: *Olympia* (flag), *Baltimore, Raleigh, Petrel, Concord*, and *Boston.*

About 5.05 the Luneta and two other Manila batteries opened fire. Their shots passed well over the vessels. It was estimated that some had a range of seven miles. Only the *Boston* and *Concord* replied. Each sent two shells at the Luneta battery. The other vessels reserved their fire, having in mind my caution that, in the absence of a full supply of ammunition, the amount we had was too precious to be wasted when we were seven thousand miles from our base. My captains understood that the Spanish ships were our objective and not the shore fortifications of a city that would be virtually ours as soon as our squadron had control of Manila Bay.

With the coming of broad daylight we finally sighted the Spanish vessels formed in an irregular crescent in front of Cavite. The *Olympia* headed toward them, and in answer to her signal to close up, the distance between our ships was reduced to two hundred yards. The western flank of the Spanish squadron was protected by Cavite Peninsula and the Sangley Point battery, while its eastern flank rested in the shoal water off Las Pinas.

The Spanish line of battle was formed by the *Reina Cristina* (flag), *Castilla, Don Juan de Austria, Don Antonio de Ulloa, Isla de Luzón, Isla de Cuba,* and *Marqués del Duera.*

The *Velasco* and *Lezo* were on the other (southern) side of Cavite Point, and it is claimed by the Spaniards that they took no part in the action. Some of the vessels in the Spanish battle-line were under way, and others were moored so as to bring their broadside batteries to bear to the best advantage. The *Castilla* was protected by heavy iron lighters filled with stone.

Before me now was the object for which we had made our arduous preparations, and which, indeed, must ever be the supreme test of a naval officer's career. I felt confident of the outcome, though I had no thought that victory would be won at so slight a cost to our own side. Confidence was expressed in the very precision with which the dun, war-colored hulls of the squadron followed in column behind the flag-ship, keeping their distance excellently. All the guns were pointed constantly at the enemy, while the men were at their stations waiting the word. There was no break in the monotone of the engines save the mechanical voice of the leadsman or an occasional low-toned command by the quartermaster at the conn, or the roar of a Spanish shell. The Manila batteries continued their inaccurate fire, to which we paid no attention.

The misty haze of the tropical dawn had hardly risen when at 5:15, at long range, the Cavite forts and Spanish squadron opened fire. Our course was not one leading directly toward the enemy, but a converging one, keeping him on our starboard bow. Our speed was eight knots and our converging course and ever-varying position must have confused the Spanish gunners. My assumption that the Spanish fire would be hasty and inaccurate proved correct.

So far as I could see, none of our ships was suffering any damage, while, in view of my limited ammunition supply, it was my plan not to open fire until we were within effective range, and then to fire as rapidly as possible with all of our guns.

At 5:40, when we were within a distance of 5,000 yards (two and one-half miles), I turned to Captain Gridley and said:

"You may fire when you are ready, Gridley."

The Battle of Manila Bay

While I remained on the bridge with Lamberton, Brumby, and Stickney, Gridley took his station in the conning-tower and gave the order to the battery. The very first gun to speak was an 8-inch from the forward turret of the *Olympia*, and this was the signal for all the other ships to join the action.

At about the time that the Spanish ships were first sighted, 5.06, two submarine mines were exploded between our squadron and Cavite, some two miles ahead of our column. On account of the distance, I remarked to Lamberton: "Evidently the Spaniards are already rattled."

However, they explained afterward that the premature explosions were due to a desire to clear a space in which their ships might manoeuvre.

At one time a torpedo-launch made an attempt to reach the *Olympia*, but she was sunk by the guns of the secondary battery and went down bow first, and another yellow-colored launch flying the Spanish colors ran out, heading for the *Olympia*, but after being disabled she was beached to prevent her sinking.

When the flag-ship neared the five-fathom curve off Cavite she turned to the westward, bringing her port batteries to bear on the enemy, and, followed by the squadron, passed along the Spanish line until north of and only some fifteen hundred yards distant from the Sangley Point battery, when she again turned and headed back to the eastward, thus giving the squadron an opportunity to use their port and starboard batteries alternately and to cover with their fire all the Spanish ships, as well as the Cavite and Sangley Point batteries. While I was regulating the course of the squadron, Lieutenant Calkins was verifying our position by crossbearings and by the lead.

Three runs were thus made from the eastward and two from the westward, the length of each run averaging two miles and the ships being turned each time with port helm. Calkins found that there was in reality deeper water than shown on the chart, and when he reported the fact to me, inasmuch as my object was to get as near as possible to the enemy without grounding our own vessels, the fifth run past the Spaniards was farther inshore than any preceding run. At the nearest point to the enemy our range was only two thousand yards.

There had been no cessation in the rapidity of fire maintained by our whole squadron, and the effect of its concentration, owing to the fact that our ships were kept so close together, was smothering, particularly upon the two largest ships, the *Reina Cristina* and *Castilla.* The *Don Juan de Austria* first and then the *Reina Cristina* made brave and desperate attempts to charge the *Olympia*, but becoming the target for all our batteries they turned and ran back. In this sortie the *Reina Cristina* was raked by an 8-inch shell, which is said to have put out of action some twenty men and to have completely destroyed her steering-gear. Another shell in her forecastle killed or wounded all the members of the crews of four rapid-fire guns; another set fire to her after orlop; another killed or disabled nine men on her poop; another carried away her mizzen-mast, bringing down the ensign and the admiral's flag, both of which were replaced; another exploded in the after ammunition-room;

and still another exploded in the sick-bay, which was already filled with wounded.

When she was raised from her muddy bed, five years later, eighty skeletons were found in the sickbay and fifteen shot holes in the hull; while the many hits mentioned in Admiral Montojo's report, and his harrowing description of the shambles that his flag-ship had become when he was finally obliged to leave her, shows what execution was done to her upper works. Her loss was one hundred and fifty killed and ninety wounded, seven of these being officers. Among the killed was her valiant captain, Don Luis Cadarso, who, already wounded, finally met his death while bravely directing the rescue of his men from the burning and sinking vessel.

Though in the early part of the action our firing was not what I should have liked it to be, it soon steadied down, and by the time the *Reina Cristina* steamed toward us it was satisfactorily accurate. The *Castilla* fared little better than the *Reina Cristina*. All except one of her guns was disabled, she was set on fire by our shells, and finally abandoned by her crew after they had sustained a loss of twenty-three killed and eighty wounded. The *Don Juan de Austria* was badly damaged and on fire, the *Isla de Luzón* had three guns dismounted, and the *Marqués del Duero* was also in a bad way. Admiral Montojo, finding his flag-ship no longer manageable, half her people dead or wounded, her guns useless and the ship on fire, gave the order to abandon and sink her, and transferred his flag to the *Isla de Cuba* shortly after seven o'clock.

Victory was already ours, though we did not know it. Owing to the smoke over the Spanish squadron there were no visible signs of the execution wrought by our guns when we started upon our fifth run past the enemy. We were keeping up our rapid fire, and the flag-ship was opposite the centre of the Spanish line, when, at 7:35, the captain of the *Olympia* made a report to me which was as startling as it was unexpected. This was to the effect that on board the *Olympia* there remained only fifteen rounds per gun for the 5-inch battery.

It was a most anxious moment for me. So far as I could see, the Spanish squadron was as intact as ours. I had reason to believe that their supply of ammunition was as ample as ours was limited.

Therefore, I decided to withdraw temporarily from action for a redistribution of ammunition if necessary. For I knew that fifteen rounds of 5-inch ammunition could be shot away in five minutes. But even as we were steaming out of range the distress of the Spanish ships became evident. Some of them were perceived to be on fire and others were seeking protection behind Cavite Point. The *Don Antonio de Ulloa*, however, still retained her position at Sangley Point, where she had been moored. Moreover, the Spanish fire, with the exception of the Manila batteries, to which we had paid little attention, had ceased entirely. It was clear that we did not need a very large supply of ammunition to finish our morning's task; and happily it was found that the report about the *Olympia's* 5-inch ammunition had been incorrectly transmitted. It was that fifteen rounds had been fired per gun, not that only fifteen rounds remained.

Feeling confident of the outcome, I now signalled that the crews, who had had only a cup of coffee at 4 A. M., should have their breakfast. The public at home, on account of this signal, to which was attributed a nonchalance that had never occurred to me, reasoned that breakfast was the real reason for our withdrawing from action. Meanwhile, I improved the opportunity to have the commanding officers report on board the flag-ship.

There had been such a heavy flight of shells over us that each captain, when he arrived, was convinced that no other ship had had such good luck as his own in being missed by the enemy's fire, and expected the others to have both casualties and damages to their ships to report. But fortune was as pronouncedly in our favor at Manila as it was later at Santiago. To my gratification not a single life had been lost, and considering that we would rather measure the importance of an action by the scale of its conduct than by the number of casualties we were immensely happy. The concentration of our fire immediately we were within telling range had given us an early advantage in demoralizing the enemy, which has ever been the prime factor in naval battles. In the War of 1812 the losses of the *Constitution* were slight when she overwhelmed the *Guerrière* and in the Civil War the losses of the *Kearsarge* were slight when she made a shambles of the *Alabama*. On the *Baltimore* two officers (Lieutenant F. W. Kellogg and Ensign N. E. Irwin) and six men were slightly wounded. None of our ships had been seriously hit, and every one was still ready for immediate action.

In detail the injuries which we had received from the Spanish fire were as follows:

The *Olympia* was hulled five times and her rigging was cut in several places. One six-pound projectile struck immediately under the position where I was standing. The *Baltimore* was hit five times. The projectile which wounded two officers and six men pursued a most erratic course. It entered the ship's side forward of the starboard gangway, and just above the line of the main deck, passed through the hammock-netting, down through the deck planks and steel deck, bending the deck beam in a wardroom state-room, thence upward through the after engine-room coaming, over against the cylinder of a 6-inch gun, disabling the gun, struck and exploded a box of three-pounder ammunition, hit an iron ladder, and finally, spent, dropped on deck. The *Boston* had four unimportant hits, one causing a fire which was soon extinguished, and the *Petrel* was struck once.

At 11:16 A. M. we stood in to complete our work. There remained to oppose us, however, only the batteries and the gallant little *Ulloa*. Both opened fire as we advanced. But the contest was too unequal to last more than a few minutes. Soon the *Ulloa*, under our concentrated fire, went down valiantly with her colors flying.

The battery at Sangley Point was well served, and several times reopened fire before being finally silenced. Had this battery possessed its four other 6-

inch guns which Admiral Montojo had found uselessly lying on the beach at Subig, our ships would have had many more casualties to report. Happily for us, the guns of this battery had been so mounted that they could be laid only for objects beyond the range of two thousand yards. As the course of our ships led each time within this range, the shots passed over and beyond them. Evidently the artillerists, who had so constructed their carriages that the muzzles of the guns took against the sill of the embrasure for any range under two thousand yards, thought it out of the question that an enemy would venture within this distance.

The *Concord* was sent to destroy a large transport, the *Mindanao*, which had been beached near Bacoor, and the *Petrel*, whose light draught would permit her to move in shallower water than the other vessels of the squadron, was sent into the harbor of Cavite to destroy any ships that had taken refuge there. The *Mindanao* was set on fire and her valuable cargo destroyed. Meanwhile, the *Petrel* gallantly performed her duty, and after a few shots from her 6-inch guns the Spanish flag on the government buildings was hauled down and a white flag hoisted. Admiral Montojo had been wounded, and had taken refuge on shore with his remaining officers and men; his loss was three hundred and eighty-one of his officers and crew, and there was no possibility of further resistance.

At 12.30 the *Petrel* signalled the fact of the surrender, and the firing ceased. But the Spanish vessels were not yet fully destroyed. Therefore, the executive officer of the *Petrel*, Lieutenant E. M. Hughes, with a whale-boat and a crew of only seven men, boarded and set fire to the *Don Juan de Austria, Isla de Cuba, Isla de Luzón, General Lezo, Coreo,* and *Marqués del Duero,* all of which had been abandoned in shallow water and left scuttled by their deserting crews. This was a courageous undertaking, as these vessels were supposed to have been left with trains to their magazines and were not far from the shore, where there were hundreds of Spanish soldiers and sailors, all armed and greatly excited. The *Manila,* an armed transport, which was found uninjured after having been beached by the Spaniards, was therefore spared. Two days later she was easily floated, and for many years did good service as a gun-boat. The little *Petrel* continued her work until 5.20 PM., when she rejoined the squadron, towing a long string of tugs and launches, to be greeted by volleys of cheers from every ship.

The order to capture or destroy the Spanish squadron had been executed to the letter. Not one of its fighting-vessels remained afloat. That night I wrote in my diary: "Reached Manila at daylight. Immediately engaged the Spanish ships and batteries at Cavite. Destroyed eight of the former, including the Reina Cristina and Castilla. Anchored at noon off Manila."

As soon as we had sunk the *Ulloa* and silenced the batteries at Sangley Point, the *Olympia*, followed by the Baltimore and *Raleigh*, while the *Concord* and *Petrel* were carrying out their orders, started for the anchorage off the city. The Manila batteries, which had kept up such a persistent though impotent firing all the early part of the day, were now silent and made no attempt to reopen as our ships approached the city.

Consul Williams was sent on board a British ship moored close inshore near the mouth of the Pasig River, with instructions to request her captain to be the bearer of a message to the Spanish captain-general. This message was taken ashore at 2 p. m., in the form of a note to the British consul, Mr. E. H. Rawson-Walker, who, after the departure of Mr. Williams, had assumed charge of our archives and interests, requesting him to see the captain-general, and to say to him, on my behalf, that if another shot were fired at our ships from the Manila batteries we should destroy the city. Moreover, if there were any torpedo-boats in the Pasig River they must be surrendered, and if we were allowed to transmit messages by the cable to Hong Kong the captain-general would also be permitted to use it.

Assurance came promptly that the forts would not fire at our squadron unless it was evident that a disposition of our ships to bombard the city was being made. This assurance, which was kept even during the land attack upon the city, some three months later, led me to drop anchor for the first time since we had entered the bay. From the moment that the captain-general accepted my terms the city was virtually surrendered, and I was in control of the situation, subject to my government's orders for the future. I had established a base seven thousand miles from home which I might occupy indefinitely. As I informed the secretary of the navy in my cable of May 4, our squadron controlled the bay and could take the city at any time. The only reason for awaiting the arrival of troops before demanding its surrender was the lack of sufficient force to occupy it.

In answer to the other points of my message, the captain-general, Don Basilio Augustin Davila, said that he knew of no torpedo-boats in the river, but that if there were any his honor would not allow him to surrender them. As there were none, he was quite safe in making this reservation, which did not affect the main fact, that his capital was under our guns. He refused my request about the cable. As a result he found himself cut off from all telegraphic communication with the outside world on the next morning, because I directed the *Zafiro* to cut the cable.

As the sun set on the evening of May 1, crowds of people gathered along the water-front, gazing at the American squadron. They climbed on the ramparts of the very battery that had fired on us in the morning. The *Olympia*'s band, for their benefit, played "La Paloma" and other Spanish airs, and while the sea-breeze wafted the strains to their ears the poor colonel of artillery who had commanded the battery, feeling himself dishonored by his disgraceful failure, shot himself through the head.

During the mid-watch that night a steam-launch was discovered coming off from Manila. The crews went to quarters and search-lights and guns were trained upon her until she approached the *Olympia*, when she was allowed to come alongside. A Spanish official was on board. He desired permission to proceed to Corregidor to instruct the commanding officer that none of the batteries at the entrance to the bay were to fire on our ships when passing in or out. Permission was granted and he was told to return the following morning. When he came he was put on board the *Raleigh*, which was sent, with the *Baltimore* as escort, to demand the surrender of all the defences at the entrance to the bay. The surrender was made and the garrisons disarmed. The next day I had the *Boston* and *Concord* land parties, who disabled the guns and brought their breech-plugs off to the ships. All the ammunition found, as it was of a calibre unsuited to any of our guns, was destroyed.

Meanwhile, to my surprise, on the morning of May 2, the Spanish flag was seen to be again flying over the Cavite arsenal. Captain Lamberton was sent at once to inquire what it meant, and to demand a formal surrender. He went over to Cavite in the *Petrel*, and upon leaving her to go on shore gave instructions that in case he did not return within an hour she was to open fire on the arsenal. Upon landing he found the Spanish soldiers and sailors under arms, and in answer to his inquiry, what was meant by this and by the hoisting of the Spanish colors, he was informed by the Spanish commandant, Captain Sostoa, that the colors had been lowered the day before only as token of a temporary truce. Captain Lamberton's reply to this evasive excuse was an ultimatum that if the white flag were not hoisted by noon he would open fire.

Captain Sostoa then asked for time in which to refer the matter to Madrid, and this being refused, for time to refer it to the authorities at Manila. But he was informed that only an unconditional surrender of officers, men, and arms would be considered. Captain Lamberton then returned to the *Petrel*, and at 11:35 the white flag was hoisted by the order of Admiral Montojo; and it was this order, peculiarly enough, and not the loss of his squadron, that led to his court-martial upon his return to Spain. Shortly afterward all the Spanish officers and men evacuated the place. Possibly imperfect knowledge of each other's language by Captain Lamberton and Captain Sostoa led to a misunderstanding of our terms by the Spaniards. In a way this was fortunate for us, as we were in no position to take care of prisoners. We had what we needed: possession of the arsenal, with its machinery, workshops, and supplies, as a base for future operations.

It was not until May 4, however, when all the aftermath of the details of the victory had been cared for, that I found it convenient to send the *McCulloch* to Hong Kong to transmit to Washington the complete news of what the squadron had accomplished, where already many misleading reports had been received from Spanish sources. Before the cable was cut the captain-general, in a communication to his government, had acknowledged his severe loss, yet intimated that the American squadron had been repulsed; while other "cables affirmed that our casualties were heavy. [4]

But the newspapers of May 2 had had a brief announcement of the victory, one of which had been sent by the operator at the Manila cable station before the cable was cut. Senator Redfield Proctor, of Vermont, who had been responsible for my assignment to the command of the Asiatic Squadron, felt that he had a personal cause for jubilation, and on the morning of the 2d he wrote the following note, in his characteristic vein, to President McKinley:

"I feel well this morning.

"You may remember that you gave, at my earnest request, the direction to Secretary Long to assign Commodore Dewey to the Asiatic Squadron. You will find you made no mistake; and I want to say that he will be as wise and safe, if there are political duties devolving on him, as he is forcible in action. There is no better man in discretion and safe judgment. We may run him against you for President. He would make a good one."

The President now gave me the same rank of acting rear-admiral that Captain Sampson, commanding the North Atlantic Squadron, had already received. Congress passed a vote of thanks to the squadron commander, its officers and men, and all anxiety for the safety of the Pacific coast was relieved. One of the most gratifying cables was this: "Every American is your debtor. Roosevelt."

Not until many weeks later, when the mails began to arrive, did I fully realize how the victory had electrified the whole United States. One of the first congratulatory letters received I particularly prize. It was written by my old friend John Hay, then ambassador to England, in the delightful phrase of which he was a master. He spoke of the "mingled wisdom and daring" of our entrance into the bay, which has always seemed to me as fine a compliment as any naval officer could receive.

The victory had put a stop to the talk of European intervention. It had set a pace to be followed in the operations on the Atlantic coast and had checked the mendacious slanders about our navy which had been circulated broadcast throughout continental Europe. There were reports of utter lack of discipline and that our crews were entirely foreign mercenaries. Perhaps, in comparison with some foreign navies, we lacked the etiquette of discipline, which is immaterial if the spirit of discipline exists. We had the spirit — efficient, dependable, and intelligent. "The man behind the gun" was not a foreigner. With the development of the new navy the percentage of American-born seamen had rapidly increased. It was about eighty per cent in my squadron.

In his war proclamation, April 23, 1898, the Spanish captain-general had declared that the North American people were "constituted of all the social excrescences." He spoke of us as a "squadron manned by foreigners possessing neither instruction nor discipline," which was "unacquainted with the rights of property" and had come "to kidnap those persons whom they consider useful to man their ships or to be exploited in agricultural or industrial labor...Vain designs! Ridiculous boastings! ...They shall not profane the tombs of your fathers, they shall not gratify their lustful passions at the cost of your wives' and daughters' honor, or appropriate the property your industry has accumulated as a provision for your old age."

The author of this proclamation, I was told, was not the captain-general himself, but the Archbishop of Manila, who as head of the church in the Philippines was *ex officio* a member of the general council of the colony. Some months later I had the pleasure of entertaining him on board the *Olympia*. In his honor I had the ship's company paraded. As he saw the fine young fellows march past his surprise at their appearance was manifest.

"Admiral, you must be very proud to command such a body of men," he said finally.

"Yes, I am," I declared; "and I have just the same kind of men on board all the other ships in the harbor."

"Admiral, I have been here for thirty years," he concluded. "I have seen the men-of-war of all the nations, but never have I seen anything like this" (as he pointed to the *Olympias* crew).

In view of the language of the proclamation, I considered this generous admission very illuminating.

But better than winning the esteem of foreigners was winning that of our own people. They could have had none too great confidence in their navy at the outbreak of the war, or else there would not have been such a popular cry to have the Atlantic coast guarded against possible ravages by Cervera's squadron.

It was the ceaseless routine of hard work and preparation in time of peace that won Manila and Santiago. Valor there must be, but it is a secondary factor in comparison with strength of material and efficiency of administration. Valor the Spaniards displayed, and in the most trying and adverse circumstances. The courageous defence made by all the vessels of the Spanish squadron, the desperate attempt of the *Reina Cristina* to close with the *Olympia*, and the heroic conduct of her captain, who, after fighting his ship until she was on fire and sinking, lost his own life in his attempt to save his wounded men, can only excite the most profound admiration and pity.

But what might not have been accomplished had this courage been properly directed and had there been appreciation of the importance of preparation? For three months war had been imminent, and although the Spanish government was highly reprehensible for its unaccountable inertia, and Spanish indolence and climatic influences must bear their share of blame, nothing can excuse the Spanish authorities in the Philippines for neglecting to utilize the materials of defence already in their possession.

The approach of our squadron had been reported from Bolinao in the morning and from Subig in the afternoon the day before the battle, yet the Spanish admiral that very evening left his flag-ship and went over to Manila, five miles distant, to attend a reception given by his wife. He was driving back to Cavite by carriage at the same hour that our squadron was passing through the Boca Grande. Many of his officers, following his example, passed the night ashore and were seen returning to their ships early on the morning of the battle, after the firing had actually begun.

To us it seems almost incomprehensible that the guns of Caballo and Corregidor and Punta Restinga failed to fire on our ships; that when our vessels were hampered by the narrow waters of the entrance there was no night attack by the many small vessels possessed by the Spaniards; and that during the action neither the *Isla de Cuba* nor the *Isla de Luzón,* each of them protected by an armored deck and fitted with two torpedo-tubes, made any attempt to torpedo our ships.

Naturally, the Spanish government attempted to make a scape-goat of poor Admiral Montojo, the victim of their own shortcomings and maladministration, and he was soon afterward ordered home and brought before a court-martial. It was some satisfaction to know that a factor in influencing the court in concluding that he had fulfilled his duty in a courageous manner was a letter from me [5] testifying to his gallantry in the action, which I was glad to give in response to his request.

[1] Lieutenant John M. Ellicott, U. S. N., who was one of the officers of the Baltimore, in his article upon "The Defences of Manila Bay," published in the *Proceedings of the U. S. Naval Institute,* June, 1900, says:

"In the face of all evidence the existence of mines at the entrance to the bay can scarcely be doubted. A chart was captured at Cavite next morning with lines of torpedoes marked on it in Boca Chica, and off San Nicolas Shoal, and with marginal memoranda about the spacing and number of mines. In the articles of capitulation signed by the Governor of Corregidor it was stated that mines existed in Boca Grande. The testimony of nearly every Spanish officer interviewed by the writer after the fall of Manila was to the same effect. If these mines were contact mines they had become innocuous from barnacles or sea-weed or badly adjusted moorings; if they were electro-controlled the firing devices had not been installed or were defective."

[2] Appendix C.

[3] Appendix C.

[4] Last night, April 30, the batteries at the entrance to the port announced the arrival of the enemy's squadron, forcing a passage under the obscurity of the night. At daybreak the enemy took up position, opening with a strong fire against Fort Cavite and the arsenal. Our fleet engaged the enemy in a brilliant combat, protected by the Cavite and Manila forts. They obliged the enemy with heavy loss to manoeuvre repeatedly. At nine o'clock the American squadron took refuge behind the foreign shipping on the east side of the bay." — (Cablegram of the Spanish captain-general to Madrid, May 1, 1898.)

[5] Appendix D.

Chapter Sixteen - After the Battle

There was little leisure or rest, either for myself or my subordinates, in the early days of May. We had to inaugurate a system to meet the conditions which were the result of the battle. The blockade of Manila must be established and enforced; immunity from surprise or attack by the Spaniards insured; Cavite arsenal must be occupied, its stores protected, and its precincts policed; and, generally, American supremacy and military discipline must take the place of chaos.

About 11 A. M., on the 2d of May, the British consul, Mr. E. H. Rawson-Walker, who was acting as gerant of United States consular affairs, came on board the *Olympia* to make an official call. During many weeks to come he was to perform a most valuable service in his efforts to render the lot of the foreign residents as little onerous as possible under what, to them, were most trying conditions. I asked him to remain to luncheon with me. While we were waiting for it to be announced and he was telling me about the condition of affairs in the city, I was informed that the shore batteries of Manila were being manned. As a matter of precaution, the ships were signalled to go to general quarters; but at the same time I told the consul he need have no fear of the batteries opening fire. So we sat down to our meal, which was not interrupted by any shots.

This incident had its effect. The consul agreed with me that, in view of the possibility of some irresponsible person in the batteries firing on the ships and thus precipitating a bombardment of the city, it would be advisable to remove the temptation. Late that afternoon the ships all took up an anchorage nearer our base off the Cavite arsenal, which was retained until the attack on Manila in the following August.

During the night, between the departure of the Spaniards and the landing of our guards at Cavite, there had been some looting on the part of the natives. But the next morning the place was well policed by our forces and all disorder checked. Commander E. P. Wood, of the *Petrel*, was placed in charge of the arsenal, government buildings, and stores; the machinery, docks, and workshops were utilized for our ships, and, later, the many resources of the place were employed not only in keeping our squadron in good condition, but also in making repairs upon the other naval vessels and army transports which later arrived from home.

Working parties were at once landed to bury the dead, and all our surgeons were sent ashore to aid in attending the Spanish sick and wounded. Arrangements were soon made to send the sick and wounded, numbering four hundred and ninety, to Manila. Captain Lamberton took charge of their removal upon the captured steamer *Isabel,* flying the Red Cross flag, and later of their transfer to the Spanish authorities. A detail of marines was sent to act as stretcher-men in moving those unable to walk from the hospital to the steamer. The sisters, who were acting as nurses, received the marines with every sign of abject fear and horror. They had read the Spanish captain-general's proclamation about the fiendish nature of the American barbarian, and fully expected to be subjected to outrage.

In establishing the blockade all merchant-vessels in the bay were assigned an appropriate anchorage outside the zone of possible naval operations. All arriving merchant-vessels were boarded off the Bocas as soon as sighted in the offing, informed of the blockade and warned off, unless laden with coal.

In that event they were allowed to enter and their cargoes taken for our squadron at the current market rate.

Men-of-war of various nationalities soon made their appearance. They were allowed to enter without hindrance other than being boarded to establish their identity, thoroughly informed of the actual conditions of affairs, given an anchorage off the city, and permitted to communicate with their countrymen and with the Spanish officials. They were allowed to carry the mails for Manila, and, with a single exception, the consideration which I tried to show was never abused. Commercially, the blockade was always vigorously enforced, and from May 1 until the surrender of the city on August 13 the great trade of Manila was entirely suspended.

When, on May 4, I sent the *McCulloch* to Hong Kong with my cable reporting the victory [1] the Boston and *Concord* convoyed her beyond the Bocas. This precaution, taken in view of the fact that there were known to be over twenty Spanish gunboats stationed in various parts of the Philippines, was soon deemed unnecessary, and all subsequent trips were made without fear of molestation. When she returned, on May 11, bringing the news of my promotion, with the congratulations of the President and the secretary of the navy, the broad pennant of a commodore was hauled down and a rear-admiral's flag hoisted on board the *Olympia*.

Incidentally, I may say that the bundle of congratulatory cables from chambers of commerce, clubs, corporations, and individuals showing the enthusiasm at home was even more surprising to my officers than to me. There was a feeling in the squadron that, after all, we were away from the main theatre of war, which was in the Atlantic, where our battle-ship squadron was also looking for the Spaniards. Professional opinion sharing none of the public's fear of the outcome, we were certain of the decisive success of Rear-Admiral Sampson's squadron in any engagement. But I had reminded my officers that if ours were really the first blow of the war, it must be appreciated at home. In view of the evident gratification of the government and the public at what we had accomplished, I hastened to recommend that Lamberton, my chief of staff, and all my captains be advanced ten numbers. Their aid had made success possible.

On May 12 an amusing incident occurred. A Spanish gun-boat, the *Callao*, was sighted coming in. The *Raleigh* was promptly under way to overhaul her, and, joined by the *Olympia* and *Baltimore,* fired a few shots before she surrendered. She had sailed from some remote spot in the islands where it was not known that war existed between the United States and Spain, and her commander was utterly dumfounded when he was received with shotted guns from foreign men-of-war in Spanish waters.

He was a young fellow, and his crew were mostly natives, including only three or four Spaniards. I told him that all could take their parole, but he answered that the Spanish regulations would not permit the acceptance of a parole.

"You, sir," he said quite dramatically, "who are old enough to be my father, advise me what to do in this emergency. If I go to Manila saying that I have been paroled, I shall be shot."

"Then you may go without parole," I said, as he and his crew would be only an encumbrance as prisoners.

The very next day the *Callao*, commanded by Lieutenant Tappan, was doing duty as a gun-boat in our service by boarding vessels off the Bocas. We also commissioned the armed transport *Manila,* under command of Lieutenant-Commander Frederic Singer. The *Barcelo, Rapido, Hercules,* and other small craft that had been captured were all transformed into auxiliaries which became valuable on patrol and messenger duty.

My instructions sent by Acting-Secretary Roosevelt had said that I was to conduct offensive operations in the Philippine Islands. My idea first and last was to obey them in spirit and letter until I was otherwise ordered. While we remained at war with Spain our purpose must be to strike at the power of Spain wherever possible. The question of making the Philippine Islands United States territory was one of policy for the nation at home to decide, which had nothing to do with my duties as a naval officer.

When I sent the *McCulloch* to Hong Kong again, on May 13, in my report of conditions I once more emphasized the fact that I could take the city at any moment; and now I impressed upon the government at home the necessity, if it were our intention to occupy Manila, that a force of occupation should immediately be sent. For this purpose I estimated that five thousand well-equipped troops would be necessary, and they would have been sufficient if we had had to deal alone with the Spaniards and not with a native insurrection. We had the city under our guns, as Farragut had New Orleans under his. But naval power can reach no farther ashore. For tenure of the land you must have the man with a rifle.

The position of the squadron was one of peculiar isolation. It must be six days by way of Hong Kong before I could receive an answer to any communication to Washington. The supply ship *Zafiro*, which came to be regularly employed for these trips, invariably had one of our officers in charge. His authority gave the vessel an official character, enabling her to fly a pennant and insuring her an immunity from the many red-tape restrictions and charges to which merchant-vessels are subjected. She brought from China delicacies which greatly mitigated the discomforts of blockade duty, with its attendant seafare. In Manila Bay a little fruit or a few fresh eggs might occasionally be purchased from the natives, but in such small quantities as to admit of no general distribution.

In the purchase of supplies, however, the officer in charge of the *Zafiro* had to exercise discretion, and particularly in their embarkation. The British authorities were personally so cordial and so inclined to be fair in their construction of the laws of neutrality that I thought we should be very careful, on our side, to commit no act that could be misconstrued. Both fresh meat and vegetables were bought by Chinese compradors from Chinese mer-

118

chants, and sent off to the *Zafiro* in small quantities under cover of night. Happily, we had the fact in our favor that the British part of Hong Kong harbor only extends to a certain limit; beyond this the Chinese authorities have control. Therefore the *Zafiro* could be anchored in the Chinese zone whenever she took on board coal or provisions.

Of course the Spanish consul at Hong Kong was on the lookout. Indeed, his activity, if it could have been transmitted to the Spanish army and navy in the Philippines during the period of preparation for war, might have made the victory of May 1 less easily won. At one time the British colonial authorities made a point that our use of the cable for military purposes was a breach of neutrality and could not be permitted. Lieutenant Walter McLean, the officer then in charge of the *Zafiro*, having made proper representations in answer, was allowed to be the judge or censor of our cablegrams. Thus, all that he chose to pass would be accepted and forwarded.

Only by efficient enforcement of the blockade could we be certain that no contraband of war reached the Spaniards in Manila. The glint of a sail or a trail of smoke on the horizon was quickly detected by our lookout. No sooner was either one reported than the signal flags from the *Olympia* despatched a vessel to overhaul and investigate the stranger.

Upon one occasion a small craft emerged from an inlet of the bay and was seen making for Manila. The *McCulloch*, being sent in chase, soon overhauled and captured her. She proved to be the Spanish gun-boat *Leyte,* which we immediately utilized for our service. She had fled from the scene of action on May 1, and with some refugees on board had run up one of the rivers to the northward and westward of the city. Her commander had hoped to escape out of the bay by night, but finding us so watchful and himself short of provisions and harried by the insurgents, he finally decided to make for Manila, or, failing that, to surrender.

Our squadron was maintained in constant readiness to resist attack and every ship was prepared to get under way at a moment's notice. Many merchant-steamers, tugs, launches, and coastwise vessels were lying in the harbor in enforced idleness and available for any purpose. Meanwhile, the officers and crews of Admiral Montojo's sunken squadron were in the city. Presumably they must chafe under the recollection of their defeat. The officers had shown their courage in battle. It stood to reason that they would not hesitate at any desperate undertaking of the kind that made Cushing's destruction of the *Albemarle* so notable, in order to strike a blow for their country. Moreover, they would have the technical knowledge essential for the use of torpedoes.

Indeed, it was inconceivable to our own officers that any service could show such professional inertness as that of the Spaniards during the blockade. We were always apprehensive lest their apparent inaction was merely a ruse to lull us into a sense of security. At all events, it was my duty to take every precaution against any form of surprise which I would take against the most energetic enemy.

Meanwhile, I received from time to time alarming rumors and reports. On May 20 the insurgents brought me circumstantial information that the Spaniards would try to recover Cavite by an attack from the land side that night. The *Petrel* and *Callao* were ordered into a position commanding the navy yard, and the rest of the squadron was on the qui vive; but morning came without a sign of any movement on shore. Again, toward the middle of June, there was a circumstantial warning of a torpedo attack. All preparations were made to receive it. Steam was kept up on the small boats, while the *Boston, Concord*, and *Callao* were sent at 3 a. m. to search the waters of the bay in the vicinity of Manila. But, as usual, nothing happened.

It was about this time that our continual watchfulness was actually tested by a German man-of-war's steam-launch. This was the first and only occasion that any launch of the numerous foreign men-of-war in the harbor which had gathered to observe the operations had approached one of our vessels after dark; for, naturally, it was known that any squadron in time of war will take no risks in allowing small craft to approach it at night. When the German launch was picked up by the search-lights of our vessels she continued to advance. Her true nature was not readily determined at once, and, as I had observed her myself from the quarter-deck, I ordered a six-pounder shot fired over her, while the marine watch on duty opened a small-arm fire. She stopped, and then we identified a small German flag being waved by her coxswain.

A picket was sent to inspect her and to bring her officer to the flag-ship. He appeared rather flurried by his narrow escape. Apparently he was impressed when I informed him of the great danger that any small craft ran in approaching a squadron after dark in time of war. I expressed the hope that hereafter German boats would be sent only during the day, as otherwise a distressing accident might unavoidably occur.

Being thus constantly upon the alert by night, while by day, in spite of the tropical heat, the crews were continually exercised at sub-calibre practice and ship drills, and still further taxed by the necessity of sending working parties on shore to the Cavite arsenal machine-shops, the intervening months between the victory and the occupation of Manila by the troops proved very trying to officers and men. But they had in mind the fate of the *Maine* when lying at anchor in a Spanish harbor, and there was no inclination to relaxation of vigilance on their part.

As for myself, I have ever been a very early riser. I was always about the ship before daylight, while Chief of Staff Lamberton and Flag-Lieutenant Brumby divided the night between them into watches. The strain had soon told upon Captain Gridley, and on May 25 he was condemned by a medical survey and started for home, where he was never to arrive alive. Captain Lamberton succeeded him in command of the flag-ship, but still remained a close adviser, while heavier duties devolved upon Brumby, to whose unswerving industry, loyalty, and high intelligence I owe an everlasting debt.

Among the situations with which I had to deal promptly as they arose, when I could not delay to consult Washington, the most complicated was that of the Filipino insurgents. Before the squadron had left Hong Kong a cable, dated April 24, had been received from our consul-general at Singapore, saying that Emilio Aguinaldo, the insurgent chief, was at Singapore and would proceed to Hong Kong to see me if I so desired. I requested him to come, as it was possible that he might have valuable information to impart at a time when no source of information was to be neglected.

He came to Hong Kong, but did not arrive until after the departure of our squadron. Upon the first visit of the *McCulloch* to Hong Kong, he and several other insurgent leaders applied for transportation to Cavite. In the absence of any orders on the subject, Lieutenant Brumby refused to grant the request, but promised to take up the matter with me. On the second trip of the *McCulloch* I sent Ensign Caldwell, with instruction to allow Aguinaldo and three or four of his colleagues passage on board her to Manila.

Aguinaldo had been at one time a copyist in the Cavite arsenal under the Spanish regime. He was not yet thirty, a soft-spoken, unimpressive little man, who had enormous prestige with the Filipino people. Obviously, as our purpose was to weaken the Spaniards in every legitimate way, thus hastening the conclusion of hostilities in a war which was made to free

CAPTAIN CHARLES V. GRIDLEY, CAPTAIN OF THE "OLYMPIA"

COMMANDER B. P. LAMBERTON, ADMIRAL DEWEY'S CHIEF OF STAFF

Cuba from Spanish oppression, operations by the insurgents against Spanish oppression in the Philippines under certain restrictions would be welcome. Aguinaldo was allowed to establish himself in the arsenal, where he opened negotiations with his compatriots.

Soon, however, the marine officer in charge of the guard of the naval station was complaining about the constant traversing of his lines by scores of natives, who, of course, might be friends, but might equally well be enemies. As a result, I sent for Aguinaldo and informed him that he must leave the arsenal, but I would allow him to take up his quarters in Cavite town.

From my observation of Aguinaldo and his advisers I decided that it would be unwise to co-operate with him or his adherents in an official manner. Aside from permitting him to establish himself ashore, the only aid rendered him was a gift of some Mauser rifles and an old smooth-bore gun that had been abandoned by the Spanish. He mounted the 'gun on a float, but I declined to grant his request that our launches tow it across the bay. In short, my policy was to avoid any entangling alliance with the insurgents, while I appreciated that, pending the arrival of our troops, they might be of service in clearing the long neck of land that stretches out from Cavite Peninsula to the environs of Manila. [2]

Their numbers increasing by daily additions, the Filipinos slowly but surely drove the Spaniards back toward the city. By day we could see their attacks, and by night we heard their firing. We had some negotiations with them in regard to the disposition of Spanish prisoners and the transfer of Spanish women and children who had fallen into their hands; and again, at the request of the Spanish captain-general, Don Basilio Augustin Davila, I asked Aguinaldo's good offices in securing free passage through the insurgent lines for Don Basilio's own family, and other Spanish families who were cut off from Manila.

His answer expressing his willingness to grant my request, if it were in his power, was interesting because of its quaint English. [3]

The insurgents fought well. Their success, I think, was of material importance in isolating our marine force at Cavite from Spanish attack and in preparing a foothold for our troops when they should arrive. By the end of May they had entirely cleared Cavite Province of the enemy, and had so nearly surrounded Manila as to cause a panic among the inhabitants. The foreign consuls, acting for their apprehensive compatriots, now appealed to me to allow refugees of the various nationalities to leave the limits of the city and find asylum under my protection. Already, upon application of the British consul and of Captain Edward Chichester, of the British cruiser *Immortalité,* the senior British naval officer present, I had permitted several Europeans and some four hundred and fifty Chinese to embark in an English steamer bound for Amoy; and I was now equally willing to grant this new request.

At first I designated Cavite town as a place of refuge; but after further consideration I decided that, as all the quarters and facilities of Cavite would be needed for our own troops upon their arrival, it would be better to employ some of the many vessels then lying idle off Manila. Accordingly, ten of these were chartered by the different consuls and placed under the flags of their respective countries, in charge of the different men-of-war assembled off the city. Later, three more, one being assigned to the authority of the British, one to the French, and one to the German men-of-war, were added for the Spanish women and children.

I was also glad to consent to the request of the Spanish authorities that a number of their wounded then in a military hospital at Guadalupe should be transferred to a ship in the bay in charge of Captain Chichester; and through my good offices the insurgents who held the territory between this hospital and the sea allowed the wounded to pass through the lines for embarkation.

It was my aim to do everything consistent with military wisdom to minimize the rigor of the blockade.

As early as May 16 the navy department had informed me that the *Charleston* and transports with troops would soon be despatched. A week later the *Peking, Australia,* and *City of Sidney,* with a force of twenty-five hundred men under command of Brigadier-General Anderson, sailed from San Francisco for Honolulu, bringing for the squadron a supply of ammunition which I had earnestly requested. After the depletion of our magazines and shell-rooms by the battle, I felt the inevitable solicitude of any commander in the midst of war who is without sufficient ammunition to meet the emergencies of an engagement. This solicitude developed into anxiety when not only had Spain despatched a stronger naval force than my own, with a view to retrieving the disaster of May 1, but another nation was gathering a powerful squadron in Manila Bay.

The effect of the victory had precipitated a new element in the mastery of the Pacific and in the international rivalry for trade advantage in the populous Orient. Hitherto the United States had been considered a second-class power, whose foreign policy was an unimportant factor beyond the three-mile limit of the American hemisphere. By a morning's battle we had secured a base in the Far East at a juncture in international relations when the parcelling out of China among the European powers seemed imminent. This intrusion of an outsider could hardly be welcome in any quarter where there was opposition to the policy of the "open door" and the integrity of China which was advocated by us.

I knew that the intervention of any third power or group of powers while Sampson had yet to engage *Cervera,* or in the critical event of any set-back to our arms, might have brought grave consequences for us, while the Philippines were a rich prize for any ambitious power; or, if they remained Spanish, they were still under the sovereignty of a nation which could hardly be expected to play an important part in the affairs of China.

[1] Appendix B.
[2] Appendix E.
[3] GOBIERNO DICTATORIAL FILIPINAS
Kavite, 14th *June,* 1898.
Rear-Admiral
      George Dewey, *U. S. Navy.*
Dear Sir:
    I would have great satisfaction in pleasing you what you are asking me to allow the free return to Manila some Spanish families resident in Pampanga specially the General Mr. B. Augustin's.

I must remember you that the said Province my forces have not taken yet, but only surrounded; reason of which I see the impossibility to may garantee the free pass that you ask.

Notwithstanding I give to my subordinates terminal orders that as soon as they get in their hands the said families, not only keep the habit considerations among the civilizes nations, and also treat them as friends and carry them to Manila, as soon as the way will be safed from any risk, so as the families and their conveyers and the plan of operations would allow.

I am. Dear Sir,

Yours respectfully,

E. Aguinaldo.

Chapter Seventeen - A Period of Anxiety

At a dinner given me at the White House upon my return home President McKinley mentioned the repeated statements in the press about the friction in my relations with Vice-Admiral von Diedrichs, in command of the German Asiatic Squadron.

"There is no record of it at all on the files," he said.

"No, Mr. President," I answered. "As I was on the spot and familiar with the situation from day to day, it seemed best that I look after it myself, at a time when you had worries enough of your own."

Every officer who had served in the Civil War had had some experience with blockade, and some observation, if not experience, of the international questions which it had precipitated. Moreover, international law had been one of my favorite studies. Before the declaration of war with Spain I had not only considered the preparations for the battle, but my position in the event of victory. (In the event of defeat no ship of our Asiatic Squadron would have been afloat to tell the story.)

I foresaw that I must establish a blockade, cutting off the enemy's commerce as the first natural step in weakening the enemy. Inevitably the foreign nations would send their men-of-war to the bay for purposes of observation. During the Civil War English and French cruisers were always going and coming up and down the coast to see if the blockade were being maintained. There was rarely more than one, and never more than two off one port at a time. The appearance of a British or a French naval force larger than Dahlgren's off Charleston, or larger than Farragut's off Mobile, would have been considered a serious demonstration. I must maintain the blockade of Manila thoroughly and impartially if I were to avoid remonstrances. This I aimed to do from the moment of its establishment.

One might have thought that the activity shown by each foreign power would be regulated by the extent of its commercial interests and the number of its subjects on shore. The British had an overwhelming preponderance in trade, in investment, and in the number of their subjects resident in the Philippines. They had the largest naval force in Far Eastern waters of any power. But they never had more than three ships in Manila Bay at one time during the blockade.

In view of my isolation from a home base, and a desire to avoid any difficulties which should cause the government concern, it was bound to be a
matter of policy, if not of personal predilection, to allow visiting naval vessels
every privilege consistent with the principles of international law in relation
to neutrals. As I have previously stated, they were allowed to enter the bay
without any requirement other than the simple formality of being boarded,
in order to establish their identity, to inform them of the condition of affairs,
and to assign them an anchorage where they would not be in the way of operations if I had to engage the enemy's batteries or defend the squadron from
any improvised night torpedo attack.

Among the early arrivals of foreign men-of-war, besides the British ships
Linnet (May 2) and *Immortalité* (May. 7), were the French cruiser *Brieux*
(May 5), the Japanese cruiser *Itsukushima* (May 10), and the German cruisers
Irene (May 6) and *Cormoran* (May 9). Our flag-ship was off Cavite, our colors
were flying over the Cavite naval station, and our authority was paramount
in the bay. In view of these facts, the British, French, and Japanese saw and
acted on the obvious propriety — as foreign men-of-war did in the Civil War
— of reporting to the commander-in-chief of the blockading force and asking
where they should anchor.

The *Irene* had come from Nagasaki. Although she may not have heard the
news of the victory before leaving Japan, she definitely had the information
from an English steamer the morning of her arrival. Nevertheless, she
steamed by the *Olympia* without stopping and dropped anchor where she
chose.

I regarded this as an oversight which was a breach of naval etiquette, of
course, but not to be taken seriously unless I were inclined to insist on punc-
tiliousness. It was only natural to reason that the captain of the *Irene* might
not be familiar with the customs and the laws of blockades. I knew the German naval officers were very self-reliant, keen to take offence about their
rights, and most ambitious to learn by observation, which I always liked to
think explained their subsequent proceedings. On my part, despite the exag-
gerated reports which should be set at rest, let me repeat that my only object
was enforcement of the blockade in such a manner as should safeguard my
squadron, and leave no room for complaint of favoritism.

The second German ship, the *Cormoran,* came in at three in the morning.
Naturally, at night it was our business to be on the alert. When her lights
were seen a steam launch was sent to board her. She gave no heed to the
steam launch's hail. Even though a man-of-war flew a German flag, it was
possible that she was Spanish, using the German flag as a ruse. According to
the laws of blockade it was our right and duty to board and identify her.

In order to get the attention of the *Cormoran* the *Raleigh* fired a shot
across her bows. Then she promptly came to. Her captain was surprised at
our action, but our boarding officer explained the law, and also the risk that a
man-of-war was running in coming into the harbor at night. We had no
thought of being discourteous and no desire to rouse any ill feeling, and fully

appreciated how our point of view had not occurred to the captain of the *Cormoran* when he ran straight in toward our squadron in the dark. The shot across the bow was not provocative, but simply a form of signal when other signals had failed.

As early as May 20 the navy department had cabled me that the *Carlos V, Pelayo,* and *Alfonso II* and some transports were reported to have left Spain for the East. I replied that in event of their arrival our squadron would endeavor to give a good account of itself. On May 27 and 30 I received further cables announcing that the monitors *Monterey* and *Monadnock* would be sent to reinforce me.

On the 12th Vice-Admiral von Diedrichs arrived in his flag-ship, the *Kaiserin Augusta.* This made three German cruisers in the harbor. I learned that another was expected. Already, on the 6th, a German transport, the *Darmstadt,* bringing fourteen hundred men as relief crews for the German vessels, had appeared. Such a transfer, for which I readily gave permission, while it might have been unusual in a blockaded harbor, might at the same time be easily explained as a matter of convenience for the German squadron which was absent from its regular base at Kiau Chau. The *Darmstadt,* however, with her force of men nearly equal to the total number of my own crews, remained at anchor for four weeks.

As my rank was inferior to Vice-Admiral von Diedrichs's, I made the first call, in the usual exchange of visits. In the course of conversation I referred to the presence of the large German force and to the limited German interests in the Philippines (there was only one German commercial house in Manila), and this in a courteous manner, amounting to a polite inquiry which I thought was warranted, particularly in view of the fact that six days had elapsed without the *Darmstadt* transferring her men. To this the vice-admiral answered:

"I am here by order of the Kaiser, sir"; from which I could only infer that I had expressed myself in a way that excited his displeasure.

In the course of a cable to the navy department on June 12 I requested that the *Monadnock* and *Monterey* be expedited. Meanwhile, I had heard nothing further of the reports of the departure of a Spanish squadron to the Far East, which I might set down as a rumor that had been unconfirmed.

In a cable of June 18 from Washington, which was brought to Manila by the *McCulloch,* which had taken mine of the 12th, I was informed that Camara's squadron, consisting of "two armored cruisers, six converted cruisers, four destroyers, reported off Ceuta, sailing to the East, by the United States consul at Gibraltar. If they pass Suez, Egypt, will cable you. The *Monterey* and collier sailed for Manila from San Diego on June ii. The *Monadnock* and collier will follow on June 20, if possible...."

Within a week there were five German men-of-war in the port, two of them having a heavier displacement than any of my own ships. The *Kaiser* came in after dark on June 18. She paid no attention to the launch sent to board her. However, the next morning she steamed over to Cavite and for-mally reported her arrival.

My idea of the Spaniards was that at the first sign of the offensive in any direction Camara would take the defensive. In answer to the announcement that he had sailed I cabled the department from Hong Kong, June 27, that in my judgment "if the coast of Spain were threatened the squadron of the en-emy would have to return." Peculiarly enough, this reached the department a few hours after the board of strategy had advised that Commodore Watson be sent with a squadron to make the demonstration on the coast of Spain, which it was never necessary for him to undertake.

On the 26th Camara was at Port Said, from which his arrival was reported to me as promptly as the information could reach me when I was three days from any working cable station. He had the two powerful cruisers *Pelayo,* of 9,000 tons, and *Carlos V,* of 9,200 tons, while the total displacement of my whole squadron was only 19,098 tons. They were so well protected as to be in the armored class. They had two 12.6-inch and four 11-inch guns, while my largest calibre was 8-inch. Alone, they were an equal antagonist for my squadron.

Therefore, my desire for the prompt arrival of at least one of the monitors was even more keen than when I had expressed it in the cable of June 12. On account of their low freeboard, scarcely meant for transoceanic cruises, the monitors must make very slow progress. But once the *Monterey* arrived I had an armored vessel with two 12 and two 10-inch guns, which, though it could manoeuvre at only eight knots, was able to deliver telling blows and with-stand a fire which would have been most damaging to my unarmored cruis-ers.

With a superior squadron of the enemy coming, with the many perplexi-ties of the blockade, while I waited on the arrival of the monitors and the transports with troops, the latter days of June were full of care for myself and staff. In every cable from Washington we looked for fresh news about Cama-ra and hoped for decisive action by our troops and our squadron at Santiago which would effectually dispose of Cervera's squadron, thus leaving Admiral Sampson's ships ready for any fresh emergency. Once Camara was past Suez, with sufficient coal for the rest of the cruise, there could be no question but that I must be prepared to engage him.

Characteristic of bold journalism was the direction of Mr. Hearst to one of his staff to sink a ship in the canal to delay Camara, which, however, his sub-ordinate did not carry out. Mr. Watts, our consul-general at Cairo, was most active in his representations to Lord Cromer, the British adviser of the Egyp-tian government, for the enforcement of the neutrality laws. Thanks to his efforts and those of Ambassador Hay, in London, the Egyptian government prohibited the sale of coal to the Spanish vessels other than enough to take them back to Spain, and limited their stay in port to the usual period of twen-ty-four hours.

However, even after this decision by the Egyptian government, Camara remained at Port Said for some days attempting to purchase coal, and, upon this being refused him, to transship coal from his own colliers. He also tried to enlist a force of stokers, but Mr. Watts's renewed remonstrances brought forth a peremptory order for him to depart at once.

After passing through the canal he made a stop at Suez, but being warned off he left the harbor and anchored five miles offshore, where he was well outside the three-mile limit and thus free of Egyptian authority. He was still in condition to continue his voyage, it being an easy matter for him to have coaled from his colliers in the smooth waters of some of the ports of the Red Sea, where neutrality restrictions would not have been enforced.

In the event that Camara should arrive before the *Monterey,* as I had reason at one time to fear that he would, my plan was not to wait in Manila Bay for him, as Montojo had waited for our squadron, but to take up my position in the southern part of the Philippine archipelago, from which I should have steamed out to strike the enemy's ships, hopefully by surprise, when they were hampered by their transports, thus throwing them into disorder at the outset of the engagement. One source of great confidence lay in my veteran crews. They had already fought the Spaniards in one battle.

But the necessity of another action was averted. The department had cabled on June 29: "Squadron under Watson, Iowa, *Oregon, Yankee, Dixie, Newark,* and *Yosemite a*nd four colliers, preparing with all possible despatch to start Spanish coast. The Spaniards know this." The knowledge had the effect intended. On July 8, after the victory of Santiago, when the whole of Sampson's squadron was free to go to the coast of Spain, Camara's squadron re-entered the Suez Canal, and on July 11 it left Port Said for Cartagena. Meanwhile, on June 30, the transports with the first lot of our troops had arrived. They were escorted by the cruiser *Charleston*, which was a valuable reinforcement to my squadron and brought the supply of ammunition which was vitally important if I were to engage Camara.

In the latter part of June and the early days of July the Germans, with the industry with which they aim to make their navy efficient, were keeping very busy. I saw that they did not mean to accept my interpretation of the laws of blockade. German officers frequently landed in Manila, where they were on the most cordial terms with the Spaniards, who paid them marked attention; and, the wish fathering the thought, the talk of the town was that the Germans would intervene in favor of Spain. It was well known that ViceAdmiral von Diedrichs had officially visited the Spanish captain-general in Manila, who had returned the call at night. No other senior foreign naval officer had exchanged visits with the captain-general. Other Spanish officials called on the Germans and were saluted by the German vessels, these salutes being returned by the Spanish batteries on shore; but they did not call on the other senior officers present so far as I know, and certainly were not saluted if they did. One foreign consul in Manila, I know, had orders from his government to report the actions of the Germans in cipher.

Not only did the German officers frequently visit the Spanish troops and outposts, thus familiarizing themselves with the environs of Manila, but a Prince Löwenstein was taken off to the *Kaiserin Augusta* by one of Aguinaldo's staff. This came to our knowledge through the fact that the prince and his escort had to seek refuge on board an English man-of-war in a heavy sea. German man-of-war boats took soundings off Malabon and the mouth of the Pasig River, and German seamen were sent to occupy the lighthouse at the mouth of the Pasig for some days.

These extracts from the *Olympia's* log are illuminating as to the activities of the German ships which were continually cruising about the bay and running in and out:

"June 27 — Irene returned from Mariveles, During first watch at night saw searchlight at entrance of bay. *Kaiserin Augusta* got under way from Manila anchorage and stood down the bay.

"June 28 — *Kaiser* came in.

"June 29 — I*rene* got under way, steamed about the upper bay and returned. Later again left the harbor. *Prinzess Wilhelm* came in and anchored. *Cormoran* got under way and stood down to Mariveles.

"June 30 — *Kaiserin Augusta* came in and anchored off Manila. *Callao* was sent over to Manila to board her. *Trinidad* with coal for German Squadron arrived.

"July I — *Cormoran* and P*rinzess Wilhelm* came in.

"July 2 — *Cormoran* and German collier left.

"July 3 — *Kaiser* left harbor."

Finally, without my permission, they landed their men for drill at Mariveles harbor opposite Corregidor and Boca Chica at the entrance to the bay and took possession of the quarantine station, while Admiral von Diedrichs occupied a large house which had been the quarters of the Spanish officials. On July 5 I hoisted my flag on the *McCulloch* and steamed around the German ships anchored in Mariveles, without, however, communicating with the German admiral, while I trusted that he might understand that I did not view his proceeding with favor.

On the 6th I was informed by the insurgents that the Germans had been interfering with their operations against the Spaniards in Subig Bay. This was, of course, contrary to my policy to allow the insurgents to weaken the Spaniards as far as possible, and it was, besides, a breach of neutrality by a neutral power. I despatched the *Raleigh* and *Concord* to Subig to inquire into the truth of this report. They found a force of Spanish troops intrenched on Isla Grande, and under siege by the insurgents. There was not a German subject in the place. When the German cruiser *Irene* appeared her captain had visited the Spaniards and then informed the insurgents that they might not use a small steamer which was in their possession to assist in their operations against the Spaniards. However, when the *Raleigh* and *Concord* steamed into the harbor at daylight the *Irene* promptly steamed out.

Captain J. B. Coghlan, of the *Raleigh*, being the senior officer present, concluded that Isla Grande, on account of its strategic importance in commanding the entrance to Subig Bay (which might furnish Camara a refuge if he should escape us), ought not to be in the possession of the enemy. After we fired a few shots from the light guns of the two cruisers the Spaniards, six officers and five hundred men, surrendered. As Coghlan had no means of caring for the prisoners, he turned them over temporarily to the insurgents, with express instructions that they must be well treated.

Even before our flag was flying over Isla Grande, although we had not yet received the news, Americans at home were rejoicing over our naval victory at Santiago and Camara had been recalled to Spain, I was glad of an opportunity of stating my own position with perfect candor to Admiral von Diedrichs, yet in a diplomatic fashion which could not be personally offensive to him, however positive he was in his views about the rights of neutrals in a blockaded port. Already there had been a correspondence between us in which, in keeping with the accepted authorities on international law, [1] including the German Perels, who had lectured at the Imperial German Naval Academy at Kiel, I maintained my right of blockade in boarding all vessels, including men-of-war. Or, in my own words, in one letter to ViceAdmiral von Diedrichs:

"As a state of war exists between the United States and Spain, and as the entry into this blockaded port of the vessels of war of a neutral is permitted by the blockading squadron as a matter of international courtesy, such neutrals should necessarily satisfy the blockading vessels as to their identity. I distinctly disclaim any intention of exercising or claiming the *droit de visite* of neutral vessels of war. What I do claim is the right to communicate with all vessels entering this port, now blockaded with the forces under my command. It could easily be possible that it was the duty of the picket vessel to notify incoming men-of-war that they could not enter the port, not on account of the blockade, but the intervention of my lines of attack."

Vice-Admiral von Diedrichs, in denial of the right, had notified us that he would submit the point to a conference of all the senior officers of the men-of-war in the harbor. But only one officer appeared. Captain Chichester, of the British *Immortalité*. He informed the German commander that I was acting entirely within my rights; that he had instructions from his government to comply with even more rigorous restrictions than I had laid down; and, moreover, that as the senior British officer present he had passed the word that all British men-of-war upon entering the harbor should first report to me and fully satisfy any inquiries on my part before proceeding to the anchorage of the foreign fleet.

However, Vice-Admiral von Diedrichs was unconvinced. When, later, the *Cormoran*, which was an old offender, was sighted coming up the bay Flag-Lieutenant Brumby was sent to make sure that she stopped to report, in keeping with the custom of other foreign men-of-war. When the *Cormoran* saw the *McCulloch* approaching she turned and steamed toward the northern part of the bay, compelling the *McCulloch* to follow. Brumby first hoisted the international signal, "I wish to communicate." No attention was paid to this by the *Cormoran*. Then Brumby fired a shot across her bows, which had the desired effect.

On the following day Vice-Admiral von Diedrichs sent a capable, tactful young officer of his staff to me with a memorandum of grievances. When I had heard them through I made the most of the occasion by using him as a third person to state candidly and firmly my attitude in a verbal message which he conveyed to his superior so successfully that Vice-Admiral von Diedrichs was able to understand my point of view. There was no further interference with the blockade or breach of the etiquette which had been established by the common consent of the other foreign commanders. Thus, as I explained to the President, after the war was over, a difference of opinion about international law had been adjusted amicably, without adding to the sum of his worries.

[1] Appendix F.

Chapter Eighteen - The Taking of Manila

On the way across the Pacific the bloodless capture of Guam was effected by the first expeditionary force. Brigadier-General Anderson, who was in command, had his troops quartered ashore soon after his arrival. On July 17 a second contingent of thirty-six hundred men came in under command of Brigadier-General Francis V. Greene. The next day they were landed at Paranaque, a position more than half-way between Cavite and Manila, which the insurgents had reached in their persistent advance. The captured vessels *Rapido* and *Isabel* and some cascoes (lighters), which I had obtained for the purpose, were utilized in landing General Greene's command, while the gunboat *Callao* covered the disembarkation which was not in any way opposed, as the Spaniards kept to their agreement with me and made no demonstration during the operation.

Within three days the whole force, with their provisions, equipage, ammunition, and field-guns, were all in camp on some open ground protected on one side by the beach and on the other by rice paddy fields and dense tropical undergrowth. Although within range of the Spanish artillery, they were beyond that of the Spanish rifles and without any interference by the Spaniards were able to settle down to the business of accustoming themselves to the heat, insect life, and torrential rains of their new surroundings.

Manila at this time was garrisoned by some thirteen thousand troops, stationed either within the fortifications or in the lines of trenches and defensive works around the city. The insurgents had been at work only two months with an organization of the flimsiest character, yet by means of guerilla warfare, developed from years of experience in their resistance to Spanish domination, had not only advanced their lines along the beach almost to the fortifications, but had invested the city on the inland side as well. Thanks to their advance, we were able to land our troops within easy striking distance of their objective.

When Major-General Merritt arrived on July 25 to take supreme command of the army, he agreed with me that it was not good policy to make any movement that would precipitate a conflict with the Spaniards or tend to bring on a general engagement before the chosen moment for a combined attack. My wishes were rather emphatic on this subject, and rightly so, I still think. I was already conducting negotiations with the Spanish captain-general which I felt sure would result in a practically peaceful surrender of Manila, with a saving of life on both sides.

However, with two armed forces facing each other in time of war it is difficult to prevent a clash; and it was not long before the inevitable happened. General Merritt decided that the attack should be made along the shore, and also that the insurgents, who were between our troops and the Spaniards, must be drawn to one side. His instructions, in common with mine, were to avoid all sign of alliance with the insurgents. Therefore, without holding any direct communication with Aguinaldo, he directed General Greene to persuade the Filipinos to move out of the way. This Greene tactfully accomplished, and our men soon occupied part of the trenches built by the insurgents. Had they remained in this position there might have been no bloodshed. But on the plea that these trenches were not well located they pushed ahead and began fortifying themselves in a new position nearer Fort San Antonio, garrisoned by the Spaniards, which was only a thousand yards distant.

This work was continued for three days before the Spaniards made a move of any kind. Then they appeared to realize that a new line of intrenchments three hundred yards in length, much more formidable than the shallow rifle-pits used by the insurgents, was becoming a serious menace to the fort, and on the night of July 31 they suddenly opened fire on our troops.

To our naval officers, thoroughly accustomed to such night alarms, this firing as heard out on the bay seemed only a habitual proceeding between the Spaniards and the insurgents. But to our raw volunteers the sudden burst of bullets in the midst of intense darkness, blinding rain, and flooded trenches and generally exotic surroundings formed a real test of discipline and courage. The Spaniards made no advance. Their efforts were entirely confined to the rifle and artillery fire, which continued for two hours. Our volunteers stood their ground during their baptism of fire with the nonchalance of veterans, and suffered a loss of ten killed and thirty wounded.

Meanwhile, in anticipation of some such affair as a result of my observation of the course of events ashore, I had directed that the *Boston* should anchor near our camp, less than a mile from shore. The captain was instructed to open fire if so requested by General Greene. At the same time I strongly expressed my desire that this should be avoided unless considered absolutely necessary.

A less experienced officer than General Greene might have readily been misled into thinking the situation alarming; but, fortunately, and much to my satisfaction, he did not call upon the *Boston* for assistance. Three more of these night attacks occurred during the ensuing week; but in keeping with our mutual understanding, General Merritt had given positive orders that the Spanish fire should not be returned unless the Spaniards left their works to attack us. This order was not implicitly obeyed, as it was finally impossible to restrain our spirited infantry from returning some of the compliments which they were receiving from the enemy.

On July 31 Brigadier-General Arthur Mac Arthur with four thousand additional troops arrived, and after some delay, owing to bad weather and a heavy surf, they were added to the numbers under General Greene's command. Three days be-fore this was effected, however, on August 4, the *Monterey* steamed into the harbor, and with her as a reinforcement my squadron was stronger than any squadron in the bay.

The U. S. S. Monterey

Our troops were now chafing at restraint. They could see no reason for further delay. Even General Greene earnestly requested that the attack should be delivered forthwith. However, I pointed out to him the risk and loss of prestige in a premature attack, arguing that neither the army nor the navy was ready for an engagement. The storm which had delayed the landing of MacArthur's brigade had also prevented the landing of ammunition, of which there was a shortage on shore, while the *Monterey* after her long voyage needed a few days' overhauling. Moreover, I was sanguine of the successful issue to negotiations for a peaceful capitulation which I had initiated with the Spanish captain-general through the medium of M. Edouard André, the Belgian consul in Manila.

Owing to the restriction of the blockade and to the investment of the city on the land side by the insurgents, the people of Manila were in a bad way for supplies. Soon after the victory of May 1, as I have already stated, General Don Basilio Augustin Davila, through the British consul, Mr. Rawson-Walker, had intimated to me his willingness to surrender to our squadron. But at that time I could not entertain the proposition because I had no force with which to occupy the city, and I would not for a moment consider the possibility of turning it over to the undisciplined insurgents, who, I feared, might wreak their vengeance upon the Spaniards and indulge in a carnival of loot.

During July the British consul was very ill. His death, in fact, occurred early in August. When the negotiations with the captain-general tending to a surrender were again broached it was M. André who acted as intermediary, transmitting all messages (always verbal ones) from the captain-general to me and from me to the captain-general. I was almost alone in believing in the sincerity of these negotiations. General Merritt was sceptical, but ready to defer to my judgment, and so were my chief of staff and my flag-lieutenant. Nevertheless, I felt confident of the outcome, in which I consider that I was fully justified by later events.

While M. André's work had begun with Don Basilio on July 24, a cable from Madrid had summarily dismissed Don Basilio from office, with orders to turn over his authority to General Firmin Jaudenes. This cable presumably was sent to the Spanish consul in Hong Kong, whence it was transmitted through the mails, reaching Don Basilio about August I. It was in reply to a message from Don Basilio to the home government, in which he had pointed out the critical condition of affairs in Manila and the hopelessness of its defence, the exhausted state of his troops, the shortness of provisions in the city, the rapid augmentation of the American forces, and the utter despair that existed on all sides since the receipt of the news of Camara's return to Spain. In view of these considerations he declined the responsibility of the situation, and the government's answer was his relief from command.

However, André continued with General Jaudenes the negotiations begun with Don Basilio. These progressed with varying success and numerous side issues, but always with the stipulation on the part of the Spaniards that if they surrendered the insurgents should be kept out of the city. Finally, without making any definite promise, General Jaudenes agreed that, although he would not surrender except in consequence of an attack upon the city, yet, unless the city were bombarded, the Manila batteries would not open on our ships. Moreover, once the attack was begun he would, if willing to surrender, hoist a white flag over a certain point in the walled city from which it could be seen both from Malate and from the bay.

In other words, his attitude differed from that of Don Basilio only in that he wished to show the form of resistance for the sake of Spanish honor; or, as the Chinese say, to "save his face."

It was also understood that before this white flag was shown the *Olympia* should fly the international code signal "D. W. H. B.," meaning "Surrender," and a sketch of the signal flags to be hoisted was given by M. Andre to General Jaudenes. Although there were some further negotiations concerning the terms of surrender, nothing was definitely agreed upon; while it was impressed on General Jaudenes that the generosity of the terms granted would depend upon the brevity of his resistance. Indeed, these pourparlers continued until the day before the capture of the city.

At first General Merritt and myself decided upon August 10 as the date of the attack. On the 7th we sent the usual forty-eight hours' notice preparatory to a bombardment to General Jaudenes. [1] He answered that, being surrounded by insurgent forces, he had no place of refuge for the wounded and sick and the women and children except within the walls of the city. In reply we pointed out how helpless was his position and how clearly it was his duty to save the city from the horrors of bombardment. He demurred and begged time in which to consult his government, a request which was promptly refused.

In keeping with our assurance on the 7th that the city would not be fired upon for at least forty-eight hours the desultory firing between the infantry forces on either side ceased. On the 9th the foreign men-of-war and the refugee steamers under their charge were notified to shift their anchorages so as to be out of the line of fire. It was noticeable that while the German and French vessels took up a position to the northward of the city, the English and Japanese came over to Cavite and anchored near our squadron. Later in the day the *Concord* and *Petrel* were sent over in the vicinity of the German vessels. On the following morning they closed in to within one mile of the breakwater at the mouth of the Pasig River. This position they maintained until the city surrendered.

On the morning of the loth all preparations were complete for any emergency. Boats and extra gear had been sent on shore to the arsenal. The ships were cleared for action with steam up, and waited only on the word to get under way. But the signal run up to the *Olympia*s yard-arm was, "The attack is postponed." General Merritt had come on board the flag-ship to report that the army was not quite ready.

However, on the 12th it was announced that the attack would be delivered upon the following morning. The 13th dawned as a typical Manila day, after intervals of rain during the night. The air was lifeless, the thermometer in the 8o's, and everything was steaming with humid heat. But at eight o'clock the sky partially cleared and a light breeze sprang up. At 8.45 the ships got under way and moved in to their stations — the *Charleston, Boston,* and *Baltimore* off the Luneta battery, the Monterey farther inshore and nearer the batteries of the city proper, the *Concord* off the mouth of the Pasig, and the *Olympia, Raleigh,* and *Petrel,* with the *Callao* and *McCulloch,* opposite the Malate fort, where they could not only reduce the fort but enfilade the Spanish lines.

As we got under way the officers and men of the British ship *Immortalité* crowded on the deck, her guard was paraded, and her band played "Under the Double Eagle," which was known to be my favorite march. Then, as we drew away from the anchorage from which for over three months we had watched the city and bay. Captain Chichester got under way also and with the *Immortalité* and the *Iphigenia* steamed over toward the city and took up a position which placed his vessels between ours and those of the foreign fleet. We broke our battle flags from the mast-heads with the conviction that we were to see the end of the story which we had begun when they were broken out on the morning of May 1.

At 9.35 the *Olympia, Raleigh, Petrel,* and *Callao* opened fire on Fort San Antonio, on the flank of the Spanish intrenchments, which was continued slowly for about an hour, without any response from the fort. Meanwhile, we could see our troops on shore advancing through the fields and along the beach. As they came into view, sturdily breasting their way through the shallow water and meeting all obstacles with enthusiastic cheering, the flag-ship signalled to cease firing, and shortly afterward, followed by the *Raleigh* and *Petrel*, steamed to the northward to assume a position off the town. With the *Callao*, under Lieutenant Tappan, and the little *Barcelo*, in charge of Naval Cadet White, keeping ahead of them and sweeping the beach and Spanish trenches with their machine guns, the troops gallantly rushed to the assault and soon were seen swarming over the parapet of Fort San Antonio. At 10.35 the Spanish colors disappeared from the fort and our own were hoisted.

In the meantime the other vessels of the squadron had awaited developments in their position commanding the heavy batteries of the city itself. Few on board, and, indeed, few of the junior officers of the army, had any inkling of an agreement with the Spaniards, so that all were firmly convinced that they were going into action. But my captains were directed not to fire unless fired upon, and not one of the enemy's thirty-nine heavy guns having the range of our ships was discharged.

As the *Olympia* and her consorts approached the other vessels the flag-ship was flying the international signal "D. W. H. B." for "Surrender"; but, although sharp eyes on the bridge of the flag-ship scrutinized the forts for a sign of the return signal, the background was so indefinite that for a time nothing was sighted. Finally, however, it was my fortune to be the first to make out a white flag flying on the appointed place on the southwest bastion of the city wall. Our own signal had been hoisted at 11 AM., and it was not until 11:20 that we distinguished the answer.

Flag-Lieutenant Brumby and Colonel Whittier, of General Merritt's staff, with M. André, were now landed in the city and were met by General Jaudenes and Admiral Montojo, and the preliminary articles of capitulation were promptly drawn up. [2] General Jaudenes had saved his honor by a formal show of resistance. At 2:20 Brumby returned to the flagship with his report and I signalled the squadron: "The enemy has surrendered." I directed the ships, which had been kept under way in readiness for any failure of the compact with the Spaniards, to anchor off the water-front of the city, where they commanded it with their guns. Meanwhile, the army had entered the city from the side of the Luneta, and with some difficulty had also prevented the insurgents from coming in.

Probably the army officers were so completely absorbed in their work that they did not notice that the Spanish flag was still flying over the citadel. From the ships, however, it was strikingly apparent, and I concluded that before the sun went down our colors must float over the city. So I sent Brumby on shore again with the largest American ensign we had on the flag-ship, accompanied only by a couple of young signal boys. He had to push his way through the crowded streets and enter a citadel filled with Spanish soldiers not yet disarmed to accomplish his task.

At 5:43 I saw the Spanish flag come down and then our own float in its place. The guns of all our ships thundered out a national salute, while the band of one of our regiments, which happily chanced to be passing the citadel, played the "Star-Spangled Banner," the troops saluted, officers uncovered, and the Stars and Stripes, as it was raised for the first time over Manila, was greeted with all the honor so punctiliously given the flag on ceremonious occasions both by the army and the navy. The next morning the foreign men-of-war were officially notified that the city had been occupied and the port was open. Of all the foreign commanders, only Captain Chichester acknowledged the notification by firing the national salute of twenty-one guns with the American ensign at the main.

The details of the surrender [2] were determined on the 14th by a joint commission, on which my chief of staff. Captain Lamberton, was our naval representative. The Spanish troops surrendered the city and its defences with all the honors of war, laying down their arms and referring the question of their future status and repatriation to the government at Washington; officers were allowed to retain their side-arms, horses, and private property; all public property and public funds were turned over to United States authority; and Manila, with its inhabitants, churches, educational institutions, and private property, was placed under guard of the American army.

I paid my first visit to the city two days later, and found conditions absolutely tranquil and orderly. The people had already resumed their peaceful avocations, and if it had not been for the colors over the citadel, the American sentries posted here and there, and the presence in the streets of the tall, stalwart, good-natured Western volunteers, who made the little Filipinos seem diminutive in contrast, one would never have imagined that a state of war had lately existed or that the sovereignty of centuries had been changed.

News of the signing of the peace protocol, with instructions to occupy the city pending the conclusion of a treaty of peace [3] and to suspend hostilities and the blockade, arrived in Manila on the 16th, and so did the monitor *Monadnock*. But now one was as useless as the other was unnecessary. On the night of August 14, for the first time since April 25, the ships were not shrouded in darkness. That afternoon I had given the welcome signal, "All restrictions on lights revoked," which meant an immense difference in the comfort of the officers and men of the squadron.

Had not the cable been cut there would have been no attack on the 13th, for while our ships — counting the twelve hours' difference in time between the two hemispheres — were moving into position and our troops were holding themselves in readiness for a dash upon the Spanish works the protocol was being signed at Washington. The absence of immediate cable connection had allowed no interruption to the fateful progress of events which was to establish our authority in the Philippines. On August 21 the cable was raised and spliced, and Manila was no longer isolated from daily cable communication with the rest of the world.

[1] Appendix G.   [2] Appendix H.
[3]   Washington, *August* 12, 1898.

Dewey, Hongkong:

Peace protocol signed by President. Suspend all hostilities and blockade.
Allen.

Washington, *August* 12, 1898.

Dewey, Hongkong:

The protocol, signed by the President today, provides that the United States will occupy and hold the city, bay and harbor of Manila pending the conclusion of a treaty of peace which shall determine the control, disposition and government of the Philippines. This is most important.
Allen, *Acting.*

Chapter Nineteen - Since Manila

On August 20, seven days after the taking of Manila, I said, in the course of a cable to the department: "I trust that it may not be necessary to order me to Paris. Should very much regret to leave here while matters are in their present critical condition."

As the one person who had been continuously in touch with the Philippine situation from the moment that it was precipitated, I considered it my duty to remain on the scene as long as there was any opportunity for service. Hostilities had ceased with the signing of the protocol, but the final terms of a treaty of peace remained to be negotiated. Our government had yet to decide whether or not to keep the Philippines.

If we decided to keep them, there was the question of our policy of administration the urgent importance of which was readily realized by one on the spot, while it was difficult to make it realized by those in Washington who had had no experience of Oriental countries. General Merritt was ordered to report to our delegates at the Paris Peace Conference, bringing along with his own suggestions any that I had to communicate.

Philippine Commission, 1899 – Jacob G. Sherman, Admiral George Dewey, Dean C. Worcester

Mr. McKinley, after sounding public opinion at home, decided not to haul down the flag, and Spain, in return for relinquishing sovereignty of the islands, was paid the sum of twenty millions. At the time the delegates to the Peace Conference scarcely comprehended that a rebellion was included with the purchase. We were far from being in possession of the property which we had bought. Manila was only the capital city of the most important of a group of many islands, with many capitals, in all of which we must establish authority. With the native population welcoming us this would have been only a formal task. But outside Manila Aguinaldo was continuing to recruit his forces, while his agitators spread hostility to us throughout the archipelago. Gradually our troops in Manila under command of Major-General E. S. Otis, who had succeeded General Merritt, were finding themselves invested by the insurgents, while they rested inactive under strict orders not to provoke a conflict.

The Filipinos, particularly as we could have no official relations with the Aguinaldo dictatorship, could not believe in our good intentions. Mr. McKinley's proclamation of "benevolent assimilation" fell on ears which had long since learned to distrust the beneficent and grandiloquent proclamations of which the Spanish were masters. It was a time for statesmanship if we were to avoid a conflict. As Washington seemed to be in the dark about the real situation on shore, I cabled on January 7, 1899, stating that affairs were very disturbed and that a small "civilian commission composed of men skilled in diplomacy and statesmanship should be sent to adjust differences."

At the same time I wrote to Senator Proctor, expressing my fear that, despite General Otis's forbearance, we were drifting into a war with the natives. "This appears to me an occasion for a triumph of statesmanship rather than of arms. Should the President decide to do as I suggest, I hope that you will be a member of the commission. These people are afraid of us, navy and army, but would listen to you while they would not to us. They should be treated kindly, exactly as you would treat children, for they are little else, and should be coerced only after gentler means of bringing them to reason have failed."

President McKinley acted promptly on my advice. Secretary Long cabling me on January 12: "Schurman of Cornell, Worcester of Ann Arbor, Denby, late Minister to China, go soon to Manila with instructions. They with you and Otis constitute commission." But in less than a month after their appointment the growing anger of the natives had broken into flame. Now, after paying twenty millions for the islands, we must establish our authority by force against the very wishes of the people whom we sought to benefit. Once the early fighting with the insurgents was over and their capital at Malolos taken, the problem was one of successive occupation of towns and provinces against all the exasperations of guerrilla warfare, in which the navy could be of assistance only by protecting landing forces and the use of its small gunboats in shallow waters.

In requesting the appointment of the Schurman commission I had taken the first step toward the development of a system of civil administration and the application of the principles of enlightened representative government in an Oriental country under the tutelage of a Western nation. It is for other pens to write of the later history of the Philippines, with its entail of vigilance, danger, and hardships for our troops and of faithful service by our teachers and administrators, which have brought to the Filipino people the benefits of modern education and progress and the opportunity for industrial development.

Admiral Dewey Receiving Rear-Admiral Sampson on Board the "Olympia", New York

On March 2, 1899, Congress had authorized the President "to appoint by selection and promotion an admiral of the navy, who shall not be placed upon the retired list except by his own application; and whenever such office shall be vacated by death or otherwise the office shall cease to exist." President McKinley named me for this unique rank.

Ten months had now elapsed since I entered Manila Bay. I had not once left it, even to take advantage of the brief climatic change to Hong Kong which I was able to give all my officers. Whatever merit there was in untiring devotion to work while there was work to do, I might rightfully claim as an expression of gratitude for the honor which my country had bestowed upon me. But I was weary and in poor health, while I could not help being deeply affected by the necessity of the loss of life and the misery which the pacification of the islands imposed.

A year after the victory, confident that my presence was no longer necessary, the flag-ship weighed anchor, leaving the Asiatic Squadron in command of Captain A. S. Barker (now rear-admiral, retired), who had brought out the battle-ship *Oregon.*

President McKinley had left it to me to choose my time of departure and my route homeward. From all parts of the United States had come requests for a journey across the country by rail. Our inland cities seemed to be vying with one another in plans for magnificent receptions. Towns, children, and articles of commerce were named after me. I was assured that nothing like the enthusiasm for a man and a deed had ever been known. But my health was unequal to any such triumphal progress.

As one friend warned me, although I had survived the running of the batteries of Forts Jackson and St. Philip, the batteries of Port Hudson and the battles of Fort Fisher and Manila Bay, I could never survive the hospitality from the Pacific to the Atlantic coast. Therefore, I decided that I would land in New York, after cruising leisurely homeward by way of the Mediterranean.

Now, when I entered a foreign harbor, it was with my four-starred flag in place of the commodore's broad pennant, entitled to a salute of nineteen guns, and at any public function the commander of the Asiatic Squadron need not take second place. At Hong Kong for the first time in a year I enjoyed the luxury of sleeping on shore in a hotel free from ship's routine. After stops at Colombo and Singapore, where the

The Temporary Triumphal Arch Erected In New York in Admiral Dewey's Honor Upon His Arrival from the Philippines

British officials showed me every honor, and at the same time with characteristic consideration appreciated my desire for rest, I proceeded through the Suez Canal.

My fondness for the Mediterranean, which had begun with my midshipman cruise, had never waned. In its bracing air I found the tonic that I needed; Many old associations were renewed, many old memories aroused, among them those of Farragut's tour. The Civil War had sent its admiral with the message of a nation reunited by force; and the Spanish War had sent its admiral with the message of a country reunited in sentiment and become a world power. I could be as proud of the *Olympia* for the victory she had won as I had been as a midshipman of the *Wabash*; and where as captain of the *Pensacola* I knew that we had a navy of antiquated ships, now I knew that we had a navy of ships that were fully abreast of the progress in naval science.

I was happy in the thought of duty done in a way to win praise and at the thought of seeing my own country again, even if I were unequal to all the banquets that had been offered me. After calls at Trieste, Naples, Leghorn,

141

and Villefranche, while I forewent all except formal official functions in my honor, I finally sailed from Gibraltar for New York early in September.

Even the accounts in the newspapers, the invitations from cities and corporations and civic and patriotic organizations, did not fully prepare me for the splendor of the attentions awaiting me. They were overwhelming. My career as a hard-working naval officer scarcely equipped me for a role as the central figure of public applause. On the 30th of April, 1898, I had been practically unknown to the general public. In a day my name was on every one's lips. The dash of our squadron into an Oriental bay seven thousand miles from home had the glamour of romance to the national imagination.

I knew what to do in command of the Asiatic Squadron, but being of flesh and blood and not a superman, it seemed impossible to live up to all that was expected of me as a returning hero. Had I died on the way across the Atlantic, there would have been an outpouring of subscriptions which would have promptly rebuilt the temporary arch in my honor in Madison Square in marble. If I were to feel later, when the "triumph and shouting" had abated, that the people had misunderstood me, I knew that I had not misunderstood their thought in their exuberant pride over the way that the Asiatic Squadron had conducted "offensive operations" in the Philippine Islands.

Dewey arches, Dewey flags, and "Welcome Dewey" in electric lights on the span of the Brooklyn Bridge! The great city of New York made hol-

President McKinley and Admiral Dewey Reviewing the Parade after the Presentation of the Sword Given by Congress

iday. Its crowds banked the piers, the roofs, and Riverside Drive when the *Olympia*, leading the North Atlantic Squadron, which won Santiago, proceeded up the North River; and they packed the streets for the land parade in token of public emotion, while the gold loving-cup which came to me with the freedom of the city expressed the municipality's official tribute. In the presence of the spectacle, which was without equal, my emotion was indescribable. I was no less deeply affected when I stood on the steps of the State House at Montpelier with the grounds filled with Vermont "home folks," and when, on the steps of the east front of the Capitol, I received from the hands of the President the sword of honor which Congress had voted me.

On October 5, 1899, my flag was hauled down from the *Olympia*; but I was to raise it again on the Southern drill grounds for the manoeuvres, when I had under my direction the most powerful fleet which we had ever mobilized up to that time. A gratifying feature of the rank of admiral of the navy, which Congress had given me, was that I was to remain in active service for life. While I lived there would be work to do.

Before the Spanish War we had had no central advisory authority in determining our naval policy, which was therefore subject to the recommendations of the different bureaus directly under the secretary of the navy, with the result that there was not a harmonious purpose. We had been making our appropriations without a proper regard for their expenditure to the definite end of developing a fighting force as an efficient whole; we had been building ships without regard to homogeneity. Now it was my pleasure not only to see the recommendations which I had made to Secretary Tracy carried out by the concentration of our battle-ships in home waters, but by the establishment of the General Board, which was to prepare war plans, recommend the types and armament of ships for the annual building programme, and act as a clearing-house for all questions of naval policy. I was made President of the Board — a position which I still occupy, and where I am in daily association with some of the finest minds in the service. Naturally, my new assignment required my presence in Wash-

The Dewey Medal, designed by Daniel C. French

ington, the city with which I had the most associations, and where I preferred to settle.

For many years during my residence in Washington before going to the East Mrs. Mildred (McLean) Hazen and I had been friends. Upon my return from the East she did me the honor to become my wife. To her companionship I owe my happiness in later years.

Among all the tokens of the honors that the people paid me the simplest one is valued as much as the costly loving-cup; and I rejoice in having been able to pass the great mile-stone of threescore and ten in vigor, still able to appear at my office every morning as a naval officer on the active list, who can keep in touch with the living science of naval warfare in a responsible position, and whose experience in two wars and through many stages of naval progress I trust is of some value.

My good friend the late John Hay said that one could not boast of his triumphs in love and diplomacy. This is true of the work of the General Board. War, which would bring a test of its results, will find, unless I am mistaken in my knowledge of our officers, men, and ships, the spirit of Jones, Perry, and Farragut still dominant, with the certainty that our commanders will go into action not only with a sufficiency of ammunition but with the confidence that they are a part of a well-prepared force.

143

Appendices

Appendix A - Resume of Ships Which Took Active Part in Action

SHIP	DISPLACE-MENT	MAIN BATTERY	SECONDARY BATTERY (RAPID-FIRE GUNS)	TORPEDO TUBES	COMPLE-MENT ON BOARD	COMMANDING OFFICER
Olympia.............	5870	4 8", 10 5"	21	6	381	Captain C. V. Gridley
Baltimore............	4413	4 8", 6 6"	8	....	328	Captain N. M. Dyer
Petrel..............	892	4 6"	3	....	110	Commander E. P. Wood
Boston..............	3000	2 8", 6 6"	6	....	230	Captain F. Wildes
Raleigh.............	3213	1 6", 10 5"	12	2	252	Captain J. B. Coghlan
Concord............	1710	6 6"	6	....	155	Commander A. Walker
McCulloch[1].........	1280	....	4	....	68	Captain D. B. Hodgsdon

[1] Not engaged.

SHIP	DISPLACE-MENT	MAIN BATTERY	SECONDARY BATTERY (RAPID-FIRE GUNS)	TORPEDO TUBES	COMPLE-MENT	COMMANDING OFFICER
Reina Cristina........	3520	6 6.2"	13	5	352	Captain L. Cadarso
Castilla..............	3260	4 5", 2 4.7"	14	2	349	Captain A. Algado
Isla de Cuba.........	1045	4 4.7"	4	2	156	Commander I. Sidrach
Isla de Luzón........	1045	4 4.7"	4	2	156	Commander I. L. Human
Don Antonio de Ulloa..	1160	4 4.7"	6	....	159	Commander E. Robión
Don Juan de Austria...	1159	4 4.7"	8	2	179	Commander I. de la Concha
Marqués del Duero....	500	1 6.2", 2 4.7"	...	....	96	Lieutenant S. M. de Guerra
General Lezo[1]........	520	2 4.7"[2]	1 3.5" 1 Nord.	1	115	Lieutenant R. Benavente
Velasco[1]..............	1152	3 5.9"[3]	2 3" 2 Nord.	....	145	....
El Cano[1].............	560	3 4.7"	2 Nord. 1 H. R. C.	1	115	....
Argos[1]...............	508	1 3.5"	....	....	87	....

[1] Not engaged.   [2] Battery said to be on El Fraile Island.   [3] Battery said to be on Caballo Island.
The Spanish ships are given their allowed complements; the number actually on board was said to be much greater.

TOTALS	AMERICAN	SPANISH
Number of ships.............	6	7
Displacement.................	19,098	11,689
Guns over 4-inch.............	53	31
Guns under 4-inch............	56	44
Torpedo tubes...............	8	13
Officers and men.............	1,456	1,447

Appendix B

U. S. Naval Force on Asiatic Station, Flagship "Olympia,"
Cavite, Philippine Islands, *May* 4, 1898. Sir:

I have the honor to submit the following report of the operations of the squadron under my command:

The squadron left Mirs Bay on April 27, immediately on the arrival of Mr. O. F. Williams, United States consul at Manila, who brought important information and who accompanies the squadron.

Arrived off Bolinao on the morning of April 30 and, finding no vessels there, proceeded down the coast and arrived off the entrance to Manila Bay on the same afternoon.

The Boston and *Concord* were sent to reconnoiter Port Subic, I having been informed that the enemy intended to take position there. A thorough search of the port was made by the Boston and *Concord*, but the Spanish fleet was not found, although from a letter afterwards found in the arsenal (inclosed with translation), it appears that it had been their intention to go there.

Entered the Boca Grande, or south channel, at 11:30 PM., steaming in column at distance at 8 knots. After half the squadron had passed, a battery on the south side of the channel opened fire, none of the shots taking effect. The *Boston* and *McCulloch* returned the fire.

The squadron proceeded across the bay at slow speed, and arrived off Manila at daybreak, and was fired upon at 5:15 AM. by three batteries at Manila and two at Cavite and by the Spanish fleet anchored in an approximately east and west line across the mouth of Bakor Bay, with their left in shoal water in Canacao Bay.

The squadron then proceeded to the attack, the flagship *Olympia*, under my personal direction, leading, followed at distance by the *Baltimore, Raleigh*, *Petrel*, *Concord*, and *Boston,* in the order named, which formation was maintained throughout the action. The squadron opened fire at 5:41 AM. While advancing to the attack, two mines were exploded ahead of the flagship, too far to be effective.

The squadron maintained a continuous and precise fire at ranges varying from 5,000 to 2,000 yards, countermarching in a line approximately parallel to that of the Spanish fleet. The enemy's fire was vigorous, but generally ineffective.

Early in the engagement two launches put out toward the *Olympia* with the apparent intention of using torpedoes. One was sunk and the other disabled by our fire and beached before an opportunity occurred to fire torpedoes. At 7 AM. the Spanish flagship *Reina Cristina* made a desperate attempt to leave the line and come out to engage at short range, but was received with such galling fire, the entire battery of the *Olympia* being concentrated upon her, that she was barely able to return to the shelter of the point. The fires started in her by our shell at this time were not extinguished until she sank.

At 7:35 AM., it having been erroneously reported to me that only 15 rounds per gun remained for the 5-inch rapid-fire battery, I ceased firing and withdrew the squadron for consultation and a redistribution of ammunition, if necessary.

The three batteries at Manila had kept up a continuous fire from the beginning of the engagement, which fire was not returned by this squadron. The first of these batteries was situated on the south mole head at the entrance to the Pasig River, the second on the south bastion of the walled city of Manila, and the third at Malate, about one-half mile farther south. At this point I sent a message to the Governor-General to the effect that if the batteries did not cease firing the city would be shelled. This had the effect of silencing them.

At 11:16 AM., finding that the report of scarcity of ammunition was incorrect, I returned with the squadron to the attack. By this time the flagship and almost the entire Spanish fleet were in flames, and at 12:30 PM. the squadron ceased firing, the batteries being silenced and the ships sunk, burnt, and deserted.

At 12:40 PM. the squadron returned and anchored off Manila, the *Petrel* being left behind to complete the destruction of the smaller gunboats, which were behind the point of Cavite. This duty was performed by Commander E. P. Wood in the most expeditious and complete manner possible.

The Spanish fleet lost the following vessels:

Sunk — *Reina Cristina, Castilla, Don Antonio de Ulloa.*

Burnt — *Don Juan de Austria, Isla de Luzón, Isla de Cuba, General Lew, Marques del Duero, El Correo, Velasco,* and *Isla de Mindanao* (transport).

Captured — *Rápido* and *Hércules* (tugs) and several small launches.

I am unable to obtain complete accounts of the enemy's killed and wounded, but believe their loss to be very heavy. The Reina Cristina alone had 150 killed, including the captain, and 90 wounded.

I am happy to report that the damage done to the squadron under my command was inconsiderable. There were none killed, and only seven men in the squadron very slightly wounded. As will be seen by the reports of the commanding officers which are herewith inclosed, several of the vessels were struck and even penetrated, but the damage was of the slightest, and the squadron is in as good condition now as before the battle.

I beg to state to the Department that I doubt if any commander-in-chief, under similar circumstances, was ever served by more loyal, efficient, and gallant captains than those of the squadron now under my command. Captain Frank Wildes, commanding the *Boston,* volunteered to remain in command of his vessel, although his relief arrived before leaving Hongkong. Assistant Surgeon C. P. Kindleberger, of the *Olympia*, and Gunner J. C. Evans, of the *Boston,* also volunteered to remain after orders detaching them had arrived.

The conduct of my personal staff was excellent. Commander B. P. Lamberton, chief of staff, was a volunteer for that position and gave me most efficient aid. Lieutenant T. M. Brumby, flag lieutenant, and Ensign W. P. Scott, aid, performed their duties as signal officers in a highly creditable manner. The *Olympia* being short of officers for the battery, Ensign H. H. Caldwell, flag secretary, volunteered for and was assigned to a subdivision of the 5-inch battery. Mr. J. L. Stickney, formerly an officer in the United States Navy, and now correspondent for the New York *Herald,* volunteered for duty as my aid, and rendered valuable service.

While leaving to the commanding officers to comment on the conduct of the officers and men under their commands, I desire especially to mention the coolness of Lieutenant C. G. Calkins, the navigator of the *Olympia*, who came under my personal observation, being on the bridge with me throughout the entire action, and giving the ranges to the guns with an accuracy that was proven by the excellence of the firing.

On May 2, the day following the engagement, the squadron again went to Cavite, where it remains. A landing party was sent to destroy the guns and magazines of the batteries there. The first battery, near the end of Sangley Point, was composed of two modern Trubia B. L. rifles of 15 centimeters caliber. The second was one mile farther down the beach, and consisted of a modern Canet 12-centimeter B. L. rifle behind improvised earthworks.

On the 3d the military forces evacuated the Cavite arsenal, which was taken possession of by a landing party. On the same day the *Raleigh* and *Baltimore* secured the surrender of the batteries on Corregidor Island, paroling the garrison and destroying the guns.

On the morning of May 4 the transport Manila, which had been aground in Bakor Bay, was towed off and made a prize.

Very respectfully, your obedient servant,

George Dewey,
Commodore, U. S. Navy,
Commanding U. S. Naval Force on Asiatic Station.
The Secretary of the Navy,
Washington, D. C.

Appendix C - Official Report of Admiral Montojo

Departure for Subic

On the 25th of April, at 11 p. m., I left the bay of Manila for Subic with a squadron composed of the cruisers *Reina Cristina*, *Don Juan de Austria, Isla de Cuba, Isla de Luzón,* despatch boat *Marqués del Duero,* and the wooden cruiser *Castilla.* This last could merely be considered as a floating battery, incapable of maneuvering, on account of the bad condition of her hull. The following morning, being at Subic, I had a conference with Captain Del Rio, who, though he did not relieve my anxiety respecting the completion of the defensive works, assured me that they would soon be finished.

In the meanwhile the cruiser *Castilla*, even on this short cruise, was making much water through the bearings of the propeller and the opening astern. They worked day and night to stop these leaks with cement, finally making the vessel nearly water-tight, but absolutely impossible to use her engines.

On the morning of the 27th I sailed with the vessels to cover the entrance to the port of Subic. The *Castilla* was taken to the northeast point of Isla Grande to defend the western entrance, since the eastern entrance had already been closed with the hulls of the *San Quintin* and two old merchant vessels which were sunk there.

With much disgust, I found that the guns which should have been mounted on that island were delayed a month and a half. This surprised me, as the shore batteries that the navy had installed (with very little difficulty) at the entrance of the bay of Manila, under the intelligent direction of Colonel of Naval Artillery, Senor Garces, and Lieutenant Venavente, were ready to fight twenty-four days after the commencement of the work.

I was also no less disgusted that they confided in the efficacy of the few torpedoes which they had found feasible to put there.

The entrance was not defended by torpedoes nor by the batteries of the island, so that the squadron would have had to bear the attack of the Americans with its own resources, in 40 meters of water and with little security. Our vessels could not only be destroyed, but they could not save their crews. I still held a hope that the Americans would not go to Subic, and give us time for more preparations, but the following day I received from the Spanish consul at Hong Kong a telegram which said: "Enemy's squadron sailed at 2 PM. from the bay of Mira, and according to reliable accounts they sailed for Subic to destroy our squadron, and then will go to Manila."

This telegram demonstrated that the enemy knew where they could find my squadron and that the port of Subic had no defenses.

The same day, the 28th of April, I convened a council of the captains, and all, with the exception of Del Rio, chief of the new arsenal, thought that the situation was insupportable, and that we should go to the bay of Manila in order to accept there the battle under less unfavorable conditions.

THE RETURN TO MANILA

I refused to have our ships near the city of Manila, because, far from defending it, this would provoke the enemy to bombard the plaza, which doubtless would have been demolished on account of its few defenses. It was unanimously decided that we should take position in the bay of Cañacao, in the least water possible, in order to combine our fire with that of the batteries of Point Sangley and *Ulloa*.

I immediately ordered Del Rio to concentrate his forces in the most strategic point of the arsenal, taking every disposition to burn the coal and stores before allowing them to fall into the power of the enemy. I sent the *Don Juan de Austria* to Manila to get a large number of lighters filled with sand to defend the water line of the *Castilla* (which could not move) against the enemy's shells and torpedoes. At 10 AM. on the 29th I left Subic with the vessels of my squadron, towing the Castilla by the transport Manila.

In the afternoon of the same day we anchored in the Gulf of Cañacao in 8 meters of water. On the following morning we anchored in line of battle, the *Cristina, Castilla, Don Juan de Austria, Don Antonio de Ulloa, Luzón, Cuba,* and *Marques del Duero,* while the transport Manila was sent to the Roads of Bacoor, where the *Velasco* and *Lezo* were undergoing repairs.

At 7 PM. I received a telegram from Subic announcing that the enemy's squadron had entered the port at 3, reconnoitering, doubtless seeking our ships, and from there they sailed' with course for Manila.

The mail steamer *Isla Mindanao* arrived in the bay. I advised her captain to save his vessel by going to Singapore, as the enemy could not get into the entrance probably before midnight. As he was not authorized from the trans-Atlantic he did not do so, and then I told him that he could anchor in shallow water as near as possible to Bacoor.

At midnight gun fire was heard off Corregidor, and at 2 on the morning of the 1st of May I received telegraphic advices that the American vessels were throwing their search lights at the batteries of the entrance, with which they had exchanged several shots. I notified the commanding general of the arsenal, Señor Sostoa, and the general-governor of the plaza, Captain Señor Garcia Pana, that they should prepare themselves. I directed all the artillery to be loaded, and all the sailors and soldiers to go to their stations for battle, soon to receive the enemy.

This is all that occurred since I sailed to Subic until the entrance of the American squadron into the bay of Manila.

THE ARRIVAL OF THE ENEMY

The squadron being disposed for action, fires spread, and everything in proper place, we waited for the enemy's arrival. All the vessels, having been painted dark gray color, had taken down their masts and yards and boats to avoid the effects of projectiles and the splinters, had their anchors buoyed and cables ready to slip instantly.

At 4 AM. I made signal to prepare for action, and at 4:45 the *Austria* signaled the enemy's squadron, a few minutes after which they were recognized, with some confusion, in a column parallel with ours, at about 6,000 meters distant; the flagship *Olympia* ahead, followed by the *Baltimore, Raleigh, Boston, Concord, Helena, Petrel*, and *McCulloch*, and the two transports *Zafiro* and *Nanshan*.

The force of these vessels, excepting transports that were non-combatant, amounted to 21,410 tons, 49,290 horsepower, 163 guns (many of which were rapid fire), 1,750 men in their crews, and of an average velocity of about 17 miles. The power of our only five effective ships for battle was represented by 10,111 tons, 11,200 horsepower, 76 guns (very short of rapid fire), 1,875 crew, and a maximum speed of 12 miles.

THE FIRE FROM SHORE

At 5 the batteries on Point Sangley opened fire. The two first shots fell short and to the left of the leading vessel. These shots were not answered by the enemy, whose principal object was the squadron.

This battery had only two Ordoñez guns of 15 centimeters mounted, and but one of these could fire in the direction of the opposing fleet.

In a few minutes one of the batteries of Manila opened fire, and at 5:15 I made signal that our squadron open fire. The enemy answered immediately. The battle became general. We slipped the springs and the cables and started ahead with the engines, so as not to be involved by the enemy.

THE BATTLE

The Americans fired most rapidly. There came upon us numberless projectiles, as the three cruisers at the head of the line devoted themselves almost entirely to fight the *Cristina,* my flagship. A short time after the action commenced one shell exploded in the forecastle and put out of action all those who served the four rapid-fire cannon, making splinters of the forward mast, which wounded the helmsman on the bridge, when Lieut. Jose Nunez took the wheel with a coolness worthy of the greatest commendation, steering until the end of the fight. In the meanwhile another shell exploded in the orlop, setting fire to the crews' bags, which they were fortunately able to control.

The enemy shortened the distance between us, and, rectifying his aim, covered us with a rain of rapid-fire projectiles. At 7:30 one shell destroyed completely the steering gear. I ordered to steer by hand while the rudder was out of action. In the meanwhile another shell exploded on the poop and put out of action nine men. Another destroyed the mizzen masthead, bringing down the flag and my ensign, which were replaced immediately. A fresh shell exploded in the officers' cabin, covering the hospital with blood, destroying the wounded who were being treated there. Another exploded in the ammunition room astern, filling the quarters with smoke and preventing the working of the hand steering gear. As it was impossible to control the fire, I had to flood the magazine when the cartridges were beginning to explode.

Amidships several shells of smaller caliber went through the smokestack and one of the large ones penetrated the fire room, putting out of action one master gunner and 12 men serving the guns. Another rendered useless the starboard bow gun; while the fire astern increased, fire was started forward by another shell, which went through the hull and exploded on the deck.

The broadside guns, being undamaged, continued firing until there were only one gunner and one seaman remaining unhurt for firing them, as the guns' crews had been frequently called upon to substitute those charged with steering, all of whom were out of action.

THE DESTRUCTION OF OUR SHIPS

The ship being out of control, the hull, smoke pipe, and mast riddled with shot or confused with the cries of the wounded; half of her crew out of action, among whom were seven officers. I gave the order to sink and abandon the ship before the magazines should explode, making signal at the same time to the *Cuba* and *Luzón* to assist in saving the rest of the crew, which they did, aided by others from the *Duero* and the arsenal.

I abandoned the *Cristina,* directing beforehand to secure her flag, and accompanied by my staff, and with great sorrow, I hoisted my flag on the cruiser *Isla de Cuba.*

After having saved many men from the unfortunate vessel, one shell destroyed her heroic commander, Don Luis Cadarso, who was directing the rescue.

The *Ulloa*, which also defended herself firmly, using the only two guns which were available, was sunk by a shell which entered the water line, putting out of action her commander and half of her remaining crew, those which were only remaining for the service of the two guns stated.

The *Castilla,* which fought heroically, remained with her artillery useless, except one stern gun, with which they fought spiritedly, was riddled with shot and set on fire by the enemy's shells, then sunk, and was abandoned by her crew in good order, which was directed by her commander, Don Alonzo Algado. The casualties on this ship were 23 killed and 80 wounded.

The *Austria,* very much damaged and on fire, went to the aid of the Castilla. The *Luzón* had three guns dismounted, and was slightly damaged in the hull. The *Duero* remained with one of her engines useless, the bow gun of 12 centimeters and one of the redoubts.

At 8 o'clock in the morning, the enemy's squadron having suspended its fire, I ordered the ships that remained to us to take positions in the bottom of the Roads at Bacoor, and there to resist to the last moment, and that they should be sunk before they surrendered.

THE SINKING

At 10:30 the enemy returned, forming a circle to destroy the arsenal and the ships which remained to me, opening upon them a horrible fire, which we answered as far as we could with the few cannon which we still had mounted.

There remained the last recourse to sink our vessels, and we accomplished this operation, taking care to save the flag, the distinguishing pennant, the money in the safe, the portable arms, the breech plugs of the guns, and the signal codes.

After which I went with my staff to the Convent of Santo Domingo de Cavite, to be cured of a wound received in the left leg, and to telegraph a brief report of the action, with preliminaries and results.

It remains only to say that all the chiefs, officers, engineers, quartermasters, gunners, sailors, and soldiers rivalled one another in sustaining with honor the good name of the navy on this sad day.

The inefficiency of the vessels which composed my little squadron, the lack of all classes of the personnel, especially master gunners and seamen gunners; the inaptitude of some of the provisional machinists, the scarcity of rapid-fire cannon, the strong crews of the enemy, and the unprotected character of the greater part of our vessels, all contributed to make more decided the sacrifice which we made for our country and to prevent the possibility of the horrors of the bombardment of the city of Manila, with the conviction that with the scarcity of our force against the superior enemy we were going to certain death and could expect a loss of all our ships.

Our casualties, including those of the arsenal, amounted to 381 men killed and wounded.

Appendix D

Office of the Commander-in-Chief of the Navy in the Philippines.

Personal.   Manila, 26 *September,* 1898.

To His Excellency,
Rear-Admiral Dewey.

My dear Sir:

With all my consideration and special respect, I present my earnest thanks for the amiable reply which you took occasion to send to my letter in your communication of the 24th ultimo, regretting also that the circumstances in which we find ourselves do not permit me to convey my feelings by conversation.

Being called to Madrid to make answer to the charges which may be made against me, principally for going to Subic and for the loss of my squadron at Cavite, I have to defend myself from the calumny which may be raised against me; for this purpose it would be of the greatest utility and much force if I were able to offer the highly valuable testimony of the authorized opinion of yourself, the distinguished Commander-in-Chief of the squadron which I had the honor of engaging.

For this purpose I am compelled to put on record:

1. That the port of Subic was without shore fortifications or submarine torpedoes at its entrance.

2. That the destruction of my squadron, given the superiority of yours, would have been far more complete at Subic than at Cavite because the depth of water being much greater in the former port, ships and men would have sunk, causing great loss of life.

3. That you did not find us unready at the entrance of Manila Bay and still less so at Cavite, and if fortune did not favor the Spaniards it was not for lack of valor but principally because we had poor ships.

I know that my temerity in making this request of you is very great; but invoking the fact that we belong to the same profession and remembering that you have more than once had the kindness to praise my conduct, I force myself to believe that this will be well received.

The affair has an immense importance for me since it is closely related to my honor and personal reputation.

I have another request to make of you, and that is in favor of Captain Del Rio, old and sick, late naval commandant at Subic, and the officers, sailors and soldiers who are with him in the power of the insurgents, and very badly treated. If you would consent to arrange for their transfer to Manila, continuing as prisoners, they would be satisfied.

For my part, after begging your pardon a thousand times for the liberty which I am taking, I hope that you will kindly grant my request, for which your faithful servant will be eternally grateful.
Patricio Montojo.

Rear-Admiral Montojo,
    Manila.
My dear Sir:
It gives me pleasure, replying to your letter of the 26th instant, to record my testimony in favor of a gallant foe.

1. In regard to the port of Subic, it was carefully reconnoitred on the 30th of April by three of my ships, two of which made the complete circuit of the bay without finding anything to oppose them.

2. Your statement as to the probability of greater loss of life in a deep bay like that of Subic than in shoal water as at Cavite, appears to me to be incontrovertible.

3. Although without accurate knowledge as to the condition of your ships, I have no hesitation in saying to you what I have already had the honor to report to my government, that your defense at Cavite was gallant in the extreme. The fighting of your flagship, which was singled out for attack, was especially worthy of a place in the traditions of valor of your nation.

In conclusion, I beg to assure you that I very much regret that calumnies have been cast at you, and am confident that your honor cannot be dimmed by them.

With assurances of my highest consideration,
Very sincerely,
George Dewey,
Rear-Admiral, U. S. N., Comdg. Asiatic Station.

Appendix E

Washington, *May* 26, 1898.
Dewey (care American Consul) Hongkong:
    You must exercise discretion most fully in all matters, and be governed according to circumstance which you know and we cannot know. You have our confidence entirely. It is desirable, as far as possible, and consistent for your success and safety, not to have political alliances with the insurgents or any faction in the islands that would incur liability to maintain their cause in the future.   Long.

Washington, *June* 14, 1898.
Dewey (care American Consul) Hongkong:
    Report fully any conferences, relations, or cooperations, military or otherwise, which you have had with Aguinaldo, and keep informed the Department in that respect.   Long.

Hongkong, *June* 6, 1898 (Cavite, *June* 3).
Secretary of Navy, Washington:
    Receipt of telegram of May 26 is acknowledged, and I thank the Department for the expression of confidence. Have acted according to the spirit of Department's instructions therein from the beginning, and I have entered into no alliance with the insurgents or with any faction. This squadron can reduce the defenses of Manila at any moment, but it is considered useless until the arrival of sufficient United States forces to retain possession.
Dewey.

Hongkong, *June* 27, 1898.
Secretary of Navy, Washington:
    Receipt of telegram of June 14 is acknowledged. Aguinaldo, insurgent leader, with thirteen of his staff, arrived May 19, by permission, on *Nanshan*. Established self Cavite, outside arsenal, under the protection of our guns, and organized his army. I have had several conferences with him, generally of a personal nature. Consistently I have refrained from assisting him in any way with the force under my command, and on several occasions I have declined requests that I should do so, telling him the squadron could not act until the arrival of the United States troops. At the same time I have given him to understand that I consider insurgents as friends, being opposed to a common enemy. He has gone to attend a meeting of insurgent leaders for the purpose of forming a civil government. Aguinaldo has acted independently of the squadron, but has kept me advised of his progress, which has been wonderful. I have allowed to pass by water recruits, arms and ammunition, and to take such Spanish arms and ammunition from the arsenal as he needed. Have advised frequently to conduct the war humanely, which he has done invaria-

bly. My relations with him are cordial, but I am not in his confidence. The United States has not been bound in any way to assist insurgents by any act or promises, and he is not, to my knowledge, committed to assist us. I believe he expects to capture Manila without my assistance, but doubt ability, they not yet having many guns. In my opinion, these people are far superior in their intelligence and more capable of self-government than the natives of Cuba, and I am familiar with both races.

Dewey.

Filipinos:

The great North American nation, the cradle of genuine liberty, and therefore the friend of our people, oppressed and enslaved by the tyranny and despotism of its rulers, has come to us manifesting a protection as decisive as it is undoubtedly disinterested toward our inhabitants, considering us as sufficiently civilized and capable of governing for ourselves our unfortunate country. In order to maintain this high estimate granted us by the generous North American nation we should abominate all those deeds which tend to lower this opinion, which are pillage, theft, and all sorts of crimes leading to persons or property, with the purpose of avoiding international conflicts during the period of our campaign.

I decree as follows:

Article I. The lives and property of all foreigners, Chinese being included in this denomination, shall be respected, as well as that of all Spaniards who neither directly nor indirectly contributed to carry on war against us.

Article II. Enemies who lay down their arms must also be respected in like manner.

Article III. All hospitals and ambulances must likewise be respected, as well as all persons and goods found therein, including the staff on duty, unless they manifest hostility.

Article IV. Those who disobey what is prescribed in these preceding articles shall be tried by summary process, and put to death if the said disobedience has resulted in murder, robbery, or rape.

Given in Cavite, the 24th of May, 1898.

Emilio Aguinaldo.

Appendix F

The following extracts from the writings of well-known authorities on the subject are given in Stockton's Manual of Snow's International Law:

It may be a serious disadvantage, if not positive injury, to a blockading belligerent to have a blockaded port subject to frequent or sympathetic visits of a neutral vessel of war. The tendencies favor a limitation of such visits which usage permits as a matter of courtesy alone. The vessel of war desiring to enter the blockaded port should, in seeking permission, if necessary, establish her identity to the blockading vessels. Quotations from authorities upon this subject follow here:

Perels, a German authority, makes the following statement upon the subject, which is the more interesting from his position as lecturer at the Imperial Naval Academy at Kiel. In his work, translated into French by Arendt, he says, on page 203:

"La fermeture de la place bloquée doit être respectée par les navires de guerre et de commerce neutres; il n'est pas rare, cependant, que les navires de guerre neutres soient exceptes de la prohibition d'entrer....Le Gouvernement français avait adopté une règle contraire en 1838, lorsqu'il fit mettre, par sa flotte, les côtes de la république Argentine en état de blocus. Le département des affaires étrangères rendit alors le decret suivant: 'Les bâtiments de guerre neutres se présentant devant un port bloqué doivent aussi être invités à s'éloigner; s'ils persistent, le commandant du blocus a le droit de s'opposer à leur entrée par la force, et la responsabilité de tout ce qui peut s'en suivre pésera sur les violateurs du blocus.'"

Captain Testa, of the Portuguese navy, professor at the naval school in Lisbon, in the French translation of his work, by M. Boutiron, states on page 225 that —

"D'accord avec les principes admis, le blocus établit le droit de prohiber l'entrée des points bloqués tant pour les navires de guerre que pour les navires de commerce. Cependant, les puissances qui établissent le blocus autorisent souvent la libre entrée et la sortie des navires de guerre neutres par la considération qu'il n'est pas présumable d'après leur caractère, qu'ils aillent aider le belligérent bloqué; et qu'en outre, la fin principale du blocus étant d'interdire le commerce par mer, l'entrée ou la sortie des navires de guerre impartiaux et non commerçants ne porte pas préjudice à ce but."

Calvo says, in section 2561, page 97, of volume 4, that —

"En droit l'accés et la sortie d'un port bloqué sent interdits aussi bien aux bâtiments de guerre qu'aux navires de commerce.

"'Un bâtiment de guerre,' dit Wheaton, 'n'a pas le droit d'entrer dans un port bloqué ni d'en sortir, a moins qu'il n'y fut deja à l'époque où a commencé le blocus.' ..."

Mr. J. H. Ferguson, formerly of the Netherlands royal navy, and at one time minister of the Netherlands in China, says in his manual, volume 2, page 486, article 276:

"During the continuance of the state of blockade no vessels are allowed to enter or leave the blockaded place without special license or consent of the blockading authority. Public vessels or vessels of war of neutral powers are all equally bound by the same obligation to respect the blockade. When the public vessel of a neutral state wishes to have communication with a blockaded place, the neutral commanding officer is obliged to observe strict neutrality and to comply with the conditions under which such permission has been granted to cross the lines of the blockading belligerent...."

Walker, on page 522, says:

"The stringency of a blockade may indeed be relaxed in two peculiar cases. After the expiration of the period appointed for the withdrawal of ordinary neutral private vessels, and at any time during the continuance of the investment men-of-war flying the flags of neutral powers are commonly by courtesy permitted to communicate with the blockaded ports, and to maintain the public correspondence of their own or other neutral governments with their respective consular or diplomatic agents. It behooves such licensed carriers, however, to see to it that their privilege does not become a cloak for illegitimate dealings...."

Appendix G

Headquarters United States Land and Naval Forces, Manila Bay, Philippine Islands,
August 7th, 1898.
To the General in Chief,
    Commanding Spanish Forces in Manila.
Sir:

We have the honor to notify your Excellency that operations of the land and naval forces of the United States against the defenses of Manila may begin at any time after the expiration of forty-eight hours from the hour of receipt by you of this communication, or sooner if made necessary by an attack on your part.

This notice is given m order to afford you an opportunity to remove all non-combatants from the city.
Very respectfully,
Wesley Merritt,
Major-General, U. S. Army,
Commanding Land Forces of the United States.
George Dewey,
Rear-Admiral, U. S. Navy,
Commanding United States Naval Force on Asiatic Station.

Manila, *August* 7, 1898.
To the Major-General of the Army,
    AND THE Rear-Admiral OF THE Navy,
    Commanding respectively the Military and Naval Forces of the United States.

Gentlemen:

I have the honor to inform Your Excellencies that at half-past twelve today I received the notice with which you favor me, that after forty-eight hours have elapsed you may begin operations against this fortified city, or at an earlier hour if the forces under your command are attacked by mine.

As your notice is sent for the purpose of providing for the safety of non-combatants, I give thanks to Your Excellencies for the humane sentiments you have shown, and state that, finding myself surrounded by insurrectionary forces, I am without places of refuge for the increased numbers of wounded, sick, women and children, who are now lodged within the walls.

Very respectfully, and kissing the hands of your Excellencies,

Fermin Jaudenes,

Governor-General and Captain-General of the Philippines.

Headquarters United States Land and Naval Forces Manila Bay, Philippine Islands

August 9, 1898.

Sir:

The inevitable suffering in store for the wounded, sick, women and children, in the event that it becomes our duty to reduce the defenses of the walled town in which they are gathered, will, we feel assured, appeal successfully to the sympathies of a general capable of making the determined and prolonged resistance which Your Excellency has exhibited after the loss of your naval forces, and without hope of succor.

We therefore submit, without prejudice to the high sentiments of honor and duty which Your Excellency entertains, that surrounded on every side as you are by a constantly increasing force, with a powerful fleet in your front, and deprived of all prospect of reinforcement and assistance, a most useless sacrifice of life would result in the event of an attack, and therefore every consideration of humanity makes it imperative that you should not subject your city to the horrors of a bombardment. Accordingly we demand the surrender of the city of Manila, and the Spanish forces under your command.

Very respectfully,

Wesley Merritt,

Major-General, U. S. A.,

Commanding Land Forces of the United States.

George Dewey,

Rear-Admiral, U. S. N.,

Commanding U. S. Naval Force on Asiatic Station.

The Governor-General and Captain-General of the Philippines.

The Governor-General and Captain-General of the Philippines to the Major-General of the Army, and the Rear-Admiral of the Navy,

Commanding respectively the Military and Naval Force of the United States.

Gentlemen:

Having received an intimation from Your Excellencies that, in obedience to sentiments of humanity to which you appeal and which I share, I should surrender this city and the forces under my orders, I have assembled the Council of Defense which declares that your request cannot be granted, but taking account of the most exceptional circumstances existing in this city which

Your Excellencies recite and which I unfortunately have to admit, I would consult my Government if Your Excellencies will grant the time strictly necessary for this communication by way of Hong Kong.

Very respectfully, Fermin Jaudenes,
Governor-General and Captain-General of the Philippines.

Headquarters United States Land and Naval Forces,
Manila Bay, *August* 10th, 1898.
To the Governor-General and Captain-General of the Philippines Islands.
Sir:

We have the honor to acknowledge the communication of Your Excellency of the 8th instant, in which you suggest your desire to consult your government in regard to the exceptional circumstances in your city, provided the time to do so can be granted by us.

In reply we respectfully inform Your Excellency that we decline to grant the time requested.

Very respectfully,
Wesley Merritt,
Major-General,
U. S. Army, Commanding United States Land Forces.
George Dewey,
Rear-Admiral U. S. Navy,
Commanding United States Naval Forces, Asiatic Station.

Appendix H

Preliminary Agreement entered into this day in regard to capitulation of the Spanish Army in the Philippines, details to be arranged by a joint commission.

The capitulation will be under the following terms:

1. The military forces of the United States shall occupy the city and the defenses of Manila until in the treaty of peace between the two belligerent powers may be agreed the final fate of the city.

2. It being impossible for the Spanish forces of the garrison to evacuate the place either by sea, on account of the lack of steamers, or by land on account of the insurgents, it is hereby agreed that all the fighting forces capitulate with the honors of war, the officers keeping their swords, guns, horses and furniture, and the troops will deposit theirs in the place agreed.

3. All persons included in the capitulation will be at liberty, being allowed to live in their abodes, which shall be respected.

4. The Spanish troops will remain in their barracks at the orders of their chiefs.

5. The authorities and the forces of North America will carefully respect the persons, their dwellings and property, of the inhabitants of Manila and its suburbs.

6. The banks, credit societies, industrial establishments, and those for educational purposes or any other, the object of which is humanity and civilization, shall continue open according to their regulations, unless modified by the authorities of the United States as circumstances may require.

7. The expenses of living of the military and navy men will be paid with the funds of the Spanish treasury if there be enough, and in the contrary they will be aided with the amount that corresponds to the prisoners of war, according to their rank.

8. The repatriation of the officers and soldiers and their families will be at the cost of the United States and also of the native officers which may desire to return to Spain.

9. The native troops will be dismissed from the service.

10. The United States authorities, to the best of their ability, guarantee and will insure the safety of the lives and properties of the inhabitants of Manila.

The 7th Article shall be construed to cover rations and necessary supplies. The United States to determine what is necessary.

Complete returns of men shall be rendered to the United States authorities by organizations, and also full lists of public property and stores in their possession.

The question of returning troops to Spain and the expenses thereof to be determined by the United States Government at Washington.

Arms will be returned to the men at the discretion of the U. S. authorities, and officers shall retain their side arms.

Fermin Jaudenes.   Wesley Merritt,
Major-General, U. S. A.

Manila, *August* 14th, 1898.

THE UNDERSIGNED, having been appointed a commission to determine the details of capitulation of the city and defenses of Manila and its suburbs, and the Spanish forces stationed therein, in accordance with the agreement entered into the previous day by Major-General Wesley Merritt, U. S. Army, American Commander-in-Chief in the Philippines, and His Excellency Don Fermin Jaudenes, Acting General-in-Chief of the Spanish Army in the Philippines, HAVE AGREED UPON THE FOLLOWING:

1. The Spanish troops, European and native, capitulate with the city and defenses, with all the honors of war, depositing their arms in the places designated by the authorities of the United States, and remain in the quarters designated and under the orders of their officers and subject to the control of the aforesaid United States authorities, until the conclusion of a treaty of peace between the two belligerent nations. All persons included in the capitulation remain at liberty and officers remaining in their respective homes, which shall be respected as long as they observe the regulations prescribed for their government and the laws in force.

2. Officers shall retain their side arms, horses, and private property.

3. All public horses and public property of all kinds shall be turned over to staff officers designated by the United States.

4. Complete returns in duplicate of men by organizations, and full lists of public property and stores, shall be rendered to the United States within ten days from this date.

5. All questions relating to the repatriation of officers and men of the Spanish forces and of their families and of the expenses which said repatriation may occasion, shall be referred to the Government of the United States at Washington. Spanish families may leave Manila at any time convenient to them.

6. Officers included in the capitulation shall be supplied by the United States, according to their rank, with rations and necessary aid, as though they were prisoners of war, until the conclusion of a treaty of peace between the United States and Spain. All the funds in the Spanish treasury and all other public funds shall be turned over to the authorities of the United States.

7. This city, its inhabitants, its churches and religious worship, its educational establishments, and its private property of all descriptions, are placed under the special safeguard of the faith and honor of the American army.

F. V. Greene, *Brig. Gen. of Volunteers, U. S. Army.*
B. P. Lamberton, *Captain, U. S. Navy.*
Charles A. Whittier, *Lieut. Col. and Inspector General.*
E. H. Crowder, *Lieut. Col. and Judge Advocate.*
Nicolas de la Peña, *Auditor General Excmo.*
Carlos Reyes, *Coronel de Ingenieros.*
Jose Maria Olaquen Felín, *Coronel de Estado Mayor.*

United States Naval Force on Asiatic Station
Flagship *Olympia*,
Manila, P. I., *August* 18, 1898.
Sir:

1. I have the honor to report that at 9 a. m. on August 13th, the Squadron left its anchorage at Cavite and took position off the city of Manila.

2. The flagship *Olympia*, *Raleigh* and *Petrel* then proceeded to shell the magazine, fort, and entrenchments at Malate, an army column attacking from the southward at the same time, accompanied by the gunboat *Callao* and tug *Barcelo*, well inshore. Commenced firing at 9.35 and ceased firing at 10.32, the fort being silenced and the enemy retreating into the city closely followed by the army advancing along the beach, with the *Callao* and *Barcelo* on its flank.

3. The other vessels of the squadron took the positions assigned them opposite the principal batteries along the water front, as did also the *Olympia*, *Raleigh* and *Petrel* after the reduction of the fort at Malate.

4. At 11 AM. hoisted the international signal. Do you surrender? and at 11:20 a white flag was seen on the city wall. After preliminary conference, General Merritt landed with 600 troops and arranged the terms of surrender.

5. The Spanish flag was hauled down by Lieutenant Brumby of my staff, who hoisted the United States flag at 5:43 PM. A company of troops with a regimental band happening to be marching past, saluted the colors as they went up and played the national air. The vessels of the Squadron fired a national salute.

6. I have the honor and pleasure to forward the Spanish flag to the Secretary of the Navy; also the colors of the armed transport *Cebu,* their only remaining naval vessel.

7. The forts and batteries on the bay front of the city contained the following guns:

Four B. L. R. of 24 cm. (9.4-inches), distributed as follows: two in battery north of Ermita, one outside moat near southwest angle of city wall, and one outside wall near northwest angle, opposite Fort Santiago.

Four B. L. R. guns of 14 cm. (5.5-inches) in battery near middle of west front outside walls.

Two B. L. R. bronze guns of 15 cm. (5.9-inches) on siege carriages near the preceding.

Two B. L. R. guns of 12 cm. (4.7-inches) on siege carriages in battery at the end of south mole of Pasig River.

Nine muzzle-loading rifled mortars of 21 cm. (8.3-inches), four in battery outside southwest angle of city walls, and five on the city wall between the two gates of the west front.

All these guns were mounted behind earthworks, with well-supplied and protected magazines at hand. There are also the following serviceable guns:

Eighteen M. L. R. guns of 16 cm. (6.3-inches) distributed as follows: Nine on southwest angle of city wall, five in Fort Santiago (northwest angle of city wall), two in front of flagstaff, and two in battery on outer end of south mole of Pasig River.

Eight B. L. Krupp field pieces distributed along city wall. Also numerous saluting guns and obsolete guns and mortars.

8. Under a separate cover, I forward for the information of the Department plan showing sea front of walled city and location of principal batteries as determined by special reconnaissance on August 15th, 1898.

I have the honor to be.

Very respectfully,

George Dewey,

Rear-Admiral, U. S. Navy,

Commanding U. S. Naval Force on Asiatic Station.

The Secretary of the Navy,

Washington, D, C.